PENGUIN BOOKS

More Please

BARRY HUMPHRIES

MORE PLEASE

He was always a seeker
after something in the world
that is there in no satisfying measure,
or not at all.

Walter Pater
From *Imaginary Portraits*

PENGUIN BOOKS

Author's Note

The people portrayed in this book are real
and the events described took place, but
fictional names and descriptive detail have
sometimes been used.

PENGUIN BOOKS

UK | USA | Canada | Ireland | Australia
India | New Zealand | South Africa

Penguin Books is part of the Penguin Random House group of companies
whose addresses can be found at global.penguinrandomhouse.com

Penguin
Random House
UK

First published by Viking 1992
Published in Penguin Books 2017
001

Copyright © Barry Humphries, 1992

The moral right of the author has been asserted

Pages 335–6 constitute an extension of this copyright page

Printed in Great Britain by Clays Ltd, St Ives plc

A CIP catalogue record for this book is available from the British Library

ISBN: 978-0-241-97748-4

www.greenpenguin.co.uk

MIX
Paper from
responsible sources
FSC® C018179

Penguin Random House is committed to a
sustainable future for our business, our readers
and our planet. This book is made from Forest
Stewardship Council® certified paper.

Dedicated with much love
to my sister, Barbara,
and my brothers, Christopher and Michael,
who would probably tell you
a very different story

Contents

Acknowledgements

I wish to thank the following for their encouragement and assistance in this daunting task: my wife, Lizzie Spender; my sister, Barbara, and my brothers, Christopher and Michael; Katherine Brisbane, Peter Coleman, Geoffrey Dutton, Ramona Koval, David Marr, Lewis Morley, Colin and Neil Munro, C. K. Stead, Paul Taylor and others who helped me in Australia; in America: Earl McGrath, Jean and Brian Moore, Evgenia Sands and Stephanie du Tan; in England I'm indebted to Helen Crisp, Nicholas Garland, Candida Lycett-Green, Charles Osborne, Stephen Spender, Ken Thomson, Ed Victor, my secretaries Annabel, Beverley and Nicole, and, at Penguin, the book's designer, Caz Hildebrand, my copy-editor, Judith Flanders, and especially my editor Fanny Blake, who had faith that this book might be written even when I did not.

'More please'
– the author's first coherent utterance

Alzheimer Remembers

I ALWAYS WANTED MORE. I never had enough milk or money or socks or sex or holidays or first editions or solitude or gramophone records or free meals or real friends or guiltless pleasure or neckties or applause or unquestioning love or persimmons. Of course, I have had more than my share of most of these commodities but it always left me with a vague feeling of unfulfilment: *where was the rest*? Is it possible that while still at the breast my infant gaze was fixed on the adjacent mound of nourishment fearing that it might be snatched away before I could clamp it with avid gums?

Now I have passed middle age and achieved enough fame to be sought after by hostesses, AIDS charities and a few well-meaning Australian thesis-writers. I am already the subject of two generous biographies and it is only the fear that my adventures might for a third time be profitably chronicled by another man that prompts me to relate my own story.

Vanity plays lurid tricks with our memory, as Conrad has observed, but the well-intentioned biography or earnest thesis can also play lurid tricks with the truth, as its author squeezes and pummels his subject to fit a convenient or fashionable theory.

I cannot say that this has yet happened to me, but if I do not immediately sink into obscurity or cease to be funny tomorrow, it might. I had intended to call this volume of reminiscences by the above title to illustrate the selective pathology of all such memoirs. Yet as I begin this task aspiring to total candour, it is inevitable that I will rearrange the facts of my life in an attractive tableau, in much the same way as we arrange our features when we are about to be photographed. In that fraction of a second before the shutter clicks, our faces undergo a subtle but dramatic transformation. I am sure that all authors, however bent on frankness, also perform some last-minute act of moral titivation before embarking on self-portraiture.

From time to time I have stepped into a lift or washroom, or some other chamber lined with mirror, and for a second been perplexed by the sight of a round-shouldered, middle-aged man, dewlapped and disconsolate, a few feet away from me and looking in the other direction. It is when I see he is wearing my suit and my necktie and carrying my briefcase that I know him to be my *doppelgänger*, lurking in the far corner of my field of vision; the man who will never catch my eye. Unlike the friendly fellow who confronts me from the shaving mirror with his rehearsed and jaunty grin, this, though I am pained to confess it, is the *real* me. You may meet him on these pages, but only, so to speak, when I am not looking.

The Reader will be relieved, I hope, to see that this book is not prefaced by a page of pompous epigraphs; obscure apophthegms from Kierkegaard, Borges, F. Scott Fitzgerald, Kafka, Turgenev and the letters of Arnold Schoenberg. It is an indulgence of the provincial opsimath; a highfalutin' mannerism beloved of Australian and American authors keen to parade their multi-lingual skills and sophistication in the face of strong suspicions to the contrary. I will also try to avoid a lot of unnecessary name-dropping. Thus, in the illustrated section, the *here's me with* . . . pictures will be mercifully few.

But the retrospective posture is uncomfortable. Long periods spent looking over one's shoulder can lead only to a painful case of Orpheus' Neck. So I must proceed with my story.

Alzheimer! Erinnern Sie!

Beverly Hills, November 1991

MORE PLEASE

Ghostly Golfers

I WAS BORN at Number 38 Christowel Street, in the Melbourne suburb of Camberwell, or I would have been born there had my mother not been rushed to a nearby hospital; but it was to this address that my infant self was conveyed, with throbbing fontanelle and abridged foreskin, in February 1934. A lazy breather, I had been given a good whiff of oxygen soon after my advent, and to this balsamic inhalation my mother liked to attribute my precocity – in matters of no importance.

My white wicker bassinet, shrouded with net, and later my play-pen, were usually placed in the garden under some protective bush. White cabbage moths flitted just out of reach beyond my translucent canopy, and the earliest scent I can remember is honeysuckle. A long way off, the thin nasal voice of the wireless transmitted a popular 'coon song' of 1934 called 'Oh Mona'. The melody was at once jaunty and melancholy, and the words as mysterious now as they were then.

> Down by the hen-house on my knees
> *Oh Mona!*
> I thought I heard a chicken sneeze
> *Oh Mona!*

My parents both came from the distant suburb of Thornbury, and had been at Sunday school together. Thornbury was one of

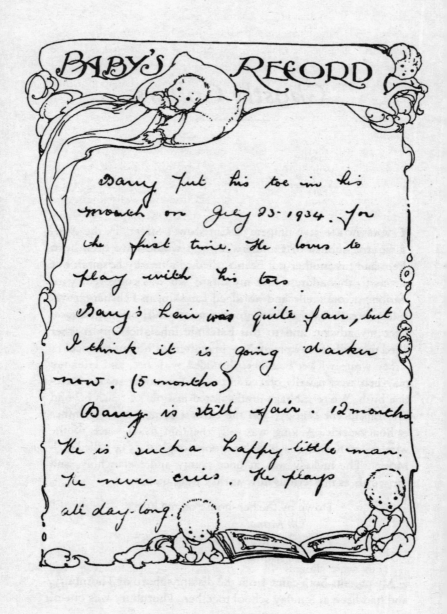

BABY'S RECORD

Barry put his toe in his
mouth on July 23·1934. For
the first time. He loves to
play with his toes.
Barry's hair was quite fair, but
I think it is going darker
now. (5 months)
Barry is still fair. 12 months
He is such a happy little man.
He never cries. He plays
all day·long.

the city's older districts, created by speculative builders in the 1880s and linked to central Melbourne by the extended cable tramline. After their marriage my mother and father made their gigantic move to the new 'garden suburb' of Camberwell. The Great Depression was receding and my father began building houses on a recently subdivided Golf Course, called somewhat anomalously – it was ten miles from the sea – the Golf Links Estate.

I can still remember those remnants of fairway, tee block, bunker and rough between the pristine brick homes, and the puckered grey golf balls we sometimes dug up as we planted our new garden. Hydrangeas, rhododendrons, geraniums, zinnias, pansies, stocks, snapdragons and phlox, all from Chandlers Nursery. There were no roses, which my mother dismissed as 'a bit old-fashioned'. Down the hill by the railway line there remained a sizeable wedge of vestigial fairway, a derelict weatherboard clubhouse and even a couple of ragged and reprieved gum trees. If that hillside were ever haunted, it would not be by the Aborigines, but by some ghostly golfer of 1910, plus-foured and Fair-Isled, prowling through those suburban gardens at dusk in search of a long-lost shanked drive.

Number 38 Christowel Street (or Christowell Street, it was spelt differently at either end of the street), in the 'Tudor style', was my father's first speculative villa and we lived there until he had built a mock Elizabethan dwelling four doors up. Soon after I was born the Tudor house was sold to two maiden ladies called the Misses Train and we moved into the Elizabethan bungalow, while my increasingly prosperous father drew up the plans for a two-storeyed cream-brick neo-Georgian monolith on the very crest of the hill. Dwarfing all its neighbours, this was to be our final family home. Or it *would* be if he got a good enough price for the Elizabethan at Number 30.

They were 'homes' in Christowel Street, Camberwell, and there was a magazine called the *Australian Home Beautiful*

SUBDIVISIONAL
AUCTION SALE

CAMBERWELL GOLF LINKS

SATURDAY 30TH APRIL

at
3 O'CLOCK

*The Spirit of the
Camberwell
Golf Links*

AUCTIONEERS

SYDNEY T. HAYNES & CO.
COMMERCIAL BANK CHAMBERS
339 COLLINS STREET · MELBOURNE

NORMAN D. MACKAY
258 RIVERSDALE ROAD, MIDDLE CAMBERWELL
PHONE CANTERBURY 1860

especially addressed to enterprising young couples who no longer wished to live in houses. 'Houses' were rather common weatherboard affairs; they were old-fashioned, dark, close to the street and sometimes joined together, or semi-detached. If you had survived the Depression and had liberated yourself from a working-class suburb like Thornbury, you deserved a nice brick home with a thirty-three-foot setback, picture windows, a terrazzo porch, a bird bath, a 'nature strip' and a driveway with 'provision for motor-car accommodation'.

In old Thornbury there were few trees, and they were mostly 'natives' – shaggy old eucalypts and pittosporums. Often in the back yards of the narrow artisans' houses there survived a few battered peppercorns, dropping their sticky aromatic drupelets or brushing the tin roofs of fowl house and outdoor dunny with their feathered leaves. Sometimes there was a perished Goodyear tyre roped up to one of the old tree's stouter boughs to make a swing for the scabby-kneed ragamuffins of that distant age, long before Thornbury became, amazingly, an Equadorian and Laotian enclave.

On the Golf Links Estate, however, the eucalypt was banished. A few, as I have said, lingered along the railway line, or survived in small parks – ghettos for gums – but in the new gardens on the hill the vernacular, even the arboreal vernacular, was considered bad manners. The New Gentility demanded silver birches, liquid ambers, pin oaks, prunus plums and magnolias, and every back garden had its lemon tree, which thrived on the sandy soil. And everyone had a Japanese maple, although after Pearl Harbor most of these were patriotically poisoned, ringbarked and extirpated.

Because the Golf Links Estate was to be a model suburb, builders had to observe special covenants ensuring that they would not erect timber dwellings and corrugated-iron roofs or paling fences within thirty-six feet of the frontage. These measures were to keep our estate respectable, free of ramshackle outhouses and, above all, chicken coops. These were emblems of a working-class background from which the young couples in Finsbury Way, Maple Crescent, Marlborough Avenue and Christowel Street had at last emancipated themselves.

Our new house had a tradesman's entrance, the only one in the street, with a discreet sign which said NO HAWKERS OR CANVASSERS. Sometimes I kept watch on the other less protected houses in the hope of glimpsing one of these strange mendicants. The hawker I imagined festooned with black birds like a sinister Papageno. On our gatepost at the entrance to the driveway was a large brass plaque and the legend:

J. A. E. HUMPHRIES
MASTER BUILDER

which my mother regularly burnished with Brasso. In the opposite gatepost there was a cavity in the brickwork containing our letterbox. Cold and slightly damp, it was the popular abode of snails which left their silver signatures on our post.

In the thirties, when our street was created, it was experimentally paved with cement, not bitumen like all the other streets in Melbourne. It felt different even to a child, living on a white road, and I can remember the many horse-drawn vehicles that clopped up and down it through my childhood. There was the ragged 'Bottle-o', with his strange yodelled call which could be heard streets away, and a Chinese greengrocer. Then the baker, with his elaborately painted van, and the milkman, whom I never saw; though if I woke early I could always hear the sound of his draught-horse snorting outside the house, the chink of the bottles and the snap of the tradesman's hatch. There was a brightly decorated ice-cream cart too, drawn by a pony with a tinkling bell, which on a hot summer afternoon made the slowest progress of all up our street. In spite of the warning on the Tradesman's Entrance, we had a procession of tradesmen to the front door from whom my mother might buy something, depending on whether they wore an ex-serviceman's badge, or how few fingers they had. We had a Honey man, a Needle-and-Thread man, a Scissor man and a Rawleigh man, who carried a small Globite suitcase of Rawleigh's medicaments, like Ready Relief and Goanna Salve, which my mother always purchased, and never used.

Over our new back fence of wooden palings coyly camouflaged with a brushwood screen, was a dark alleyway paved with bluestone and smelling of a dank ferment. If you scrambled up the fence and looked beyond this lane, you could see the broken back fences and the old unpainted weatherboard houses in Bellett Street. Once on the fringe of Melbourne, these were now the houses my parents and their neighbours literally turned their backs on. They had flaking red tin corrugated roofs, collapsing back verandas, grimy windows and their rusted fly-wire kitchen doors were constantly being slammed open and shut by ragged kids and mongrel dogs. The lazy rhythm of the lawn-mower which chattered through every summer afternoon of my childhood was never heard in those derelict back yards with their coarse and piebald grass, and their clutter of improvised fowl houses, ramshackle sheds and lopsided dunnies overgrown with Morning Glory. There, at our back door, was another world; the world of the poor!

We stared at each other sometimes, the poor and I. Me, on the top rung of my cherry-red ladder propped against the brushwood, and they, across that sour narrow lane through the gaps in their disintegrating fence and a tangle of briars and rusted hoop-iron. We never spoke, just stared. They always seemed to have very healthy brown faces and bloody kneecaps. The boys wore knotted handkerchiefs giving them an insolent piratical appearance and, with their heads on one side, they gawked at me for a while before running off to scrabble once more in the dirt amongst the dogs and chooks. Once an unkempt urchin-girl gave me a sheepish smirk before grinding her nose with the back of a frayed knitted wrist and releasing a trapeze of lettuce-green mucus.

Family snapshots show me romping around in the back garden at Christowel Street in various exotic disguises. From an early age I had a 'dress-up box' and my parents' little black

Kodak captured me coyly posturing in the costume of red Indian, sailor, cowboy and Chinaman. My first memories are of the garden in these small black-and-white photographs. The poplar and tulip trees newly planted, the big hydrangeas merely cuttings, the beds of phlox, pansies and petunias only seedlings, and the new English lawn, a timid gramineous haze.

My father had installed an elaborate underground sprinkler system to maintain both front and back gardens in a state of perpetual verdure, even through the most scorching summer. It must have been one of the first of its kind in Melbourne and it did away with the need for an unruly – and slightly common – garden hose. On hot afternoons we simply adjusted a series of taps, and miraculously, from nowhere, there sprang bouquets of sparkling water ticketed with rainbows. Amongst these I loved to play, bare soles squeaking on the wet grass. There were no water restrictions then; no neighbours eager to report a frivolous waste to the authorities.

We had only one set of neighbours anyway, the Train sisters who had bought our old house. To the left of Number 36 was a vacant allotment full of blackberries and coarse grass. For years afterwards my father bitterly regretted his failure to purchase this land and build a tennis court. Instead it was snapped up in 1939 by a Mr and Mrs Tootell who, to our horror, built *another* two-storey house, irritatingly like our own, and covered with a disagreeable buff stucco, like dried sick. Although we remained on polite terms with these childless architectural plagiarists until their ultimate relocation to a nearby twilight home, we exchanged no more than the most perfunctory courtesies; nor once crossed each other's threshold. Moreover, if half-cups of sugar, cream of tartar, bicarbonate of soda or any urgently needed ingredient was to be borrowed, my mother preferred to ask the furthest neighbour than importune the stand-offish couple next door.

From my earliest recollection, my father's habitual nickname for me was 'Sunny Sam' because of my blithe disposition. I was blithe, of course, for I was the centre of attention, the focus of my parents' affections and those of my many aunts and uncles. There was no brother or sister to deflect the flow of adoration which streamed towards me. Yet.

At bedtime my mother would come into my room to hear my prayers, a litany of gibbered 'Godblesses' in which I tried to mention everyone I knew. I most enjoyed prayers when my parents were going out to the pictures or to a 'card night'. Then my mother would be wearing her silver fox, its sprung tortoise-shell jaw snapped shut on its own tail, and its sly glass eyes staring into mine. With my nose buried in that musky pelt, I gabbled my vespers in my mother's perfumed embrace. The longer I protracted my prayers the longer I could bask in Evening in Paris, Charmosan face powder and the faint vulpine odour of her wrap.

I cannot remember precisely when my sister, Barbara, was born. I can only recall a day when there was suddenly and unexpectedly another focus of attention in our house. It lay on my mother's bed, shawled and swaddled, a black hairy caterpillar. My sister's arrival, when I was nearly three years of age, caused me no great concern at the time. I must have adjusted quite quickly and comfortably to this new presence, which failed seriously to challenge my position. But what was terribly worrying, inexplicable and grossly unjust was that, seven long months later, she was *still there*.

Licking the Beaters

MRS FLINT WAS my very first teacher. I have thought of changing her name in case some litigious descendant recognizes his venerated great-grandmother. But I can find no better name for her than her real name; grey quartzy sharp-edged hard. She ran a small kindergarten in her own grey pebble-dashed Californian bungalow down the hill from our place, and her two best rooms, the lounge and dining-room, to the right of her dark hallway, had been turned into a classroom for local tots. Edna, my first and favourite nanny, would escort me every morning down the steep pavement of Marlborough Avenue until after several twists and turns and carefully crossed, sparsely motored roads we arrived at Mrs Flint's front gate, already jammed with tricycles and mothers. Mrs Flint, wearing a large apron to keep the chalk off her faded if flocculous print dress, stood on the front step screwing her face into what she imagined to be a friendly and motherly grimace as she welcomed her little pupils and reassured departing parents. She was a good actress, this old battle-axe, for the mothers all went home fondly believing that their littlies were in wonderful hands in spite of the panic-stricken screams that most of Mrs Flint's pupils emitted as soon as they realized that they had been abandoned to her care. No sooner had the last mother gone and the drone of the last parental sedan faded up Orrong

Crescent than Mrs Flint's true mineral nature asserted itself. Once she was alone with her infant charges the ingratiating smile of the kindly old widow who adored children quickly faded and she would swing around from her blackboard and exhibit to the class a very different and frightening countenance on which rage, spite and ignorance jostled for supremacy.

It always took a long time for the crying to stop at Mrs Flint's kindergarten. One little girl called Jocelyn cried all the time and no amount of cajolery could stop her. In the end Mrs Flint put her out to graze in the back yard where, still bawling, she executed endless circuits on her trike. Inside we sat at miniature tables on stools enamelled cherry-red, one of the most popular hues of the late thirties. Because the classroom occupied Mrs Flint's lounge and dining room there were a few of her more substantial pieces of furniture – a Genoa-velvet couch, a bookcase and a Jacobean-style dining table with matching sideboard – shoved against the wall to make room for our small chairs and tables. Mrs Flint made it very clear that if anyone so much as laid a curious finger on one of her trumpery treacle-coloured sticks they would be put out in the yard with the eternally blubbering Jocelyn.

Mrs Flint was no great reader; except for the *Pears Cyclopaedia*, a couple of Ethel M. Dells and a Netta Muskett, her bookshelves accommodated faded family snaps and gewgaws which she called her 'ordiments'. However, every morning, seated in one of her deeper fawn-and-russet Genoa-velvet lounge chairs, with her dress hitched up so we could see her surgical stockings, she read us a story. Her favourite was Hansel and Gretel and even the least imaginative child found a painful empathy with this tale and its themes of parental abandonment and persecution by a cannibalistic crone.

There was a mid-morning break and we all filed out the back to our trikes and lugubriously circled Mrs Flint's prickly lawn. When I first saw Doré's engraving of convicts dismally revolving in their bleak exercise yard, I had only to imagine them with gaily painted Cyclops tricycles and scooters between their shanks to be grimly reminded of playtime at Mrs Flint's.

One day two bikes rammed into each other just in front of me, and my friend Graham Coles fell off his seat and crashed to the ground, breaking his arm. There was a big fuss and Mrs Flint's face nearly ruptured itself, feigning expressions of compassion and concern. Poor Graham's arm wasn't set properly and it had to be operated on again. The operation was not successful however and Graham's arm never grew. Years later when we were no longer the friends we had been in childhood I would see him as he passed our house on his way to Scotch College, one sleeve especially shortened to accommodate his bonsai appendage.

Apart from her fawning attentions to our parents and nannies there was one other human being to whom Mrs Flint displayed an amiable demeanour. Her daughter Nursie. Over half a century later I can only assume that Nursie was a nurse and that she had a real name like everyone else. But Mrs Flint always called her Nursie and something resembling warmth crept into her cold dry voice when she announced Nursie's presence in the house. For Nursie came and went, and we glimpsed her but occasionally sitting at the linoleum-covered kitchen table having a cup of tea, as we filed out to the back veranda for our play lunch. She had plucked eyebrows and a blonde perm which stuck out in a wedge at the back like Garbo's in the last scene in *Queen Christina*, or like the 'art deco' windswept hair-do of the woman whose white glass profile appeared on top of Atlantic petrol pumps; a crude commercial descendant of Lalique's opaline car mascots.

Between sips of Robur tea and puffs on her Du Maurier, Nursie flashed us a flirtatious smile while Mrs Flint fussed about refilling her cup and fetching her ginger nuts and Marie biscuits as though she were a nice person pleased to see her daughter.

Mrs Flint was keen to show parents that their children didn't just listen to stories or ride their bikes in endless circles in her back yard, so she decided we must all learn to count. I must have been the slowest to acquire this doubtful skill, for I remember being kept back while the other children played. Alone amongst the chipped cherry-red stools while Mrs Flint, terribly close so that I could smell her damp surgical stockings and her odour of stale talcum, forced me to count and count and recount until, weeping, I finally stumbled to one hundred. When would Edna come to rescue me? I wondered, peering up towards the lozenged leadlight windows through which grown-ups could be seen on their way to the front porch. But on that dreadful day each shrill chirrup of the doorbell announced someone else's mother, so that I was alone with my tormentor and all those numbers for what seemed like an eternity before deliverance finally came. Since those early struggles with innumeracy – as I believe it is now called – I have shunned every form of mathematics, leaving the counting to accountants and trusted managers, a task they have often performed with a surprising display of imagination.

I am not certain at this distance in time whether, having counted to a century, I graduated from Mrs Flint's Dame School, or whether my mother, detecting my misery, rescued me. I may well have complained, for I remember my mother saying, in her defence, what a 'refined' woman she thought Mrs Flint to be. Already at four years of age I had begun to apprehend that refinement was very often an extenuating virtue; one that excused and eclipsed almost every other unappetizing trait. But it was hard for me to share this adult view of Mrs Flint's refinement. No doubt the hag had once patronized my mother with a long word or an unfamiliar locution – a verbal crooking of the pinky – and had thereafter acquired her dubious epithet.

I preferred to be at home anyway; pampered by Edna and spoilt by Pat Bagott, our gardener and handyman. Pat was my father's favourite employee, and in Australian society of this period he was that great rarity, a childless Roman Catholic. This may have been the main reason why my mother spoke more generously of him and his little wife than she customarily did of their more fecund co-religionists.

As Mrs Flint's saving grace had been refinement, the Bagotts' was their cleanliness, not an attribute my mother's family associated with the adherents of Rome. She had made a point of seeing where the Bagotts lived; in a flat working-class suburb far from our undulant and lawned oasis. And she had pronounced the dwelling 'spotless', '*small, but spotless*'. One of her favourite saying was: 'You don't have to be well-off to be *particular*,' and she frequently attributed this apophthegm to her late mother, lending it a kind of genealogical veracity. Much as Reichsmarschall Hermann Goering sought to confer Aryan status on the Jewish tenor Richard Tauber, so my mother spared Pat Bagott her usual strictures against Catholicism. Without knowing it, the spotless and particular Bagotts were granted a unique amnesty; in my mother's eyes at least, they were honorary Protestants.

My father was a builder of sturdy suburban villas whose business reached its first peak of success in the years before the Second World War. He built houses in all the popular styles; mock Tudor, Spanish mission, neo-Georgian, Californian bungalow and moderne. In the very late thirties, if the client was especially rich and daring and my father able to procure enough glass building blocks and aubergine-coloured 'manganese' bricks, he would build them a 'jazz moderne' house with curved corner windows, a flat roof, a nautical-looking sun deck and *no front fence!* It is still odd to see in the suburban streets of Melbourne these once startling architectural hybrids; chubby colonial relations of their austere German cousins in Dessau and Stuttgart.

As a toddler, long before Mrs Flint's kindergarten, I would often be taken off by my father on his daily rounds visiting building sites. In that epoch before seat-belts I would roll around on the back seat of his streamlined putty-white Oldsmobile, or stand precariously on the hot grey leather clinging to a sturdy tassel. We would arrive at a 'job' and while my father strode fearlessly across the raw yellow joists remonstrating with brickies, or pored over flapping blueprints with the foreman, I would amuse myself with a drill and an offcut of Oregon pine. Sometimes we would arrive during the lunch break and I would see the men rolling their 'smokes' and making their billy tea over a mound of blazing wood chips on an improvised hearth. Just as the water in the blackened tin came to the boil Alec Gibson would open a sachet of wax paper his wife had packed with his doorstep sandwiches, and fling the contents of sugar and tea-leaves into the seething water.

I used to love watching the cement being mixed, as I enjoyed a similar process at home when my mother ran up a sponge. Alec warned me against getting too near the concrete mixer with a story about a nipper who had only the other day got too close to the grey-lipped maw of that relentlessly sloshing drum, and got sucked in. With a calloused finger he pointed to a small cement-encrusted boot lying amongst the builders' debris. 'That's all that's left of him, Bun,' said Alec lugubriously, 'so don't get too near that bloody doover, or *you'll* be a goner yesself!'

Alec and Pat Bagott and the other men called me 'Bun', which was probably short for currant bun; a reference to my innumerable moles. One day, at smoko, while we were sitting around on piles of bricks, eating our sandwiches and waiting for the billy to boil, Alec stood up, 'See you in a jiff, Bun, just going to strain the potatoes.' And he ambled off in the direction of the narrow galvanized iron dunny, screened with a hessian curtain. That night at dinner I rather pointedly left the table and on the way to the lavatory I called back to my mother, 'Just off to strain the potatoes.' When I returned there was an 'atmosphere' and I overheard my mother saying in the low voice children are not supposed to hear, '. . . and just make sure the more common element amongst your men watch what they say in front of little Barry, or who knows what he'll be coming out with next'.

The South Camberwell State School was a raw red-brick two-storey building in a small street off Toorak Road. It stood in an extensive asphalt wasteland, bounded by the palings of adjacent houses. This was the playground. Far away, against the back fence and partly shaded by a mutilated peppercorn, stood the only other structure in that desolate schoolground, the shelter shed. This was a sort of wooden box with one wall missing in which children presumably sheltered from the extremes of the Melbourne climate. At lunchtime on a wet day it would be packed with damp urchins delving into their sandwich tins and screaming at the tops of their voices. The noise in that confined space under a reboant tin roof was appalling, but worse was the overpowering and nauseating stench of gooey brown banana sandwiches and other nameless fillings. It did not surprise me in the least, when years later I learnt that the artless expression, 'Who opened their lunch?' was 1930s Australian slang for 'Who farted?' Only then did I realize that others before me had reeled back from the effluvia of cut lunches.

My parents sent me there for about a year until I was old enough to attend a nice Junior School. I had seen the brochure for Camberwell Grammar in my father's den. It had a sky-blue crinkly cover, embossed with the school's mitred crest, and glossy pages with pictures of some brand-new manganese brick buildings photographed from oblique angles to make them look more monumental than they actually were. It was supposed to be a 'very good school' and it charged *fees*. It catered for boys only, and mostly boys from 'comfortable homes'.

But Camberwell State, which I was forced to attend in the meantime, was free and co-ed. The hardships of life in Mrs Flint's back-yard jungle were nothing compared with the shrieking, thumping, yelling, wrestling maelstrom of human maggots into which I had been hurled.

Quickly I became aware of the gulf that divided me from them; the gulf that separated the Australian working class from the newly arisen 'affluent' middle class. It was wider, bleaker and more inimical than the grey tundra of the playground. In my effeminate little blue Aertex shirt which laced at the neck, pleated linen shorts, fawn cotton socks and leather sandals with side buckles, I felt uncomfortably alien to the other boys. Many of them wore scuffed and splitting sandshoes and a few even arrived at school barefoot. Our classroom was full of densely darned and threadbare maroon sweaters, patched britches, grubby lacunose stockings, scabby knees, bloody noses, verminous hair and ears erupting with bright pumpkin wax. The slatternly girls were no less alarming to a mollycoddled little Lord Fauntleroy from the Golf Links Estate.

The first form was presided over by a gorgon called Miss Jensen. She was the first woman I ever met with her hair in a bun, and she had a knack of making the chalk squeal on the blackboard. She favoured bottle-green 'twin sets' and fawn tweed skirts and she looked uncannily like Mrs Bun the Baker's wife in Happy Families. Miss Jensen and I took an instant dislike to one another.

We lived only about half a mile from the school, so I was mostly spared the ordeal of sandwiches in the shelter shed. Instead, punctually at 12.30, my father would collect me in the big putty-white Oldsmobile and drive me home for a peaceful lunch at my own little table on the lawn, or with my mother in the sun-room amongst her new cane furniture and shining brass knick-knacks. Everything in our house was new, or 'up-to-date' as they said in the thirties. We had a new Frigidaire with a light inside which went on when you opened the door. Every now and then it shuddered rather violently, as if from the cold. Most other people we knew still had ice-chests, and I rather envied them the iceman's visit as he shouldered those great glassy blocks up their sideways. On top of the fridge stood our new Sunbeam Mixmaster. This was a streamlined bullet-shaped appliance rather like a Buck Rogers spaceship, in the popular colour combination of cream and black. We had all the attachments and the brochure, but we only used it for juicing oranges and making cakes. When the twin whisks plunged into the bowl of glutinous sponge mixture my mother tweaked a mammiform control knob to the appropriate speed and the engine whirred into action, the whisks churning so that their blades seemed to vanish until they were just two chrome rods suspended in a fragrant yellow vortex. The kitchen filled with a miraculous aroma of heating machinery, compounded with vanilla essence. Once the Mixmaster was silenced and the whisks detached, I was allowed to lick off the ambrosial emulsion. Licking the beaters was one of the great privileges of an Australian childhood.

Our other modern appliance was a Radiola 'mantel model' wireless set. Chubbily ziggurattish in moulded brown Bakelite, it had a vertically fluted front panel rather like the fascia of a modernistic building. Behind the organ-pipe grille could be glimpsed a curtain of sheeny brown cretonne through which the music and the voices shrilly filtered. 'The Girl on the Pink Police Gazette' and 'My Merry Oldsmobile' were popular airs of the period, and it seemed strange and inexplicable that the radio could be singing so intimately about our family car.

> Come away with me Lucile
> In my merry Oldsmobile,
> Down the road of life we'll fly
> Automobubbling you and I.
> To the church we'll swiftly steal,
> Then our wedding bells will peal,
> You can go as far as you like with me,
> In my merry oldsmobile.

I had been given a toy submarine made in Japan, containing a clockwork mechanism which, when wound up, propelled it realistically along the bottom of the bath. One day I took it to school, a big mistake. It was one of those rare days when

I didn't go home for lunch, so, avoiding the hellish shelter shed, I took my sub and my sandwiches to a peaceful corner of the playground. Soon I found myself encircled by a group of rough kids who demanded my submarine. A tussle ensued in which my lunch got trodden into the asphalt and as the jeering circle of larrikins drew closer and more threatening I picked up a handful of gravel ready to defend myself. The bullies fled, but they did not disperse. They must have formed a delegation to Miss Jensen because immediately after recess she hauled me out in front of the class for 'throwing stones', a heinous violation of the school rules. I denied doing any such thing, but the testimony of the smirking yahoos carried more weight than my tearful protestations, and I was pushed in the corner for the rest of the afternoon with a sign on my back: I AM A BULLY. Much later, when the class had been dismissed for the afternoon, Miss Jensen told me that if I persisted in denying my guilt she would take me to see Mr Fraser, the headmaster, a ginger-haired functionary whom I had privately nicknamed 'Duckface'. I stuck to my guns, however, and only at the entrance to his study, and threatened with imminent expulsion, did I finally break down and recant, confessing to a crime I had never committed. Grudgingly, clemency supervened, and I was allowed to go home, my heart pounding with shame and rage. For some reason which remains obscure, I never told my parents of this incident — perhaps I feared that they might share Miss Jensen's view of the matter.

Since then I have entertained fantasies of vengeance. Supposing Miss Jensen had been, say, twenty-five at the time, she might now, in 1992, be a sprightly seventy-seven-year-old living with her daughter, sitting peacefully knitting in some honeysuckled garden bower, or quietly watching television in a Melbourne suburb. For my purposes it would be more convenient if she were installed in a sunset facility or oldsters' terminary. There I could visit her, explaining to the nursing staff that I was a concerned relation who required a few moments' privacy with the titubating inmate. I would need very little time to attach the small placard, concealed under my raincoat, to the back of old Miss Jensen's bobbing matinée jacket.

The Master Builder

MY NEW SISTER did little to spoil my excursions with my father. On the contrary, so that my mother could devote herself to this squealing, coconut-faced intruder, we spent more time together than before. Occasionally his business took him 'into town' and sometimes I would be left for what seemed like an eternity in the locked Oldsmobile while he rushed into banks and insurance companies. Once, I am told, he returned to find the car surrounded by a large crowd of amused pedestrians watching while I performed some sort of comic mime on the back seat. My father was sufficiently entertained by this incident to relate it proudly to my mother on our return home, but far from pleasing her it had, to his dismay, the reverse effect, and he was severely told off for 'neglecting' me.

When my father took me into town and he was not on business, we would often visit two places: the Museum and the Aquarium. At the Museum he would hurry me past the paintings and the stuffed bandicoots and the mineral samples, and stop only before one exhibit – Phar Lap, the famous racehorse, who stood, impeccably stuffed, in a large glass case. There was always a small group of awe-struck spectators around this mysterious effigy.

People would pop into the Museum in their lunch hour to pay their respects to the most celebrated dead horse in Australia;

some were eating sandwiches and sausage rolls as they stared up at those unblinking glass eyes. I had noticed on my visits to the city how often people seemed to eat in the street, many of them hurrying to catch a tram, but with their noses buried in paper bags, rather like the horses they so much admired. These ravenous pedestrians were not just office boys and shopgirls, but men in business suits wolfing hot pies as they stood at traffic lights, and with a spare handkerchief – this was before the age of Kleenex – unselfconsciously mopping up the sauce and scalding gravy as it trickled down their wrists. Even today, the lifts in office buildings throughout Australia reek with the smell of sandwiches, pies and pasties – and with the more exotic smells of Vietnamese and Laotian takeaway. Eating on the run may well be an atavistic custom inherited from convict days.

Our other pilgrimage was to the Aquarium, then a run-down and gloomy establishment. Few went there, however, to see the fish, just as the Museum and Art Gallery was rarely attended by the admirers of Tiepolo, Manet and Van Eyck. On a damp wall of the Aquarium hung an object which looked like an old rusty bucket, and beneath it, a larger crudely shaped carapace of dented iron; it was the bullet-grazed armour of Ned Kelly, the legendary bushranger, which he wore in his last confrontation with the police.

My father told me that Sarah Meadows, my grandmother, as a small child near Benalla, used to hide under the bed when the Kelly brothers rode by. I had the feeling that my father, and all the other people who shuffled in a silent semi-circle gazing up at this assembly of scrap iron, had rather a soft spot for Ned Kelly, though I no more understood why his armour hung amongst the fish than I comprehended why the mummy of a horse stood in an art gallery.

Apart from regular visits to building sites, he would also take me to the Camberwell market to buy oysters from a Greek 'reffo' (or refugee) whose shop window was perpetually veiled by a sheet of running water. This custom, now long obsolete, gave an illusion of freshness; as though the shoals of schnapper, whiting and flathead and the serried jars of oysters and mussels that lined the parsley-upholstered marble slab were submerged in their natural element.

Unlike the decorous little shops my mother frequented, the market was raucous and pungent, filled with the stench of fish, the scents of fruit and the acrid odour of chrysanthemums.

Sometimes we would have a haircut together and, because I was too small for the chair, Mr McGrath, the barber, would sit me on a box high up on one of his adjustable cast-iron thrones. A towelette would be tucked into my collar over which he draped a large sheet, so that, seen in the mirror, my head appeared to project from the summit of a white wigwam. From a glass-fronted cabinet bearing a crudely painted Red Cross, he then removed a greasy comb and a pair of scissors and proceeded to slice away at my hair, which fell in pale mousey stooks upon the folds of my voluminous tent. During this operation Mr McGrath conducted a loud and esoteric colloquy, mainly on sporting subjects, with the other customers, who lounged on a long pew against the wall, smoking and leafing through *Smith's Weekly* and copies of the Melbourne *Truth*.

As he snipped, Mr McGrath's white-coated tummy pressed so firmly against me that the labyrinthine progress of his lunch, and the peristaltic rills and tricklings which accompanied it, could be plainly heard.

Next came the clippers, which were kept, like all his other tools of trade, in the same magically sterile cabinet with the chipped Red Cross. I felt the steel mandible coldly gnashing at my nape and travelling ominously upwards. Finally the time came for a squirt of water and a swift anointment of cherry-coloured brilliantine. His last savage gesture with the comb never failed to decapitate a small mole on the crown of my head, which, undeterred, always managed to heal – and enlarge – by the next haircut. To this day, deep in my scalp, I can still feel that hidden wen; legacy of the McGrath method.

After the comb and the cowlick, the barber, with the flourish of a matador, would sweep the sheet off my shoulders and lift me down from my box on to the pilose linoleum.

Haircuts were frequently interrupted as Mr McGrath hurried to the counter at the front of his shop to serve customers with smoking materials. Behind the small lino-topped counter was a positive reredos of cigarette packets and smoking slogans: We too smoke Turf! Three Threes Always Please, Country Life, City Club, Temple Bar, Ardath, Craven A, Capstan and the less popular filtered lines designed to appeal to women and pansies, like Garrick and Du Maurier; names that aroused a distant resonance of sophistication even if you didn't know they were named after dead actors. Mr McGrath also did a roaring trade in Havelock Ready-rubbed Tobacco, Boomerang Cigarette Papers and, on very rare occasions, a packet of Spud, Australia's first mentholated cigarette. Spuds, as I later discovered, tasted of strong mothballs and had a habit of emitting small but startling detonations as the chunks of saltpetre embedded in the tobacco exploded.

Mr McGrath lived above and behind his shop. I was often in the chair or waiting when his two burly sons came home from school. With caps askew, grumous-kneed and with concertina socks, they stormed through the dark shop and disappeared into the mysterious sanctum beyond. Mr McGrath usually glanced up from his victim and eyed them reproachfully in the big mirror on which was painted a First World War infantry officer lighting a comrade's cigarette. Beneath was the puzzling rubric: 'The Greys is great!' On a dusty shelf below the mirror was a display of Spruco, a popular lolly-pink hair lotion of the period which came in chunky Cubist bottles distantly related to the sculptures of Henri Laurens and Archipenko.

I envied all shopkeepers. How exciting it must be to own a shop and live above it in a 'dwelling'. I had learned from my father that accommodation above shops was always called a dwelling whereas people who were slightly better off, i.e., didn't have to sell things, lived in houses and we, who were already, to employ my mother's favourite epithet, 'comfortable', lived in a home. Indeed, a *lovely home*.

My mother's unmarried sister, Elsie, was lucky enough to have a dwelling. She sold wool, cotton and knitting accoutrements in a dark but thriving little shop in Burke Road, Camberwell. While Aunty Elsie gossiped with her customers and doled out the bright skeins of wool to her zealous clientele of knitters, I, as her nephew, enjoyed the exciting privilege of going 'backstage'; parting the cretonne curtains behind the shop and entering the arcana of her premises where my grandfather sat in a small parlour smoking his pipe and listening to the wireless. Because Aunty Elsie was single, she had inherited the spinster's task of looking after her widowed father. His wife – my mother's mother – had died before I was born, but there was a large sepia photograph of her in my aunt's dwelling; a handsome, unsmiling and curiously implacable woman. It was impossible to tell, as with many women, whether she wore an expression of goodwill or disdain. As I write this, it occurs to me that nobody ever smiled in formal portraits of that period, since one could never sustain a smile for the length of the exposure. There must have been a moment in history when it became fashionable to grin unconvincingly at the camera. The age of the snap.

Papa Brown, as my mother's father was called, had a large repertoire of music-hall songs, my favourite being 'The Mystery of the Hansom Cab'.

Stop the cab, stop the cab, whoa, whoa, WHOA!
Somebody hold the horse's head and don't leave go,
But nevertheless they had to confess although they made a
    grab,
They never discovered the mystery of the hansom cab!

Many years later, I discovered Fergus Hume's mystery yarn of the same title. It was set in Melbourne in the 1880s and had a worldwide success, though I can find no record of the catchy but frustrating song it inspired.

At this time in my life, with little thought to the irreparable damage it might have upon my future character, my father willingly translated my every whim into reality. It may have been to compensate me for the unwelcome persistence of a sibling, but I was horribly spoiled. Soon his carpenters were busy in our back garden constructing my own shop, my name in flourishing cherry-red calligraphy, painted on the shingle by a professional sign-writer. I would spend every afternoon behind my counter selling miniature groceries to the neighbours' children for hard currency.

My father had always wanted to be a dentist and, whenever any of us had a loose tooth, would eagerly volunteer to separate us from it. He had only followed the building trade in obedience to the wishes of my grandfather who had set himself up in that business in the country town of Benalla soon after emigrating to Australia from Manchester in 1888. When my father was five my grandparents and their young family moved to Melbourne, but Great-Uncle Jack Meadows, my grandmother's brother, stayed in Benalla, and, with dubious credentials, opened a dental practice. In those far-off days when my mother still joked, my father's amateur extractions usually inspired a satirical comment: 'I don't know why your father never became a dentist like his Uncle Jack,' she would say, adding with a whimsical smile: 'not that *I* would ever have married a man who liked putting his fingers in other people's mouths!'

Respectability began to grow up around us like the garden, putting down its roots and stretching forth its tendrils and branches. We had special words for things which 'common people' didn't use. Indeed, my mother never employed the word 'common'; she preferred the epithet 'ordinary'. The children at South Camberwell State School, for example, were 'ordinary', but the boys at Camberwell Grammar School were, on the whole 'nice', from 'nice homes' (not houses) and their families were 'comfortable', that is to say, they had enough of the wherewithal. 'They' only had a back yard but we had a back garden. They had a wash house, we had a laundry. They pulled the chain, we flushed the toilet. They had 'blood' noses, we had nosebleeds. They had buck teeth, but my teeth were slightly prominent.

As soon as my father recognized that we had a dental problem in the family, I was whisked into town to see a specialist. This dentist occupied rooms in the T&G Building, one of Melbourne's first skyscrapers, and to reach him we had to ascend by lift to the giddy height of twelve floors. However this dentist did not merely occupy an architectural eminence, he had attained such distinction that he was no longer Dr Morris but *Mr* Morris, an elevation in rank which mystifies me as much now as it did then. Mr Morris looked at my rabbit-like incisors and recommended a long and costly treatment. But my father already had other ideas. Whatever these fancy Collins Street specialists might suggest, a second opinion must be sought. And the man to pronounce that opinion? No one more qualified – though his surgery was 120 miles away – than Uncle Jack.

At Spencer Street Railway Station, armed with tickets and, if not books, Reading Matter, we set off on the long train journey to my father's birthplace, the township of Benalla. The war had begun and the train was full of our men in uniform, smoking, shouting and endlessly filing up and down the swaying corridors. My father in his civvies looked slightly out of place and nervous amongst all that khaki. He had bought me a copy of a cheaply produced magazine called *Humour*, containing cartoons and a great number of short jokes like the ones found in Christmas crackers. Though I did not get the point of a single joke, I ploughed doggedly through its dully printed pages. I noticed when my father glanced at the same periodical that he smirked a couple of times and even laughed, so I realized that what was incomprehensible to me could be funny to adults. And I marvelled that an entire magazine could be devoted to making people laugh.

We were travelling at night and sometimes the train stopped

inexplicably for long intervals before rumbling off again on its endless journey. There were uncomfortable visits to the lavatory when we lurched down dim corridors through a gauntlet of somnambulistic soldiers until at last we reached the mephitic cubicle. Locked therein and struggling to keep my balance without crashing against a contagious surface, I watched my father fastidiously drape the wooden horseshoe with swathes of toilet paper.

Uncle Jack, dapper and rubicund, was waiting for us in the early hours as we alighted, ashen-faced, at Benalla Station. During the short drive in his old Ford through the wide dusty streets of the township, my father excitedly pointed out surviving landmarks of his boyhood: the iron-lace-verandaed Coffee Palace his grandmother had established and where my grandmother had worked as a girl, his old school and Great-Uncle Frank's tinsmith's shop. From the bridge I saw some ragamuffins diving into the Broken River. At last we arrived at Uncle Jack's abode, a rambling Victorian bungalow, shaded by big gnarled peppercorns, where an attractive woman with a long sallow face called Mrs Black ran us a deep Rexona-scented tub and prepared a large country breakfast of bacon and eggs. There was no sign of Aunty Gertie, who I gathered lived more or less permanently in Melbourne, and Mrs Black seemed somehow, even to childish eyes, a little more than a house-keeper.

Uncle Jack, donning a starched white double-breasted overall, ominously flecked with rust-coloured stains, vanished into his surgery only to reappear half-way through the toast and marmalade. 'Got the beggar out just before it burst!' he announced proudly, waving a pair of forceps under my nose. In the pincer-grip we saw an enormous nicotine-streaked molar and on its snaggled root the plump yellow sac of pus. 'Keep it as a souvenir, lad!' said Uncle Jack, dropping it with a clink on to the plate beside my toast. Soon after I was in the dentist's chair gagging horribly while my great-uncle's Solvoled[1] fingers plunged around inside my mouth. As my father listened

[1] Solvol: an abrasive soap.

devoutly, he explained his revolutionary new corrective method. Three days later I was orally fitted with this contraption. It was a plate, similar to my father's denture, which supported a metal band extending in a semi-circle under the top lip. Between this band and the front of my teeth were wedged several thin layers of rubber which pressed painfully against the rebellious incisors. The advantage of this method, apparently, was that it forced the teeth back twice as fast as traditional braces and the effeminate methods of the city. I had only to travel up to Benalla once a month for a whole year so that Uncle Jack could remove the plate and add another layer or two of rubber.

Apart from the dull ache which I constantly experienced, the taste of blood, and the difficulty I had in talking with this false red palate in my mouth, there was another inconvenience which I perceived only after drinking an ice-cream soda. Between my monthly visits I had to live with the nauseating taste and smell of rancid food trapped under Uncle Jack's inextricable device.

The damage from this amateur dentistry has caused problems that persist to this day and a very large chunk of my life has been spent, drugged and terrified, staring at the ceilings of dental surgeries throughout the world, or hunched over a spit-bowl drooling the blood-freaked detritus of yet another reamed root canal or shattered crown.

On winter nights we would always burn Mallee roots, which the woodman regularly heaped on the 'nature strip' outside our front gate. Some of them were huge, knotted and noduled, and rather than leave them burning all night in the grate, my father would, at bedtime, lift the incandescent root on a shovel and, trailing sparks, run outside and deposit it with a loud hiss in the gulley trap. In late summer if there was a hot north wind we might get 'red rain', big terracotta teardrops on all the picture windows and the car windscreens, which took hours to remove the next day with a chamois. The rain, we were told, was from the Mallee, a horrible far-away place where the firewood came from. It never occurred to me, or to many others then, that the more these roots were ripped from the soil to make our homes cosy, the more red rain would freckle our nice clean windows. It was a tasteless reminder of a place where Aborigines had once lived, where explorers had died, and where none of us need ever set foot.

Very few people we knew had gas fires, which my mother regarded as dangerous, and even slightly common. However, both my Aunty Elsie's 'dwelling', my grandparents' house and Uncle Jack's surgery smelt faintly of coal gas, an olfactory novelty to one accustomed as I to an odourless electrical home. When I stayed with my grandparents, Sarah, my father's mother, could always be found in her gas-scented kitchen cooking and making tea on her old 'Early Kooka', which, with its avian pun – an enamelled kookaburra on the oven door – was so much more interesting than mother's scentless Moffat electrical stove. At Nanna's there would always be the scratch of a match, a tweaked tap, a little *phut*, and then, miraculously, a blue lotus of fire. She was a tireless baker of cakes and pavlovas, and after a visit to my grandparents no one left without at least one passionfruit sponge and a tray of kisses, butterfly cakes and yo-yos. Whenever I stayed with them my sweet, kind grandmother spoiled me terribly, and fed me almost exclusively on those delicious confections she had learned to bake in her country girlhood, when she and her mother ran the Benalla Coffee Palace.

I had been told that my father's father was as stern as his wife was saintly, and when I bathed or cleaned my teeth in their small, Rexona-green bathroom, I saw, suspended beside the towel rail, his leather razor strop. My father had told me how he and his brothers had lived in fear of this shaving accoutrement, yet I found it hard to see my grandfather as a punitive figure. To me he was always affectionate; too affectionate in my mother's view.

'Eric,' she would say to my father, 'does Papa have to give

the children such wet kisses? I'm glad to say he doesn't do it to me any more.' And it was true, the tall Mancunian builder preserved a polite distance from his daughter-in-law.

My father's sister, Aunty Irene, lived with my grandparents before her marriage, and it was she who took me to my first motion picture. It was *The Wizard of Oz* and, apart from the Columbine caramels and the enchanting music of Harold Arlen, I recall few images from this film except that of Margaret Hamilton as the witch bicycling across a stormy sky. 'Could all women turn into witches?' I wondered on the many sleepless nights that followed my first movie matinée. *Snow White* was my next cinematic experience and for a long time thereafter, as my mother stooped tenderly over my bed to kiss me good-night, she may have been puzzled to see me looking up in terrified anticipation of a witch-like transmogrification.

The poisoned apple that Snow White nibbled greatly intrigued me and I was determined to make one myself and offer it to my sister's friend, Valerie, in the hope that it might immobilize her for many years to come. Carefully shaping some scraps of pastry left over from one of my mother's apple pies, I impregnated it with fly-spray, coloured it as realistically as possible with cochineal, and graciously presented it to my sister's pretty little playmate. Alas, I could only force her to take one bite before the odour of insecticide persuaded her that this was no ordinary Red Delicious, one of which a day would keep the doctor away. She must have shown my gift to her parents, for I was sternly rebuked and forbidden thereafter to offer artificial fruit to the neighbours' children. In vain I tried to explain that my poisoned apple was merely a gallant attempt on my part to hasten Valerie's encounter with Prince Charming.

Weatherboard Swastikas

SOME YEARS AGO I found myself in Paris in August. As might be expected at that time of the year, the city had an air of abandonment and the narrow streets on the Left Bank were almost deserted. Today, irrespective of season, one would find Japanese tourists milling about obediently photographing each other, but on this afternoon I noticed only one elderly couple peering into the window of an antiquarian shop that was clearly *fermé*. I instantly recognized, even at a distance of one hundred yards, two fellow Australians. Perhaps it was the predominant fawn and bistre of the man's attire, or the manner in which the woman's short-sleeved Orlon print frock exposed the peculiar flaccidity of her pale freckled triceps – known in our homeland as 'bye-byes', since it is in the valedictory gesture that they most noticeably wobble.

To confirm my surmise, I sidled up behind them to eavesdrop, only to discover that I knew them. Quite well. They were in the Old Wares business in Melbourne, in a modest way. I had sometimes visited their dim little shop full of over-priced gewgaws invariably labelled 'art deco' or 'art nouvé'. However, pleased with this chance encounter, we retired to a café for a celebratory drink, and after an inevitable discussion about the mind-numbing rudeness of the Parisians, Herb and Doris Prentiss confided that they had yet to arrange accommodation for the night. With a locution that only a Melbourne-born person of his generation would utter, Herb leant across the table and inquired plaintively: 'D'you happen to know a nice *guest house* in this particular suburb?'

Throughout my childhood the world consisted of homes, houses and Guest Houses. Hotels were taboo. They were 'licensed premises'; insalubrious buildings on street corners, sometimes with a gimcrack 'art deco' fascia, which I noticed from the car window when we lingered at the lights. Shabbily dressed men shuffled in and out of their doors through which I would glimpse dejected figures quaffing glasses of yellow beer. Often, drunks swayed on the kerbside outside them, a bottle of Foster's Lager in one hand and in the other a scarlet lobster swaddled in a few pages of the *Sporting Globe*.

Unlike these hotels, guest houses were nice, respectable affairs, mostly built of weatherboard, and nestled in some of Australia's more picturesque nooks and crannies.

The Warburton Chalet was one of the most famous guest houses in the environs of Melbourne. Probably built in the twenties, it was a rambling white weatherboard building in the pretty riverside hamlet of Warburton. Nearby, on the edge of the large moss-scented, bellbird-haunted forest, stood a famous sanatorium and surprisingly, in that sylvan retreat, a large modernistic factory in cream brick where Seventh Day Adventists manufactured 'Sanitarium Health Foods' (*sic*). There was little else in Warburton besides the gently purling waters of the Upper Yarra, the whispering tree ferns, and the giant eucalypts casting their shadows over the factory, the hospital and the guest house. With its peaceful atmosphere and babbling river sounds, it was the closest thing you could get in Australia to a European spa, and in 1937 the Warburton Chalet had already become a kind of half-way house for refugees from Hitler.

My mother and I stayed there just before my sister was born, and my most vivid memory is of one particular afternoon in the large chintzy sitting-room of the Chalet, where my mother sat ominously knitting something white and pink and monkey-sized. In the big 'crazy'-stone fireplace, flames fluttered around the hairy logs which drooled their amber sap. Outside the picture window the autumn sunshine slanted through a blue haze of wood-smoke. It was the afternoon tea hour, and at our end of the lounge cups clinked, and cakes and scones were silently devoured. But something strange and exotic was happening at the far end of the room. Who were those people? They seemed to huddle together in their odd clothes and spoke a little too loudly in a foreign language. There was much curious murmuring down our end amongst my mother's friends, until at last someone leant across the couch and, with her cake-crumbed lips close to my mother's ear, said in a whisper audible from one end of the room to the other, 'Jews!'

The sibilance almost riffled the chintz curtains. We all sat and stared; beyond the steaming crockery and the Devonshire teas, across the expanse of shining parquet, the rugs, the fringed standard lamps, subsiding armchairs and the toffee-coloured tables loaded with *Women's Weeklys, Home Beautifuls, Walkabouts* and *Table Talks*. Uneasily, awkwardly settling into chairs or sofas, at their own considerably draughtier end of the lounge the Jews stared back. My mother's informant, this time with a small stalactite of strawberry jam depending from her forelip, once more lurched lobeward. 'See their rings!' she hissed. '*They carry all their money on their fingers.*'

It was thirty-three years later when I returned to Warburton which, unlike so many idyllic spots outside Melbourne, had been spared the desecrations of progress. The old Chalet was a little modified by fire and fashion, and much much smaller than I had remembered it, but still there. I climbed the nearby hill and looked down on the rusting corrugated-tin rooftops of the sprawling Guest House. Its extended accommodations projected from the central structure in four crooked wings. The old building, seen in aerial perspective, had exactly the same configuration as . . . a weatherboard swastika.

Many Guest Houses still bore the name of the old homesteads, before their conversion and extension for paying holiday-

Old house at Mornington, oils, 1952 (note Norfolk Island pine)

makers. Dava Lodge at Mount Martha, and Ranelagh at Mount Eliza were two favourite seaside resorts on the Mornington Peninsula, where we often stayed in the old days before Melbourne's middle classes erected their own beach houses. Like the Chalet, they were rambling, asymmetrical structures spreading amoebically, like the private hospitals of the seventies, until their wooden tentacles annexed the old gardens, the apple orchards, the croquet lawns, the tennis courts and neighbouring allotments. After each successful season of maximum occupancy by the families from Malvern, Camberwell and Kew, another century-old Norfolk pine would be felled, another Victorian wistaria arbour deracinated, to make way for yet another wing of chilly, linoleum-floored bedrooms.

Before each meal, and all in black, with white starched apron, cap and cuffs, a maid hurried down the labyrinthine corridors sounding the dinner gong or strumming an inane tunelet on a miniature marimba, and in her wake streamed the famished families. Piebald with sunburn, sand chafing in each secret crevice, they hurtled towards the dining-room. This was located in the original part of the house, and invariably smelled of old gravy mingled with the more inviting effluvium of vanilla puddings. The walls were cheaply panelled in brown varnished wood in a debased Arts and Crafts style popular just before and after the Great War. Where the panelling stopped about eight feet up the wall, a 'curio ledge' supported a frieze of dusty knick-knacks, chipped Toby jugs and crockery with an Olde English theme. The tables, at which the elderly waitresses sullenly loitered, were all draped with white starched damask minutely foxed with old cigarette burns, and in the centre of each table on a small nickel-plated stand, beside a cut-glass vase of poppies and a fly-specked cruet, stood the day's menu card, crookedly typed on an ancient Underwood. Breakfast was always stewed fruit and rolled oats, and although we had porridge at home in the winter months – John Bull Oats, Sargeant Dan, Uncle Toby's and more refined derivatives like Creamota and Eazy-Meal, the generic 'rolled oats' was exclusively a guest-house offering, though it tasted exactly the same as ordinary porridge. With our eggs and bacon, toast would arrive; discreetly singed white triangles wedged in a tarnished chromium toast rack. As holidays progressed, there was a good deal of friendly nodding and smiling from one table to the next, and genteel 'G'mornings' as we walked the gauntlet of penguin-coloured waitresses to our table by the window.

Dinner was served from six o'clock until the late hour of eight, and in the corridors of Dava Lodge percussion instruments announced this repast twice; the first gong being a plangent reminder to bathe and dress. However, no sooner had the second xylophonic reverberation sounded at six sharp than the ravenous families, in their evening finery of skirts, cardigans and sports coats, once more stormed towards the dining-room. Soaped and scented with Cashmere Bouquet, Potter & Moore, Rexona, Cuticura, Pears, Palmolive and Faulding's Old English Lavender, the women's bouquet of aromas was modified by a medicated whiff of Lifebuoy from the menfolk.

Dinner consisted of soup, a joint, veg and pudding. The soup was usually as white as its main constituent (flour), meagrely flavoured with celery or tinned asparagus, although sometimes in the winter there might be a watery pea soup with 'sippets'. The joint was either mutton or pork, dished up with pumpkin, parsnips and an ice-cream scoop of mashed potato, submerged in coagulating umber gravy. All this was an irksome preliminary to the pudding, which was invariably steamed, and served in little glutinous igloos on a yellow lake of custard. There was Cabinet, Queen, Albert and Victoria pudding, and if these confections ever had a distinct character in the recipe books of the late nineteenth century, their identities had become blurred or lost on the way to Dava Lodge. Our desserts appeared to have been baptized quite arbitrarily; so that, for example, a 'Victoria' sponge might be seamed with delicious whorls of scalding apricot jam, and at other times studded with currants and sultanas. An 'Albert' pudding could resemble a lemon meringue pie or a treacle dumpling – or a synthesis of both – depending on a whim of the kitchen. They were all delectably viscous, adhering tenaciously to the roof of the mouth, and second helpings were generously proffered. Having spied on neighbouring tables where some impatient diners were already tucking into their sweets, I habitually ordered my second helping of dessert when I was half-way through the soup.

The point of being at Dava Lodge and Ranelagh was, of course, the beach, though in both cases it was a steep scramble through tea-tree and down a cliff path before we finally reached the sand. My father carried large tartan rugs and a beach umbrella and then there were the buckets, spades, baskets of sandwiches, thermos flasks, and presumably my infant sister. As I write this I suddenly see the portable wicker bassinet sitting in a shady corner of our beach rug, shrouded with white net on which the fat grey March flies settled like brooches. Deep beneath the milky drapery, my sister's small nut-coloured face seemed permanently puckered on the verge of tears.

We rarely holidayed without a few relations in tow, often one or two of my mother's sisters, who always doted upon me and thoughtfully paid little overt attention to the gnome-like interloper under the net. There was much uncomfortable wriggling and writhing under towels as we modestly changed into our swimming costumes on the beach. My own swimming 'togs' were made of some abrasive maroon jersey with a short 'skirt' to disguise impolite sexual contours.

We all wore sun hats with green fly veils and my mother insisted on lavishly anointing my freckle-prone beak with zinc cream. Then there were cooling applications of almond-scented sunburn emulsions before I was finally ready to paddle in the waves of Port Phillip Bay, which lapped apologetically a few feet from the fringe of our rug. At the water's edge, the waves stirred the bright lettuce-coloured weed, whilst further up the beach before the row of weatherboard bathing cabins the line of weed was dry, brown and fibrous and the sand sometimes so hot it was an agonizing dance to the water's edge.

The little crescent of beach, with its bright umbrellas and rugs like tartan islands, would be unrecognizable to a modern sunbather. There were no transistor radios, no thin crackle of pop or thumping rock 'n' roll to disturb those Kwik-Tan-scented afternoons. Strangest of all, amongst the stirring shells, cuttle fish and bleached driftwood at the tide's edge, there were no hideously writhing tatters of plastic or imperishable chunks of leprous styrofoam.

At night in the lamplit lounge, the adults sat in cracked leather chairs playing Solo or Five Hundred, reading their Ethel M. Dells, Dorothy Sayers and Angela Thirkells. We used to gather there to listen to the News, which in the early 1940s was synonymous with the War. There was much talk over the wireless of strange European countries being overrun by the Germans. It was odd to think that in the pencil case with the sliding lid which my Uncle Dick had given me, there were those beautiful hexagonally-bevelled blue and black Wolf-Staedtler HB pencils with a tiny gilded legend: *Made in Germany*. My father had boxes of them, bought before the war, which he used for drawing up his plans. He also had a drawer in his desk filled with rainbow-coloured aquarelles made in that other strange country they kept talking about on the wireless – Czechoslovakia.

In the Dava lounge there was one man who had been to some of these places before the war. Quiet and balding, he wore glasses so thick his eyes seemed to be looking at you through the bottom of a milk bottle. He smoked a pipe and was always reading a book called *Berlin Hotel* by Vicki Baum. Mr Hickman listened more intently to the news broadcasts than anyone else and every now and then explained something intricately geographical to the other less travelled guests. But politely and not like a know-all. Nevertheless, my mother, behind his back, often so described him. 'Know-all, know-nothing,' she would sagely mutter.

'Hicky', as the children called him, was in his quiet way the most popular person at the guest house. Perhaps a lonely schoolmaster, or a man of private means, nobody was quite sure. One night, he showed us some of his travel snaps including some pictures taken in Canada of a river choked with bits of wood. 'What do you make of that?' he asked me through his tobacco haze. Nobody else seemed to know. 'A beaver dam?' I said. By coincidence, I had been reading a book about beavers the day before. Hicky took another suck on his pipe and looked up at my father. 'You've got a very clever boy there, Eric,' he said, 'a very clever boy indeed.'

We were a bit upset when Hicky left suddenly without saying goodbye to anyone. None of the other adults at Dava Lodge had time to read us stories as Hicky did, or give us a push on the swings at dusk, even if his avuncular hand did sometimes accidentally slide a few inches too far up our shorts. They were all far too busy playing cards and ping-pong, though when Hicky left so inexplicably, I heard one of the men say: 'Good riddance!'

Years later, I thought I recognized Hicky, stooped and myopic, serving in a Melbourne bookshop. How many guest houses had he been expelled from since Dava? I wondered. How many boys' schools had he mysteriously quitted mid-term? Somehow I could not, under the circumstances and after such a lapse of time, bowl up out of the blue and introduce myself: the very clever boy from Dava Lodge who had beavered up on beavers.

Wilf

U NCLE WILF WAS my favourite uncle. He was married to
Aunty Violet, my mother's oldest sister, who had once
been a nurse and had tended victims of the Spanish influenza
just after the First World War. Wilf had served in the Australian
infantry in France and their house contained a number of
souvenirs of those terrible battles. On their Arts and Crafts
mantelpiece stood two gleaming brass shell-cases and, high up
in a cupboard, Uncle Wilf kept a German helmet with a spike
on it. Sometimes he showed us a sepia photograph taken from
the pocket of a dead German soldier, perhaps the same soldier
who no longer required the helmet. The picture showed a
husband and wife, she seated with a certain wistful beauty, he
in uniform standing stiffly at her side. In the background was
the blurred hint of a bourgeois parlour – no doubt a tricked-up
corner of the photographer's studio. They both gazed ap-
prehensively at the lens as though it were about to go off like a
rifle, but that would come a month or two later.

Uncle Wilf was the only person I knew who had served in
the First World War, though casualties of that legendary
catastrophe were often pointed out to me; legless lift drivers,
blind newspaper sellers, and the door-to-door salesman from
whom my mother bought our honey who always wore one stiff
black glove.

Wilf always marched on 25 April, that most important day in the Australian calendar, Anzac Day, when a great cavalcade of Diggers walked in solemn procession to the Shrine of Remembrance. Every year we, and thousands of others, would line the roadside and cheer the old soldiers, many in uniform and others in their Sunday best blazing with medals, as the military bands played 'Tipperary', 'Pack Up Your Troubles' and 'Roses of Picardy'. At the end of that long procession came the wheelchairs and the stretchers and nurses leading the gassed and the blind.

Wilf and Vi had one son, who was a spastic, and my aunt and uncle were devoted to his welfare. John loved music and had a large collection of records which he would play loudly at family tea parties. No one listened to his carefully planned recitals, they only talked louder, though occasionally someone would glance over at him as he sat by the gramophone nodding his head to the music, his poor legs in chromium callipers.

'There's no doubt about John,' they would cluck. *'He loves his music.'*

Uncle Wilf worked for Imperial Chemical Industries and my father often took me to his office in the city where I would be given small sample jars of dye manufactured by the company. At home I experimented with these wonderful pigments: purple, fuchsia and gamboge, dropping a pinch or two into a full beaker, and watching the bright streamers of colour fall through the water and spread like tendrils, or making exotically hued potions in the new laboratory which my father had built for me at the back of the garage.

Wilf and my father adored each other, and the three of us would regularly lunch at the Wool Exchange Hotel near Uncle Wilf's office. It was my first experience of a restaurant, and there was a pretty receptionist who always greeted the brothers-in-law flirtatiously and made a fuss over me as she led us between the rowdy lunchers to our special table. There were stiff, starched napkins, a cruet holding the indispensable bottle of Holbrook's Worcestershire sauce and, in the centre of the table, an oxidized nickel trumpet from which a few crumpled poppies bloomed on their hairy stems. The vegetable fritter with hot tomato sauce was one of the Wool Exchange's gastronomic specialities, as well as the more conservative T-bone steak and crumbed whiting.

It must have been during one of these lunches that the two men planned to build a weekend shack together at Healesville, a beauty spot about forty miles from town. Accordingly they bought thirty acres of virgin bush about a mile from the township, up a dusty track. There, in a small clearing with a blue view of Mount Riddell and the lavender-coloured foothills of the Great Divide, my father, assisted by Pat and Alec, built a house, known thereafter as 'the shack'. It was a rudimentary structure of weatherboard, asbestos sheeting and corrugated iron and there were none of the cosy amenities of Camberwell. No water, electricity or sewerage, so we had a galvanized-iron tank at the side of the house, spirit lamps and an outdoor dunny, built of split logs over a very deep hole. This was furnished with little more than a huge desiccated tarantula on the ceiling and, for the hygienic convenience of visitors, a mutilated Melbourne telephone book suspended by a string from a bent nail. This popular cubicle buzzed perpetually with the sound of voracious flies and reeked of some ammoniac pink powder which Papa Brown regularly ladled into the abyss.

Soon our shack in the bush became a regular weekend haven for all the relations. There were beds everywhere, and at night on my lumpy mattress in my little 'sleep-out', I could hear the adults in the living-room playing Whist and Mah-jong late into the night, smell Uncle Wilf's sweet Wayside Mixture and hear my father pumping up the kerosene lamps until the guttering mantles glowed white again. In the forties we acquired a battery-powered wireless set, and on Sunday evenings everyone listened to the Lux Radio Theatre. There was great excitement if the hour-long melodrama happened to star Thelma Scott, my mother's sole theatrical acquaintance, or Thelma's talented young friend, Coral Browne.

When war came I would lie awake in bed watching the lamplight ebb and flow through the crack under my door and hear those urgent, ominous news reports of far-away catastrophes. The voice of Winston Churchill crackled over the BBC World Service as my family sat gravely listening to the war in the silent Australian bush 13,000 miles from Westminster. There was so much distortion and explosive static on those shortwave broadcasts that I pictured Churchill himself standing at the very heart of the battlefield, perpetually under fire and growling his famous rhetoric through a lethal fusillade.

One night in about 1943 I heard them playing 'Sweet Spirit', a psychic parlour game in which I was never allowed to participate. An alphabetical circle was arranged on the table top and everyone put their finger on an upturned glass in the middle. They all took it in turns to ask the spirit questions, and there were always crescendos of laughter followed by, 'Shhh, you'll wake the children.' My father was regularly reproached for cheating. One night I heard a voice, I think it was Aunty Dorothy's, ask the spirit when Cliff Jones, Phyllis's brother, was coming home on leave, and there was a strange silence in the room as the glass, carrying everyone's fingers with it, darted from N to E to V to E to R. They never played that game again.

In the long summer vacation my father built a log fort for me and a red bark tree-house high up in a shaggy old eucalypt. My tree-house even had an old-fashioned battery-operated telephone connected to the main house, so that I could order cakes and sandwiches without ever having to leave my eyrie. Here I played for hours in my new Gene Autry cowboy suit with its fringed white kid chaps and my Gene Autry ivory-handled cap gun. Watching out for snakes, my young sister and

I would explore the bush together, while back at the house cousin John played his portable gramophone, so that wherever we were we could hear from afar those wisps of tinny music like the horns of elfland faintly blowing. It was strange sitting on a mossy log in the Australian bush and listening to Fraser Simpson's incomparable Vocal Gems from *Toad of Toad Hall* or Richard Tauber's 'Dein ist mein ganzes Herz'. Especially strange, really, to hear the illicit language of the Enemy thrillingly wafted through the saplings and the sword grass and the yellow flowering acacias and the mauve bush orchids.

The hour drive to Healesville seemed, of course, interminable to a child. Camberwell was then on the outskirts of the metropolitan area and once past Box Hill we were in open country. Near Lilydale, my father always pointed out the long and impeccably shaved hedge of green privet that concealed from the road the vast estate of Dame Nellie Melba, and Coombe Cottage, the Australian diva's legendary home. Melba and Donald Bradman were the only famous Australians I had ever heard of, and it seemed an amazing coincidence that Melba's name should so closely resemble the city of her birth.

Half-way to the shack we crossed a billabong of the Yarra River on a low pontoon bridge, and there on a kind of island almost camouflaged amongst the tangled blackberries and the sloughed bark of the huge river gums was a small swagman's encampment; a few wretched humpies built from rusty kerosene tins and hessian bags. As our Oldsmobile rolled past, a starved yellow mongrel always started up and barked until we were out of sight. My father had only once pointed to this little camp, but thereafter our noses were pressed to the car windows whenever we approached the river bank in the hope that we might glimpse one of these legendary vagabonds boiling his billy, or stuffing a jumbuck in his tucker bag like the hero of that incomprehensible song 'Waltzing Matilda'.

Half a mile from the shack on the other side of the Don Road lived a real swagman called Smithy. Smithy dwelt in an improvised hovel of galvanized iron and sacking where chooks and dogs scrabbled in the dust. He had a wife somewhere in that kennel too, who was supposed to be, according to Uncle Wilf, 'as black as your hat'. Smithy was a lanky taciturn figure with a pointed Adam's apple, a grey Kitchener moustache and an old digger's hat. He still wore the threadbare remnant of a khaki uniform and after Uncle Wilf befriended him he used to chop wood for us, and do odd jobs. Sometimes I would sit with the men at smoko and hear Smithy tell some of his old soldier's yarns. He had a great and touching nobility, like a peasant in a story by Turgenev. In September, before the morning mist cleared and the magpies were gargling in the tall saplings, Smithy would show us the paddocks where we could find the best and biggest mushrooms. They were the ones with the blue-pink gills underneath: the colour of milky cocoa.

If we were at Healesville at Christmas time, and the heat became unbearable, we would set off with rugs and picnic baskets to Badgers Creek. There, where no badger had ever set foot, amongst the pungent mosses, and sheltered by tall tree ferns, we splashed about in a dark green pool. Then we would perch on the bank watching the icy water purl and gurgle over rocks like emus' eggs, and sip raspberry vinegar from Bakelite cups, while Peter Dawson sang 'The Floral Dance' on John's wind-up phonograph.

There was a terrible week in 1939 when the great bushfires which raged throughout Victoria nearly got the shack. Wilf and my father drove back and forth from Healesville all day, through the smoke and under a dark copper sky, bringing linen and portable furniture to safety. The house and its surroundings, however, were spared, though it was a close one, and on the crest of Mount Riddell there was always, thereafter, a bald white patch of bleached burnt-out timber.

Those bush holidays provide the happiest memories of my childhood, and during the war the house was extended to furnish more bedrooms in case we decided to evacuate there when the bombs fell. For some reason it was felt that thirty-five miles from the General Post Office was a safe radius if the Japanese invaded Melbourne.

In the late 1930s the voice of Joseph Schmidt was always on the wireless, singing that evocative song of the period, 'A Star Fell from Heaven'. It was the voice of Europe before the Terror and, had I but known it, a Jewish voice. But the song which I most associate with the outbreak of war was 'South of the Border (Down Mexico Way)' crooned in the light tenor of Gene Autry. Whenever I am in Los Angeles, supping with my friend Roddy McDowall in Studio City, I gaze across his fence at the house next door where Gene Autry still lives, in the hope that I may get a glimpse of my childhood idol.

Papa Brown, my maternal grandfather, had an ominous ditty in his music-hall repertoire.

> Tramp, tramp, the boys are marching
> Knock, knock, the bobby's at the door.
> If you don't let him in
> He will knock the door right in,
> And you won't seen your daddy any more!

This cautionary refrain gave me terrible nightmares and Papa was forbidden by my mother to sing it ever again. Early in the war I must have overheard many discussions between my parents about whether or not my father should enlist. His younger brother, Dick, had joined the air force and my mother's brother was in the Australian Imperial Force, and I am sure my father, although he was just too old to be called up, had pangs of conscience about not doing 'his bit'. I can remember an argument between my parents once, when we drove past the Hawthorn recruiting station, but Wilf ultimately arranged for my father to do war work for ICI, building munition factories and nitroglycerine storage tanks at Deer Park, an outer Melbourne suburb. However, I am convinced the spectre of conscription must have hung over him during the early war years and I always feared that his father-in-law's minatory recruiting jingle would come true, and that my father might be snatched away by the army and I would never see him again.

When the war broke out he employed several very jolly Italians called the Angelo Brothers who created the terrazzo porches and bathroom floors in all his houses. They seemed to sing all the time as they worked and they wore paper hats made from Geelong cement bags to keep off the sun. But one day they disappeared and were never spoken of again. Although they had probably lived in Australia for years and had barely heard of Mussolini they were interned for the duration of the war in some dismal concentration camp outside the city. There was also a German carpenter called Fritz whom my father liked, and an attempt was made to save him from the same fate as the Dagos. One day my father asked Fritz to come into his den, put his hand on the family Bible and swear allegiance to King George. Agog, I witnessed this touching if somewhat naïve ceremony but, alas, it failed to save poor old Fritz from his inevitable sequestration.

Unlike my mother, my father sometimes spoke to foreigners, and often told a story of one of his uncles back in Benalla who had befriended a German tradesman during the Great War when the rest of the town refused to talk to him. When he finally died he left Great-Uncle Frank a house and several thousand pounds.

I had embarked on philately and I already had a large collection of British stamps, including a Penny Black. When my grandparents went back to England for the coronation of King George VI, I steamed the stamps off their many letters and postcards. I also had an exciting German section in my album thanks to a funny old lady called Mrs Vennemark who lived a few doors down Marlborough Avenue in a tapestry-brick, neo-

Tudor bungalow built for her by my father in 1938. Old Mrs Vennemark – though she was probably only about forty-five – spoke with a strange accent, which gave her an air of acerbity. Her house had quite a few 'teething problems' too, and I often heard her harsh voice on the telephone asking for my father. 'It's that Jewish woman making trouble again,' my mother would say. 'Why your father does business with them I'll never understand.' Mr Friedmann was another thorn in her side. He ran a local firm called the Suburban Timber Supply and although my father liked him, my mother was convinced that he was a cheat and a swindler. However, in spite of my mother's open hostility towards her, old Mrs Vennemark was very kind to me, giving me the stamps off all the letters she received from her family who were still in Germany. They were rather spectacular: most had swastikas on them and images of a bad-tempered-looking man with folded arms and a square moustache. I secretly hoped Mrs Vennemark's family would not come to Melbourne too soon or an important philatelic source might dry up. But as it happened she remained alone, and some time around 1940 the letters stopped.

My parents enjoyed a busy social life. Once a week they had a card night. Baize-topped bridge tables were erected in the 'best' room and my mother spent the whole day making sandwiches and cakes. Her specialities were matches – a delicious colonial millefeuille filled with jam and cream and covered with walnuts – and sponge fingers with passionfruit icing. The next morning we had what was left of the sandwiches toasted for breakfast and took the cakes to school in greaseproof paper.

When my mother took me into town on her shopping expeditions, we usually visited Mitzi of Vienna, her favourite dress shop.

The proprietrix, whose creations my mother found irresistible, was another of those exotic arrivals of the late thirties whose companions had given Melbourne chocolates, coffee lounges and chamber music. We would also visit the Myer Emporium, where my mother had once worked as a dressmaker, before she married my father. I noticed her voice changed when she spoke to the shop assistants, as though she had to make it very clear that she and they were now separated by a great distance, and the gap was getting wider. I always felt uncomfortable when she spoke in that unreal drawl, but I was coming to believe that my mother was perhaps several women; or different things to different people, and there was a life within her which excluded me.

Sometimes we lunched at Myer's in the Mural Hall, which for suburban shoppers of this, or any, period was the height of grandeur. Frequently used for fashion parades and receptions, it was decorated with large pale neo-classical frescoes by Napier Waller, a Melbourne artist who had lost his right arm in the First World War and immediately began painting with his left. More often, however, we had our lunch at the Wattle Tea Rooms in Little Collins Street. The Wattle was a long room in the Arts and Crafts style, with leadlight windows on the street, and dark wainscot within. Plates, Toby jugs and knick-knacks stood on the sempiternal curio ledge, and there were chintzy banquettes to the left and right, and white linen tables down the middle. These dark varnished surroundings emphasized the bright floral dresses and hats of the women who, talced and toilet-watered, thronged the Wattle every day, so that the whole café resembled a conservatory. Women like stocks, in mauve and heliotrope, or puffed up in brighter speckled hues like calceolarias. Blue delphinium women nodded to each other across the room and there were old ladies too, like bunches of violets and boronia huddled behind their Denby Ware tea sets, or sitting alone pecking at asparagus rolls. There was, of course, no shortage of snapdragons.

In the centre of each table at the Wattle there were real

flowers: gum-tips and luminous orange and yellow Iceland poppies in cut-glass vases, dropping their calyxes on the doilies as each new flower shook out its crumpled petals, the long hairy stems turning double-jointed in the water.

The speciality at the Wattle was Adelaide whiting, which all the ladies ordered if they didn't eat egg sandwiches or asparagus rolls. Afterwards there were scrumptious things on silver three-tiered cake stands: kisses, éclairs, butterfly cakes, neenish tarts, matches and lamingtons.

Sometimes, at the sound of too loud and imperious a voice at an adjacent table, or the appearance of a pink-cheeked man in a hound's-tooth jacket and corduroy trousers with perhaps, also, a spoilt child, behaving like a *little madam*, my mother, or one of the other seed-packets, would smile secretly at her neighbour and, with a roll of her eyes, mouth the mysterious initials, like a code: 'E.N.T.' The whisper ran around the Wattle; nudges and little moues were exchanged, serviettes would discreetly mask smiles as eyes swivelled in the direction of this rather stiff *loud* family. 'E.N.T. and no doubt about it I'm afraid, Coral!' I heard a tight-lipped Carnation exclaim to a Gladiolus. English Next Table.

Lou and Eric — my parents — belonged to the local tennis club and on Saturday afternoons I would sit in the small clubhouse with a book listening to the distant laughter from the mixed doubles and the soporific sounds of tennis floating in from the courts. After the tennis there was always an enormous tea dominated by something called a 'tennis cake'. They were carefree afternoons of perpetual sunshine which the war changed forever.

We lived quite close to the Camberwell Sports Ground and on Saturday afternoons, if I happened to be at home in bed sick, I would hear, borne with terrible clarity across the housetops, the spasmodic applause of the cricket fans and, worse, in winter, the frighteningly mindless roar of the football rabble.

Long before I was ever forced by school authorities to watch these horrible and pointless games, I had formed a lifelong aversion to them based solely on those first auditory impressions. Crowds have always frightened and appalled me unless they happen to be in a theatre during one of my engagements. Then the noise they make is benign; a great ecstatic whoosh like a fire going up a chimney or the word 'yes' chanted by a heavenly host.

My mother was always concerned about my health and the great bogy of my childhood was Infantile Paralysis. I was never quite sure how old one had to be to avoid this scourge, nor had I ever met a victim, but I willingly swallowed whatever my mother poured into a spoon and pressed to my lips. Usually it was just the sticky and delicious Saunder's Malt Extract. I had seen it advertised on a hoarding which depicted a muscular baby, decorously diapered, shouldering an enormous steel girder. A favourite tonic of my mother's was Hypol, which was a less palatable white emulsion of cod-liver oil. There was, however, one prophylactic against Infantile Paralysis and other ailments that always made me sick. It was the egg flip, a glass of milk into which a raw egg had been whisked. Threads and clots of albumen always wrapped themselves around my uvula like a tourniquet, and although I gagged horribly, favours were withheld until I drank the last drop.

The illnesses of my childhood, although brief, gave me time to lie in bed, reading and listening to the wireless. My mother put the Radiola set in my room on a table beside the bed, and between sips of barley water I would tweak the knurled Bakelite knob from station to station. Throughout the day there was a succession of what are now called soap operas. Many of them employed the same actors, so that it was disquieting to hear a familiar character in *Aunt Jenny's Real Life Stories* crop up again with a different name in *Dr Mack, Fred and Maggie Everybody, When a Girl Marries* and *Martin's Corner.* Somehow it gave all those radio melodramas a spooky homogeneity.

In the mornings, soon after *Daybreak Dan*, there was a popular programme of community singing; a type of entertainment that has almost died out. With Uncle Wilf, Aunty Vi and John, I once went to a recording of this show in a small radio auditorium in town. It was thronged with women, a few accompanied by their children. Some of the ladies had brought knitting, very often khaki socks on five needles, and others had colanders in their laps into which they absently shelled peas. Led by a radio 'personality' called Charlie Vaud, with Mabel Nelson at the piano, they all enthusiastically sang such war-time hits as 'Run Rabbit', 'We're Going to Hang Out Our Washing on the Siegfried Line', 'Hey, Little Hen', 'Berlin or Bust' and 'The White Cliffs of Dover'. There was a vaudeville interlude when two comedians called Edgley and Dawe capered before the microphone and a strange woman called Nellie Colley, dressed in top hat and tails and smoking a pipe, sang a comic song called 'Burlington Bertie'. It was my first enticing glimpse of the Music Hall.

There were humorous interludes on the radio: mostly records of pre-war British vaudeville comics like George Tilly, Sid Field, Cyril Fletcher, Jack Hulbert and Cecily Courtneidge and my favourite, Horace Kenny. I would lie there in the darkened room through measles, mumps, whooping cough and scarlet fever, with my calamine lotion and Vicks Vaporub, laughing at those wonderful old-fashioned jesters. In the voices of some of these radio comics I recognized with a start the northern intonations of my father's father, whose Lancastrian accent had hitherto seemed so unique and outlandish. Here on the wireless were men with similar voices, interrupted by explosions of laughter. I later wondered why so many of the funniest comedians came from the North of England and why the idea of a 'Kent comic' seemed so anomalous. In the forties, yodelling was popular and there were many excruciating hillbilly programmes on the wireless, but in the afternoon the children's sessions began, and I would listen to rather arch transmissions of *Chums at Chatterbox Corner* and later, around teatime, *The*

Search for the Golden Boomerang, which used as its signature tune the voluptuous hothouse melody of Tchaikovsky's 'Waltz of the Flowers'. By the end of the day the bedroom smelt strongly of my medicaments mingled with the aroma of hot Bakelite.

One morning, when I was about ten, I woke very early, and as I went to the lavatory I glanced down at the skirting board outside my bedroom door. I then got down on my hands and knees and looked at it more closely. There was a small wire staple fixed to the wood an inch or two above the carpet, through which was threaded a thin cord. There was another staple on the opposite side of the architrave, and more, as I discovered, at regular intervals between my bedroom and the door to my parents' room, into which, like Ariadne's thread, the string disappeared. It occurred to me that I could easily have tripped on this filament on my way to the bathroom, and it was a mere fluke that I had not.

That morning, I was alone with my father for a few minutes after he had made my mother's breakfast, and when I told him of my strange discovery he became agitated and evasive. Finally, swearing me to secrecy, he explained that for some weeks he and my mother had been disturbed in the middle of the night by Barbara's sleepwalking, so he had installed this ingenious system of trip cords which connected to a bell beside his bed. Thus, whatever the hour, he would be instantly alerted to my sister's noctambulations and steer her safely back to bed. I must say, he looked particularly haggard that morning so I assumed the mechanism had been working all too successfully over the past few weeks.

I could not help but admire my father's ingenuity, though only one detail puzzled me; the cord did not pass across my sister's bedroom door, but mine. A few weeks later I noticed the whole system had been dismantled without a trace, and my father looked considerably more rested in the mornings. I assumed that my unconscious wanderings had come to an end.

My father had secured a valuable contract to build a sausage factory for Mr Prince of Prince's Sausages. I went along with him to the old meat works for his first discussions. The noise in the factory was deafening and there was an appalling and nidorous smell. Very fat men in overalls and gumboots sloshed around in pink water as machines masticated huge quivering swags and chandeliers of offal; mauve, crimson and magenta. At the other end dirty pipes extruded serpents and stools of bright pink mince which the brutish men aimed into endless frankfurter skins. I remember my father had to rush away to be sick and thereafter never ate another sausage in his life. At our children's parties we always had cocktail frankfurters – from another firm – which we dunked in sauce and washed down with raspberry vinegar. These lavish teas, usually a celebration of a birthday, were held on Saturday afternoons and were preceded by a matinée at the Rivoli Picture Theatre near the Camberwell Junction. After the candles had been blown out and the last frankfurter ground into a slice of bread and butter and hundreds and thousands, there were party games in the garden until the parents arrived to escort their invariably weeping children home to be sick. Uncle Wilf always turned up at my parties and would organize the activities, which sometimes got rather rough, and he would find himself playing 'Stacks on the Mill, More on Still' flat on his back on the lawn beneath a writhing pyramid of about fifteen small boys.

> 'Stacks on the mill,
> More on still . . .'

chanted the children. My parents would exchange a glance and my mother once said, 'Poor Wilf. He loves children and he's only got John.'

Uncle Wilf always bought the latest parlour games which helped to fill in the long evenings after tea when we were up at Healesville. We loved Mah-jong until Wilf produced a pack of Belisha, a new card game inspired by British traffic signs. Each card had a picturesque view of England, Scotland or Wales painted in bright colours in a slightly primitive, Lowry-ish style. Although the cars in the pictures looked quaintly out of date, the landscapes, as green as salads, and the castles and thatched cottages, filled me with a yearning to go there.

After the family weekend at the shack, we used to drive back from Healesville in rather a long convoy, stopping occasionally for the children to go behind bushes or for Aunt Ella to be sick, or sometimes stopping too for Uncle Wilf to get out of their grey Chev and lean for a while with his elbows on the roof and his head in his hands. We would stop our car a few yards ahead and my father would watch his brother-in-law in the rear-vision mirror. 'Wilf's getting more of those headaches,' he said. 'Time he had a check-up.' A few months later he did, and had to go to hospital for a 'minor operation', as my parents, with their usual prudery about illness, described the removal of a brain tumour. I spoke to him on the telephone soon after he came home from the Alfred Hospital but he didn't seem to know who I was. When he died, leaving no will, the house and the land at Healesville had to be sold to provide money for his widow and son. And we left the bush forever.

Not long after Wilf's funeral, which I was not allowed to attend, my father and I were driving to one of his more important jobs to deliver a precious cargo of plate glass which was roped to the open boot. My father was driving a little too fast and as we went over an unexpected hump in the road there was an ominous thump and a dull crash behind the car. My father pulled over to the side of the road and got out to examine the disaster. I had never heard him swear, but this time he stood looking at the shivered panes and released a litany of curses. Then he sat on the kerb and sobbed quietly for a while. I didn't know what to do, but I felt he wasn't just grieving over the glass.

Hats and Glads

CAMBERWELL GRAMMAR SCHOOL had been built in the
grounds of a large Victorian house in an older neighbouring suburb. The original gardens were still there, including two
elephantine Moreton Bay fig trees and a tottering arbour, from
which, in its season, wistaria mauvely dripped. There was also
the inevitable Norfolk Island pine tree which every Victorian
residence of any distinction seemed to possess. They rose like
tall viridian fishbones over the suburban landscape and always
denoted the presence of an interesting old house. Today, however, though many of the trees survive, their gardens are often
subdivided and the houses demolished; replaced by nice 'units'
and practical townhouses. Mr Tonkin, the magenta-nosed
headmaster, lived in the original Victorian house in the school
grounds that also accommodated a few wretched and dispos-
sessed boarders on whom we well-fed, warmly housed day
boys gazed with pity.

My teachers in the junior school were mostly women. But
there was a bald and nervous little choirmaster called Mr
Dennis who visited the school and led us all in rousing rendi-
tions of 'Nymphs and Shepherds', 'Bird of the Wilderness'
(. . . blithesome and cumberless) and a muscular ditty called
'Clang, Clang, Clang on the Anvil' – a song that sounded
particularly odd when rendered by boy sopranos. At home

Purcell's 'Nymphs and Shepherds' became my earliest party turn, after my mother had overheard me singing it in the bath, and much to my embarrassment she insisted that I sing it to all the uncles and aunts at the next family Sunday tea party. I only agreed to this on condition I was allowed to perform behind the curtain, so that my voice was disembodied like those on the radio. Thereafter, if ever my parents wanted to cajole me into a song or recitation, they would have to say – and I wince to recall the words – *pretend to be the wireless*. Needless to say I have pretended to be the wireless on many occasions since.

After the persecutions by Miss Jensen at my former school, Camberwell Grammar was a blissful respite, though a boy called John Bromley, who seemed tall for his age and had soft white skin like a slug, used to push me over whenever he saw me, for no reason that I could ever understand. I learnt to avoid him, and many years later in adult life, and when he was least expecting it, I visited an exquisite revenge upon him which I will describe in a later chapter.

Sometimes when Bromley's capricious bullying got too much for me I would, I am afraid, seek a victim of my own. There was a perfectly nice, but rather small lad called Gifford, whom I pushed over a couple of times, on one occasion causing his mother's beautifully cut sandwiches to scatter on the dusty playground. For years afterwards I experienced a sharp pang of guilt whenever I thought of this incident until, on a recent visit to Melbourne, I could bear it no longer and decided, half a century later, to make amends. By consulting the telephone directory I discovered that there was, in fact, a Bruce Gifford who was practising architecture in the city and to my delight he answered the telephone. I came quickly to the point, explaining that I was sorry about the sandwiches and hoped he was doing well and that there were no hard feelings. A wave of relief and absolution passed over me, though as I gently replaced the receiver, I could still hear his voice exclaiming, 'Who is this? Who *is* this?'

I loved history, art and English, but I was already having

difficulty with arithmetic, which seemed to be the one subject in which my father hoped I might excel. Even then I may have been vaguely aware that he wanted me to become an architect; something better and grander than himself. If only he had known, he could have adopted little Gifford!

One morning, through the classroom window, we noticed a strange figure prowling around outside in the school playground. He wore floppy green trousers, a red shirt and a bow tie, and his hair was very long and wavy. We laughed delightedly at the sight of him; he was the oddest fellow any of us had ever seen. Miss Ewers left the classroom and went outside and we saw her talking to the peculiar stranger for a few minutes and shaking her head. They could both see our grinning faces pressed to the window and the weird man glanced at us nervously, but Miss Ewers did not seem to mind. She was blushing, and trying not to smile herself. Soon the stranger walked off towards the school gate and our teacher came back into the classroom. She sat at her desk and exploded with laughter. She was convulsed. 'Who was that, Miss?' we all asked, but Miss Ewers took some time to compose herself. 'He . . . wanted to know if we'd like him to give us theatre lessons at the school!' She could hardly get the words out before a further paroxysm. We were all laughing now and the weird man must have heard us through one of the open windows. We could see him at the gate, gazing back at the school with a pale puzzled face. 'Who is he, Miss Ewers?' we piped in chorus. Miss Ewers had gone bright red. She looked very pretty with her eyes sparkling with tears. 'An actor,' she said at last, drying her eyes with a handkerchief, 'he said he was an actor!' Our peals of merriment must surely have reached him now as he closed the gate and trudged off towards the bus stop.

Sport was my greatest problem at school. I was always perfectly healthy and yet I could never see the point of games. Paradoxically, I attribute my excellent constitution and energy today to the fact that since school I have never engaged in more than a minute of athletic activity. We all had to traipse down to

CAMBERWELL GRAMMAR SCHOOL

REPORT FOR FIRST TERM, 19 46

Name _J. B. Humphries_   Form _VB_

Conduct _Excellent_   No. of Boys in Form _17_

Days Absent _1_   Position in Form _8_

SUBJECTS	Percentage	Form Average	SUBJECTS	Percentage	Form Average
Scripture	82	63	Arithmetic	65	77
Writing	A	–	Algebra	60	75
Drawing	95	63	Geometry and Trigonometry	78	71
Reading	A	–	General Science		
Spelling	89	83	Physics		
English Grammar and Composition	74	59	Chemistry		
English Literature	100	64	Mathematics I		
French	76	70	Mathematics II		
German			Mathematics III		
Latin	85	68	Mathematics IV		
History	74	63	Com. Principles		
Geography	90	66	Commercial Practice		
Economics			Physical Education	D	Firshand

GENERAL REMARKS: _Barry is a most satisfactory pupil. He is showing a distinct leaning to the literary subjects. His Literature paper is one of the best I have corrected for a boy of this age._

Average 80.5%   _A. Brown_

H. L. Tonkin .... Headmaster

Signature of Parent or Guardian _J. B. Humphries_

a horrible building called The Gym. Here were coarse unscalable ropes, parallel bars and porridge-coloured mattresses, stained and pinguid from generations of brilliantined scalps and sweaty somersaults. This torture chamber was presided over by a man called Scotty, one of those repulsive and nuggety Caledonians with pale sandy hair and white eyelashes that gave him the look of a near-albino. Scotty was perpetually dressed in a short-sleeved Aertex, briefs and tennis shoes, which we called 'sandshoes' and 'ordinary' people called 'runners'. Scotty's piggy little eye fell on me immediately when he saw the difficulty I had in executing a pointless somersault. Much given to jocular nicknames, he decided that mine should be 'Granny Humphries', a soubriquet which met with the ribald approval of my schoolfellows. Needless to say, on subsequent sports days at which I was a reluctant participant and in the tedious brutalities of egg, spoon and sack races, the air rang with shrill cries of 'Come on Granny! Come on Granny!' As the reader may imagine, I had little affection for Mr Scott, but I am happy to say that very many years later a terrible sadness befell him in which I played a decisive, if anonymous, role.

An unpleasant concomitant of Physical Training was the cold shower we were forced to endure in a dank concrete basement near the gym. There were no lights and no proper drainage system, so we had to splash around in the dark with black water up to our knees, for no good reason that I could comprehend, except that cold showers were supposed to be 'good for you'.

There was a tuck shop at the school where two women sold pasties and pies to boys whose mothers, unlike mine, could not be bothered to cut their sandwiches or lovingly pack their leather satchels with fruit and cakes. The savoury effluvium which wafted from the tuck shop daily at twelve o'clock percolated to every corner of the school, and as I chewed my bland sandwiches I sometimes wished I was just slightly neglected, as I hankered for a succulent pasty, haemorrhaging sauce.

It would not be long before we would all be officially urged to devour something called the 'Oslo lunch'. At the time I assumed this to be identical with the lunches eaten by schoolchildren in occupied Norway. It consisted of a carrot, a slice of brown bread (in Melbourne, in those days, this was white bread coloured brown), a piece of Kraft processed cheese still half-wrapped in foil and bearing a parent's thumb print, and half a pint of milk. For a short while in the early years of the war my mother followed this edict and daily packed this austere and unappetizing collation in my satchel. However, on the journey to school the milk bottle often leaked and by the end of the term most of our school bags reeked with the smell of raw leather, ink and rancid milk. Soon, and in spite of the war effort, I persuaded my mother to supply me with a normal lunch of spaghetti sandwiches and cakes.

At the beginning of the war with Japan, trenches were dug in the gardens of the old school house and we were issued with gas masks and strange black rubber gags which, if bitten on when the bombs fell, would prevent our teeth from shattering. We all had to bring money to school to pay for these prophylactics, but I horrified the Head and was made to feel shamefully unpatriotic when, before the whole school, I innocently asked whether we would get our money back if the Japs didn't bomb us. It was a solecism I was never allowed to forget.

Meanwhile the school grounds became a muddy maze of trenches, and strips of cellophane were pasted in lattice patterns all over the windows. On the wireless Vera Lynn optimistically sang:

> When the lights go on again
> All over the world . . .

Many of our neighbours in Christowell Street were happily building air-raid shelters in their back gardens. These were exciting subterranean dwellings upholstered with sandbags, but my father refused to disfigure our back lawn and constructed an elaborate, but barely bomb-proof, bunker under the stairs. Carpenters made large hardboard panels that could be fitted to the inside of our windows in the event of aerial bombardment, though how this could be done at high speed in an air raid, and in a house that must have had at least forty windows, is difficult to imagine. Fortunately it was never put to the test. The back garden was converted from flowers to vegetables and fruits, and in a short time we were producing our own carrots, parsnips, beans, potatoes, peas, lemons, peaches and apricots.

There was some confusion, certainly amongst children, as to which war we should be worrying about: the Hitler one or the Tojo one. However, most streets had a Fat for Britain depot.

It was popularly believed that fat, or its absence, would be a decisive factor in the outcome of the European war, and that the more fat we could send to England the better her chances of victory. The dripping from every Sunday roast in Melbourne was therefore carefully decanted into suitable containers – old Farex tins, glucose canisters and jam jars – and these, hygienically sealed, were left on the front porch of Mrs Long's Spanish Mission Home on the corner of Fairmont Avenue, whence they were presumably collected, consolidated and shipped to London. To this day I have never met a recipient or beneficiary of this lardy largesse, but the Japanese sank many Fat for Britain ships and it is strange to think of this greasy residue of a million Sunday joints lying in some coral dell at the bottom of the Pacific, waiting to produce the biggest dripping slick in history.

Our vicar, Canon P. W. Robinson, was a Londoner, and his sermons rambled on at some length about the threat to what was then called The Old Country and the safety of the King, Queen and the little Princesses. To my father's disappointment, my mother always thought of some excuse for not going to church, though I knew that our sanctimonious vicar was the principal reason for her absence from Morning Prayer. My father, however, was a regular churchgoer, later a vestryman, and during the Offertory he would always slip a crunched-up pound note into the plate amongst everyone else's shillings, and insisted on saying Grace before meals: 'Forwhatweareabout-toreceivemaytheLordmakeustrulythankfulAmen.' This always embarrassed me when we had friends to stay, as my father's recitation usually caught them unawares mid-way through the first forkful. And sometimes, at night, I would see him through their half-open bedroom door – it was rarely closed – kneeling in prayer beside the bed. Canon Robinson took a great fancy to me and always patted my head vigorously after Sunday service. I had the uncomfortable feeling, later confirmed, that he envisaged some future for me in the Ministry, and at Sunday school he was always singling me out to read the lesson.

Sunday was the worst day of the week, because my father, with his north of England Methodist upbringing, forbade us to play with any other children on the Sabbath. Instead there were endless drives back and forth to St Mark's rather ugly buff-stuccoed nave, and the cold red-brick Sunday school beside it. In church, I liked the music, though I successfully resisted Canon Robinson's efforts to conscript me into the choir. However, the smell of everybody's 'Sunday Best'; the camphor, the talcum, hair oil and the toilet water, mingled with whatever disinfectant it was that the cleaners used, always made me feel like passing out as if I had inhaled carbon monoxide. Withal I struggled for some great faith; some transcendental religious experience. Great-Uncle Albert, always extolled to me as the most successful member of the Humphries family, had, back in Manchester, once written a seminal work, *The Holy Spirit in Faith and Experience* (Primitive Methodist Publishing Company, 1911), and though I attempted to read this book many times, it failed to yield up its mystery to me. Moreover, there was some evidence from its musty unopened appearance that previous readers had also abandoned their search for Truth amongst the closely printed pages.

Sunday lunch – or dinner as it was called – always consisted of a Roast; lamb, pork or beef. This was always cooked, as I still prefer it, until it was an attractive shade of grey. The roast was accompanied by potatoes, parsnips and pumpkin baked to a crisp, the pumpkin caramelized. This would be followed by tinned peaches or a steamed pudding in which apricot jam, golden syrup or sultanas were alternating constituents. Much as I looked forward to this meal throughout the tedious tracts of Canon Robinson's sermon, I dreaded the return home as well. For Sunday was the day that my parents usually had 'words'. It would be more truthful to say that they had no words at all, but there was a palpable atmosphere of tension which had no explicable origin. It may have been that my parents, to all appearances a happily married couple, found the prospect of one day in the week spent in each other's company unendurable. This oppressive atmosphere, which froze the heart of a child, may have had a purely gastric origin, as we consumed those large quantities of fat that would never find their way to Britain. Happily, the family's spirits lifted at last when we piled into the Oldsmobile and later the Buick and went for the traditional Sunday-afternoon spin.

There was nothing my parents enjoyed more than motoring around the new suburbs on the outskirts of the town looking at houses. For my father, the builder, it was an excursion of professional interest, and every now and then, as we drove down a brand-new street of villas, with their freshly planted lawns, bird baths and sickly silver birches, he might suddenly jam on the brakes and point an enraged finger at some crude, jerry-built imitation of one of his own designs. On the new roads, crescents and boulevards flanked by pristine triple-fronted cream-brick bungalows, other vehicles filled with gawking families also cruised. It was the thing everyone did on a Sunday afternoon, and it was called *Looking at the Lovely Homes*. On the hills of Ivanhoe and Eaglemont above the Yarra River, where the artists of the 1880s had painted their idyllic 'impressions', stood some of the grander new houses with tennis courts which especially interested my mother.

Mostly of brick, the colour of milky tea, they had curved nautical-looking terraces, balconies and picture windows, with satin festoon or 'veil of tears' blinds; and if these were raised, as they often were by the proud owners, there might be a glimpse within of blond veneer and peach mirror, and prowling along the window sill just inside the glass, a lithe white marble puma.

The lovely homes bored me. As we glided along in our big chubby car past the raw new houses, still smelling of wet cement, admiring the azaleas and the 'crazy' stone work, the 'feature' chimneys and the names of the houses or their street numbers scribbled across the façades in duck-egg blue wrought-iron, I hankered for hovels. There was a place I had heard of called Dudley Flats, a low-lying wasteland to the west of Melbourne, where 'slums' and *really* poor people could be found.

I begged my parents to drive me there so that I could see them for myself. But we never visited the older suburbs of Melbourne, except when we went to see my mother's sister, Ella, who still lived in a dark Victorian house in Thornbury where her parents had once lived and my mother had grown up. It had ruby and Bristol-blue glass in the panels beside the front door and a long central corridor with a curtain half-way down, so that when the front door was opened, visitors were not afforded a vulgar view of the back yard. There was even an aspidistra in the front parlour which Ella washed with milk, and I once asked my father, in the presence of my aunt and uncle, if their house was a *real* hovel.

Sometimes on Sunday afternoons we would visit the Melbourne General Cemetery with my relations on my mother's side. After much wandering through the maze of granite obelisks and tottering tombstones, overrun with skeleton weed and lantana, we came to a grave that was better kept than the rest. It looked rather like a narrow bed of grey stone, covered with marble chips, and on the headstone was my grandmother's name. My mother removed the old stalks and put some fresh flowers in a little vase buried in the gravel. Aunty Elsie pulled out the weeds and we all just stood and shuffled, looking at the grave and trying to feel something. Around us were sadly neglected plots and even a few that had caved in, so that kneeling down and peering through the cracks you might just see the skeletons of other people's grandmothers.

To earn extra pocket money I often went shopping for my mother. There was a small parade of shops not far away in Camberwell Road, and although their proprietors, Mr Hall, the grocer, Mr Ryal, the chemist, and Mr Ernie Young, the butcher, all seemed to me to be of normal height, my mother always referred to them as diminutive. 'Barry, would you please go down the street and get me a half a pound of nice lean lamb chops from my little butcher. Oh, and while you're there, pop in and ask the little man in the chemist shop for a bottle of Hypol and some Buckley's Canadiol Mixture.' I always took a basket with an orange ten-shilling note and a ration book.

There seemed to be no great shortage of anything, though butterless recipes were popular, but I would stand on the sawdust floor of little Mr Young's butcher's shop while he put his bloodied thumbs in a pair of scissors and deftly snipped a few squares off our meat-ration book. Sometimes, if there was a big card night looming, I would pick up a sponge, a lemon meringue pie or a few fairy cakes from the Misses Longmire who had the 'homemade' cake shop at the end of the Parade. There was always a delicious smell in their shop, though it puzzled me, since everything was baked on the premises, that the Misses Longmire could, with a clear conscience, describe their confections as being homemade when they were so obviously baked in a shop.

If I were not running simple errands after school, I might be in my laboratory mixing quite dangerous combinations of sulphur and potassium permanganate over a spirit burner or practising a few magic tricks. I had always had a hankering to be a magician like the top-hatted, opera-cloaked gigolo called

Mandrake who appeared regularly in a comic strip in my mother's *Women's Weekly*. Mandrake had only to 'gesture hypnotically' and people disappeared. That seemed to me to be the greatest gift imaginable; to make people and things vanish.

Sometimes, too, I might even play with my sister and her little friends, Maureen and Valerie. My mother had long ago whispered to me that Valerie was adopted, but never to say anything to her face because her adoptive parents had not yet told her. At the time this information intrigued and frightened me, since it occurred to me that I, like Val, might also be adopted and that my parents too could be keeping this a secret. It even occurred to me that my mother's confidences about Val's origins might be her way of preparing the ground for a confession of her own. It was true to say that her expressions of love for me were sometimes evasive or ambiguous. Once when I was quite young I asked her point-blank if she loved me and she seemed nonplussed and embarrassed. 'Well,' she replied evasively, 'naturally I love your father most of all, and then *my* mother and father, and after that, you and your sister, just the same.' It was clear from what she said that love had a strictly hierarchical structure, and was certainly not something that could be spontaneously experienced or bestowed. My unspoken adoption fears were not put to rest when my mother said, as she frequently did to others in my presence: 'Eric and I don't know *where Barry comes from*.' I have recorded this story as accurately as I can recollect it in order to show the warmer side of my mother's complex personality.

Every now and then there were special occasions; usually a wedding, or a dance at the tennis club. Weeks before these events my mother and I would drive to a distant suburb to the home of Miss Wilmot, my mother's dressmaker, and I would wait in the hall while she had another 'fitting'. These seemed to take forever, and from time to time, Miss Wilmot would put her head around the door and smile at me reassuringly, as if that were possible with a mouthful of pins. Taffeta was my mother's favourite fabric in that epoch; it was before the age of Thai silk. Taffeta was cool and it rustled and chafed upon itself, and before my mother's big night out it was, with a few drops of Bond Street perfume, the nicest textile to say your prayers against.

Once they went to a grand luncheon at the Town Hall, and my mother wore her best suit from Mitzi of Vienna, and a hat with a veil covered with fat black polka dots. Later I asked her what it was like. 'Lovely,' she replied. 'I'm pleased I went to a bit of trouble. It was all hats and glads.'

Gladioli, especially flesh-pink ones, were the floral symbols of respectability, success and thrusting, unquestioning

Mandrake the Magician – a fragment

optimism. They also seemed somehow to be the appropriate emblems of Mr Menzies, the reigning prime minister, who had such a nice 'speaking voice'. Never before had I heard a voice so described, and when my parents tuned in to the wireless to hear one of his public addresses I listened attentively to those sanctimonious, lah-di-dah tones, trying to detect why my parents had singled out this 'speaking voice' in particular. Did he have other more recondite voices, I wondered wickedly. A farting voice perhaps? Above all, Mr Menzies was extolled by my parents and their friends for his repartee and the swiftness with which he rebuked interjections from the Opposition supporters, whom he wittily described as 'that riff-raff at the back of the hall' to roars of laughter and applause.

His opponent, who was later victorious, was Mr Chifley, 'a pipe-smoking Labourite', who had once, Mrs Kendall whispered, 'been a *train driver*'. Certainly Mr Chifley had nothing which could be described as a 'speaking voice', and my father summed him up in three words, 'rough as bags'. 'Irish, too,' my mother added tartly. Since her only brother had married a Roman Catholic and been ostracized, my mother had little affection for the Irish. 'But didn't Nanna's mother come from Ireland?' I asked ingenuously. '*Northern* Ireland, Barry,' she averred warmly, 'that's the nice part of Ireland, and don't you forget it.'

I sometimes think I might still bear the ugly scars of my early indoctrination, when I read absurdly Anglophobic accounts of the Gallipoli Campaign and sensationalist works of Australian history like Robert Hughes's *The Fatal Shore*, where the British are uniformly depicted as shits, and the Irish convicts as misunderstood scallywags and political prisoners. 'He would write that, wouldn't he,' I reflect, 'typical revisionist Mick that he is!' A modern manifestation of this persistent sectarian split in Australian life is the Republican Movement with its cant about patriotism. It is, of course, no such thing, but just another form of pommy-bashing. One has only to glance at the names of its most vociferous champions: Keating, Keneally, Doogue, Conolly and

O'Horne. It is no surprise that the Australian Republican flag is green.

Today I keep my sweaters in a toffee-coloured chest lined with camphor wood. It is densely and rather crudely carved with dragons and ovate oriental bas-reliefs which I remember in the greatest detail from my earliest childhood. It was bought by my grandparents in Colombo as they returned from the Coronation on the Orient Line, as, indeed, were thousands more identical chests purchased by other voyagers. It used to stand in our upstairs hallway and contained my mother's best things: her furs, rugs, table linen, wedding dress, and a gold meshed evening belt encrusted with imitation rubies, sapphires and emeralds.

When I was eleven I noticed in the window of a small secondhand shop near Camberwell Junction a pair of earrings that seemed to match my mother's belt perfectly. I covertly inquired the price which, though I no longer recall it, may have been quite expensive for such cheap paste, but over a long period, and by secretly slipping into the shop and leaving small amounts, I finally paid off the earrings, brought them home and carefully hid them. As her birthday approached I wrapped the earrings, speculating excitedly on the surprise and delight they would bring. I had not even breathed a word to my sister or father.

The great morning came and my father brought my mother breakfast in bed. It was then that I proudly presented my small package. I watched my mother's face carefully as she unwrapped it, but when the tissue paper parted and she saw the earrings, she did not smile. Instead her face darkened and she turned angrily to my father. 'Where did he get these, Eric?' my mother said sharply. 'I hope he didn't pay for these out of his own money?' My father looked confused, and speechless. 'Where did you get them?' my mother asked me. 'Not from that little rogue down at the Junction, I hope. How much did they cost?' I muttered a price. 'Daylight robbery,' exploded my mother. She thrust the earrings at my father. 'Eric?' she commanded. 'I want you to go straight down to that little Jew and tell him to give Barry his money back. And you can also tell him if he goes on overcharging children for rubbish like this I'll have him reported.' Needless to say, that was one of my mother's more memorable birthdays.

My father often used to bring home carnations as a peace offering for some nameless transgression, and I always found them unsympathetic flowers: prim, sharply budded, pinked and serrated blooms in ice-cream colours, with a scent that smelled sprayed-on. They still fill me with a remote dread. Always wrapped in a cone of pink or purple tissue paper, they often lay on the hall table for a long while, depending on the time my mother had set for my father's sentence. But in the end she would always drop them in a vase and say with a smile, 'Look at the lovely carnations your father has given me.' They had worked again.

My father insisted that my mother have domestic 'help'. I had never quite recovered from the sudden departure of my first beloved nanny, Edna, who left without farewells or adequate explanations; although later there was a succession of domestics and housekeepers, they never meant the same to me. After my sister was born my mother engaged a girl from the nearby Salvation Army home, euphoniously called Valmai Grubb. Although my mother admitted that the rest of Valmai's family were almost certainly 'ordinary', Valmai, she insisted, had a very kind heart and a sweet soft nature. Why otherwise would she cry so uncontrollably when rebuked? Valmai stayed a long time and was replaced by Mrs Lane, a woman of about sixty, who came from Welshpool and whom my mother described as 'very countrified'. They took an instant dislike to each other and my mother told me that as soon as she saw the down-trodden heels of Mrs Lane's shoes she knew that she should never have engaged her. On Mrs Lane's days off my mother would inspect the floor of the shower recess in the 'help's' quarters and with some satisfaction she always found it to be dry and the room filled with a cloying scent of Three Flowers talcum powder, Mrs Lane's preferred alternative to soap and water. In the mornings, as the housekeeper trudged up the stairs with my mother's breakfast tray, my sister and I often overheard her muttering under her frequently juniper-scented breath the malediction: 'I hate her, I hate her, *I hate her.*'

Having engaged a 'home help' who had quickly proved herself unsuitable, my mother found herself unable to dismiss her, so that thereafter Mrs Lane, having failed as a housekeeper, was retained – even became indispensable – as an example of incompetence and slovenliness. 'Look at the dust,' my mother would say with some satisfaction. 'It's that grub Mrs Lane. She thinks I don't notice.' My mother confided all her complaints about Mrs Lane to Mrs Shores, the woman who came to do the washing and ironing. Mrs Shores was a garrulous lady with a shrill laugh and a husband who enjoyed a drink. She laughed immoderately, though quite genuinely, at all my mother's sardonic jokes. Whenever Mrs Shores arrived my mother would hurry to impart to her Mrs Lane's latest outrage, at which Mrs Shores would burst into peals of incredulous hilarity. It began to look as though Mrs Lane would never be sacked, but be retained forever as a grim cabaret turn and an essential topic of conversation. Mrs Shores was another comic act on the same bill who frequently interrupted her tasks in the laundry to follow my amused parent from room to room gossiping; or she would stand in the kitchen recounting some long anecdote at the top of her voice, assuming my mother was listening in the adjacent sun-room. However my mother often went upstairs, or wandered into the garden to pick a few camellias, and after a wink at me would return to the house to find Mrs Shores still cheerfully soliloquizing.

Mr Dunt, the gardener, was another incompetent hired in order to provide my mother with anecdotes of incompetence. He was an old man, though perhaps little older than the author of this memoir, who arrived on a bicycle with a large pannier attached to the handlebars and who thereafter pottered about pruning the wrong things and digging up carefully planted bulbs. Mr Dunt had a special cup and saucer for his afternoon tea, from which we were forbidden to drink since it was rather uncertain as to where Mr Dunt might have been. It was only after a few years that my father noticed that small things were missing from his workshop behind the garage. The absence of an expensive electric exhaust fan finally aroused his suspicions and a telephone call was made to Mr Dunt's family who, sure enough, discovered a large haul of unused appliances, as well as hinges, nails, trowels and hammers, under the old man's bed. We never saw him again.

One day when I was about seven my mother disappeared. My young sister and I were given no explanation of this terrible event and a kind family friend called Janet Ballantyne came to look after us. My father was rarely home, and seemed so stricken with anxiety that we were unable to demand an explanation. I would lie in bed feeling as though some calamity had taken place. Somehow it was even uncertain whether my mother would ever return. But she did. Perhaps she had only been absent for a few weeks, and quite recently I learnt that she had suffered a miscarriage and spent a period convalescing in hospital. My family were madly circumspect in matters to do with illness, sex and even reality, so that a misfortune combining all three taboos was veiled in absolute silence. To this day I can remember those feelings of childish desolation, so that if people close to me leave me now, even on shopping expeditions, I always need to know exactly where they are going, or that oppressive emotion of loss, with all its old force, comes back to me.

Dirty Hair

CANON ROBINSON PERSUADED my father to withdraw
me from Camberwell Grammar and enrol me at The
Melbourne Grammar School, an old and traditional establishment that was over six miles away. I hated the idea of changing
schools and leaving my friends, but Canon Robinson had
'pulled a few strings' and had even talked to the Bishop. It was
emphasized to me that I was jumping a long queue and should
be grateful for the opportunity of going to what was described
as a 'good' school.

My father seemed very nervous at the interview with the
headmaster. He received us in his study, in a romantically
decaying wing of the nineteenth-century bluestone school buildings. The room was tenebrous, and pale wistaria flickered
outside the lancet windows, which were screened with wire
mesh to protect them from cricket balls. Mr Sutcliffe wore a
tattered subfusc gown and spoke in chilly, unfriendly 'English'
tones, which seemed to intimidate my father, who became
tongue-tied and deferential. (Many years later and long after
his retirement, I met Mr Sutcliffe again at the Melbourne
Club and was then struck by his rather broad New Zealand
accent.) Canon Robinson had advised my father against describing himself in the enrolment application as a builder and
had recommended that he call himself an 'architectural

designer' instead. I think my father was embarrassed by this fraudulent snobbism but, since it had been recommended by a Canon of the Church, he reluctantly went along with it.

Our interview, it seemed, had been a success, and I was admitted to this famous institution. No longer could I ride my bicycle through leafy streets to school as I had done in my last few years at Camberwell Grammar. Instead there was a train to be caught and then a tram before I reached the iron gates in Domain Road, South Yarra, just in time for morning chapel.

The school uniform was a quaint version of the 1930s business suit: navy-blue double-breasted serge, remotely inspired by Ronald Colman. Just as the dinner-jacketed waiters in today's restaurants ape the formal dress of smart diners a generation ago, so the attire of schoolboys (and bank clerks) in the 1940s was a sartorial throwback, echoing the angular-lapelled and tiepinned matinée idols of a former decade. The compulsory hair-style too, a skull-cap varnished with brilliantine, crudely suggested a sleeker pre-war mode. In the school chapel one morning, soon after I had arrived, the headmaster delivered an impassioned address from the pulpit in which he fulminated against long hair. Prefects were urged to catch and punish any boy whose hair touched his collar, and I can still remember Mr Sutcliffe's peroration, delivered in tremulous pseudo-English Kiwi tones: LONG HAIR IS DIRTY HAIR. Permissible only was the abridged Etonian forelock or quiff, which schoolboys of this epoch used to toss back with an automatic flick of the head, almost like a tic. To this day I have observed old Melbourne Grammar boys of this generation, now completely bald, still twitching their heads as though flicking back a phantom forelock.

The boarders of Melbourne Grammar were of a type I had never encountered. With their own stercoraceous jargon, these oafish hobbledehoys resided in a crumbling and evil-smelling wing of the old school. They wore grey trousers and khaki shirts since, unlike the day boys, they were not required to resemble little Christian gentlemen on public transport. Yet

The author's birthplace

The author aet. two weeks

John and Sarah Humphries, the author's paternal grandparents

The only child

Dressing

up

Siblings

At Healesville

Schooldays

Barbara, Christopher and Barry Humphries

whereas many of the day boys were the children of the *nouveau-riche* middle classes, the boarders, often as not, sprang from the loins of Old Boys and their parents either lived in some remotely rural part of Australia, where they farmed, or within a mile of the school in the suburbs of Toorak or South Yarra, where they pursued a vapid social existence, released from the irksome necessity of feeding and housing a dim heir. Little wonder that these waifs, ill-favoured with intelligence and smarting from parental abandonment, should seek comfort in the muddy embrace of their football comrades, and for the rest of their lives pursue a bleak hedonism on ski slopes, golf links or behind the wheels of Porsches.

Our schoolmasters were equally unimpressive. Many of them had been hauled out of retirement during World War Two to replace teachers who had been 'called up', and most of these remained on the staff for the duration of my schooldays. Looked upon as wonderful 'characters' by sentimental Old Boys and younger staff members, and like my mother's home-helpers kept on for their eccentricities rather than their abilities, these ignorant dotards made no effort to communicate knowledge since they had no store of this article on which to draw. Basking in the titillating propinquity of small boys, they filled whole periods, terms and years with boring reminiscence, bluff and sadism. Thus, I was 'taught' mathematics and divinity by a senile football coach, art and algebra by a desiccated athletics instructor, and English literature by a Major of cadets.

Mr 'Tickle' Turner was famous for his intimate methods of corporal punishment. He would put the offending boy over his knee, hold him firmly by the nape of the neck and pat his buttocks rhythmically with a ping-pong bat for twenty minutes whilst delivering a history lecture. 'Bully' Taylor, a turnip-faced ignoramus, was retained by the school merely because he had once, long ago, been an effective football coach. He always took great delight in telling anti-Semitic jokes and then asking Nathan and Goldsmith if they'd got the point. The only schoolmaster I liked at all was Mr Albert Greed, the chapel organist, who took us for musical-appreciation classes one afternoon a week. Albert was usually in a convivial mood after lunch, having had a few beers up the road at the Botanical Hotel, and could sometimes be persuaded to break off a lesson on Schubert and, whilst still seated at the piano, launch in to a sprightly rendition of 'Nola' or 'Kitten on the Keys', during which he would blush and giggle immoderately. Albert also organized lunchtime concerts in the War Memorial Hall and to one of these he invited the Aboriginal tenor, Harold Blair. He was the first Aborigine I ever set eyes on, for if there were any of Australia's original inhabitants living in Melbourne, they were kept well out of the way of nice people; unless, of course, they could sing.

Meanwhile, beneath a cunning smokescreen of philanthropy, the school offered scholarships and endowments to talented state school boys, thus saving itself from gross academic disgrace in the public exams. My first form was something called Remove, which I took to be a class for dunces. I was still overwhelmed by the size of my new school. It was a disconcerting jump from being one of the tallest and best-known boys at Camberwell Grammar to being one of the smallest and least-known at Melbourne. I was to experience a similar emotion in adult life when I arrived in London as an obscure actor after a taste of hometown fame. I looked around the classroom and thought how unlikely it would be to ever make friends with a single one of these unprepossessing classmates, but I did. Slowly people got to know my name and the daunting scale of the beetling school buildings quietly subsided.

I missed the masters at my former school, especially Stanley Brown, who had encouraged my interest in books. I also missed the art classes. A 'real' artist called Ian Bow had come to teach us and though very few boys were interested in his subject he had become a kind of hero, arriving every day in a loudly backfiring Hillman Minx. It was rumoured that Mr Bow had *two wives*, one of whom my friend Richard Tolley had actually met. Mr Bow smelt of art, that is to say, turpentine. Sometimes he would bring his still-wet paintings to school and talk about the fun he had in painting them. He also told us stories about artists, one of whom, a Dutchman, had once cut off his ear. Mr Bow showed us some prints of this artist's work, including a picture of sunflowers which created a titter. He emphasized the need to use plenty of paint. I asked my father if I could have some oil-paints for my birthday – in advance, if possible, since my birthday was in eleven months' time!

So I came to possess my first set of Winsor & Newton student oil-paints, and a small easel which I set up in the middle of a paddock near Uncle Dick's house at Balwyn. The rolling green gorse-covered hills of this district have long since been built over and suburbanized, but then they were windswept and glorious and the nearest thing I could find to a Van Gogh corn field. Inspired by Mr Bow's exuberant example, I went on many painting expeditions; beside the Yarra River, where the Melbourne 'impressionists' used to set up their painting camps in the eighties and nineties, and on the red bluffs of Mornington, the bayside resort where my father had built us a new holiday 'shack', this time with a septic tank and a tennis court.

The beach at Mornington was unfrequented, almost private, and sometimes on hot summer days, when the bay seemed tideless, my sister and I would swim in the green glassy water, explore the cliff paths and search for shells. I liked to burst the small bladders of the antlered seaweed, or dabble languidly in the secret crannies of the rock pool, surprising the petals of the sea-anemones and feeling them sucking and nibbling at my fingertips. On such becalmed days, the tartan rugs would be drawn nearer the verge and the umbrellas planted close to the barely lapping water.

One hot afternoon I noticed on the shore, a few feet from where I floated, a dentist's wife my parents knew cooling her ankles in the water, squinting into the spangled brightness and brushing the sand from her knees. But then, suddenly, as she stretched across the picnic debris to have her Bakelite teacup refilled from the orange-flecked Thermos, I noticed how her woollen bathing costume gaped at the place on her legs where her suntan stopped; and then I saw a kind of pleat, sutured with hair like a dark V-shaped darn. Soon she drew her knees together again and, sipping her tea, squinted out to sea where I hid in the white dazzle.

Although I still painted during these summer holidays, trudging around with my portable easel searching for the Mornington correspondences with Cézanne's 'Mont St Victoire' and Van Gogh's 'Asylum at St Remy', there was no one at Melbourne Grammar to offer much encouragement. In fact, no one seemed to draw or paint at all. Some form of instruction in art must have been compulsory, or why else would poor lugubrious Mr Grant, known as 'Whizzer' because of his legendary sprinting prowess, be forced to teach, against his better inclination, this Cinderella subject? Not much happened in art class. There was general disorder which Mr Grant, sunk in a post-prandial torpor with his mind clearly on other things, did little to subdue. At least our music classes were livelier, especially if Albert had had a few.

Slowly, in spite of myself, I began to enjoy the new school with its old buildings and the nearby Royal Botanic Gardens to which we sometimes escaped during lunch hour. After school I would take the tram along St Kilda Road, lined with English plane trees, to the city and often, instead of catching the train home from Flinders Street Station, I would spend an hour browsing around some of the secondhand bookshops. At the top of Bourke Street near Parliament House, where an anachronistic hansom cab still loitered, there was the bookshop of Ellis Bird. Mrs Bird, a good-looking woman with a grey bun, and her assistant, Shirley, always seemed to be entertaining a priest whenever I entered the dusty old shop. But Mrs Bird had quickly learnt my name and always addressed me rather formally, and to my intense pleasure, as *Mr Humphries*. 'Excuse me, Father,' she would say to her sherry-sipping guest, 'but I just want to show Mr Humphries a book which I think might amuse him,' and she would produce *South Wind* or *The Green Hat* or Richard Garnett's *The Twilight of the Gods* or *The Monk* by M. G. Lewis.

On the campus of the Melbourne University beside the Conservatorium of Music was a curious brick building that seemed to be permanently closed. It was also apparently windowless. A small plaque, however, proclaimed it to be the Percy Grainger Museum, and those wishing to inspect its contents might obtain permission and a key from the secretary at the Conservatorium. Percy Grainger was Australia's most famous composer, *outside* Australia. In the United States, he was largely celebrated as a conductor and concert pianist who had, in 1928, been married to his 'Nordic Princess' in the presence of an audience of 23,000 people at the Hollywood Bowl (the couple were later photographed with Ramon Novarro). The event must have come as no small surprise to his bride, who was expecting a 'cameo' wedding, and supposed the Hollywood Bowl to be a picturesque grotto in a quiet park.

If Percy Grainger had any renown in his homeland, it was only as the composer of 'Country Gardens', a jaunty ditty which the Australian Broadcasting Commission used as a theme tune for its rural broadcasts. Grainger, undeterred by the indifference of his countrymen, had built this museum in Melbourne to house his own memorabilia, and he had designed it himself, so that its ground plan was identical, from the air, to an Icelandic burial ground. Unfortunately there were few, if any, Australians inclined to recognize this similitude, even had they been vouchsafed an aerial view of the building. Consequently, although it had been conceived as a modernist structure, it most resembled a large and inaccessible public lavatory.

About once a decade Percy would revisit Australia and spend a few days in Melbourne dusting his unfrequented museum and adding to its contents: a Greig manuscript here, a bust of Sibelius there.

There had been a small paragraph accompanied by a photograph in the *Melbourne Sun News-pictorial* announcing Grainger's latest visit, and on one of our Sunday afternoon drives I spotted him strolling along a quiet, leafy street at Kew, on a nostalgic jaunt. I asked my father to stop the car, and rather boldly accosted the maestro. I told him that I had what I thought to be a rare recording of one of his compositions for solo cello, and asked if he would accept it as a gift to the museum. He seemed very pleased and invited me to call on him the following day.

Thus was I taken on a personal guided tour of the museum's many treasures and curiosities, including a pair of breeches worn on a walking tour of Norway by the forgotten composer Balfour Gardiner. But I, a mere Melbourne schoolboy, had now shaken hands with the creator of *The Magic Flute*; for had not Percy shaken hands with Greig who had shaken hands with Liszt who had shaken hands with Beethoven who had shaken hands with Haydn, *who had clasped the hand of Mozart?*

Quite recently I revisited the Grainger Museum. Percy, being long and safely dead, was now acknowledged as an important Australian, and the museum doors stood proudly ajar. At a desk within I saw a young female archivist earnestly cataloguing the avalanche of letters to and from the composer, which Grainger had bequeathed to his own museum. It was a task for the stout-hearted, however, since Grainger's sexual vocation was, to say the least, exotic. Even as I entered the room, I observed the young woman holding an envelope at arm's length, and, with a pair of tweezers, disdainfully extracting from it a fibrous tangle of pubic hair.

Every Anzac Day there was a special assembly in the Memorial Hall, usually addressed by some purple-faced old general with a knighthood and a rainbow of ribbons on his khaki chest. Then, while the whole school stood silently to attention, a group of impetiginous prefects would recite the Roll of Honour; the Old Boys who had died in the Boer War and the Great War. There was one family called Snowball, which produced a titter every year, though the laughter died on our lips as we counted seven Snowballs. The list of the fallen was a long one, and many students fell in sympathy and had to be carted out, grey-faced, into the quad.

Over the next few years I gained friends and confidence. Some of my poems about theological doubt and pacifism were published, if in expurgated form, in the school magazine and I appeared every year in the school play, usually in a minor role, except for my most spectacular cameo as Mrs Pengard in Walter Hackett's *Ambrose Applejohn's Adventure,* a precursor perhaps of a later theatrical invention.

I became involved with the debating society also, and in my third year we sometimes debated against other schools on Friday evenings. Girls' schools. These exciting expeditions were organized by our history master, Mr Olsen, a dapper English-man who wore the first double-vented sports jacket seen in Melbourne. He had a knitted tie and an effeminate habit of tucking his handkerchief in his sleeve. He was also known to possess a pair of suede shoes, a sure sign in the Melbourne of this period of sexual ambivalence. Mr Olsen, however, had a rather vivid wife, who, it seemed, was interested in Art and completely understood, according to her husband, Paul Klee. The girls at our debates impressed me then as being much more clever and quick-witted than us; and to someone like me, whose female acquaintance was limited to my sister's friends (who hardly counted), my beautiful, fierce and witty debating opponents from Merton Hall, Lauriston, Shelford and the Methodist Ladies' College, seemed at once ravishing and unattainable.

My sister Barbara and I began to attend ballroom-dancing classes given by an Austrian couple called Meyer. No doubt they were Jewish refugees from Vienna and they seemed to move

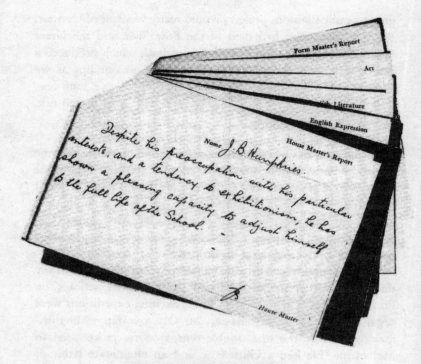

Form Master's Report

Art

...lish Literature

English Expression

House Master's Report

Name *J. B. Humphries.*

Despite his preoccupation with his particular interests, and a tendency to exhibitionism, he has shown a pleasing capacity to adjust himself to the full life of the School.

House Master

Melbourne Grammar report, c. 1948

perpetually to the tempo of the waltz. I dreaded their classes, and I was convinced that I had no dancing ability whatsoever. During these excruciating *soirées* in a rented church hall I was forced into the apprehensive embrace of all my sister's girlfriends: Valerie, Maureen, Gillian, Margot and Wendy; the latter always, it seemed, clutching in one hand a slightly damp handkerchief. At the end of what felt like an interminable evening of hopping and shuffling to a thumping piano accompaniment, Mr Meyer commiserated with my bruised and disgruntled partners, and in a last desperate attempt to inculcate in me the basic steps of the waltz or the foxtrot, would take me in his powerful arms and sweep me imperiously around the room, his chin held high, his eyes blazing and his knees locked

into mine. 'Vun two sree, vun two sree, vun two sree...'
Out of the corner of my eye I could see Mrs Meyer and the
other pupils watching this demonstration with patronizing
smirks as, growing giddier by the second, I was propelled past
them.

Most boys joined the school regiment and became known as
'cadets'. Every Tuesday afternoon after school they paraded for
hours in uniform, and the time approached when I would have
to enrol. I had been reading some of Sassoon's pacifist First
World War verse and I also knew something of Bertrand
Russell and the other conscientious objectors whom Lady
Ottoline Morrell had sheltered at Garsington, so I decided to
be a conscientious objector myself. Mr Sutcliffe, to whom I
made this rather priggish declaration, took it, to my surprise,
extremely well. He even seemed impressed and I was immediately excused from the pointless hours of drill into which
the other boys were grimly conscripted. I have a picture of
myself – not an altogether attractive one – strolling jauntily out
the school gates past a rigid platoon of my classmates, their
faces sullen with envy. Mr Sutcliffe always called me by my
first name after this and it was difficult to imagine that he was
the aloof and snobbish figure who had intimidated my poor
father years before in his office. Perhaps, I reflected, the
headmaster was a secret pacifist himself.

With a few carefully chosen friends I formed a small
subversive gang. From the back row of the classroom we would
submit some of our teachers, who were not fully the masters of
their subject, to relentless raillery. I became Secretary of the Art
Club and arranged exhibitions of work in the cricket pavilion,
in which my own paintings predominated. Some of these were
bright-hued post-impressionist oil-paintings of Mornington
views, and others, in stark contrast, were in the cubist and
Dadaist manner, designed to shock. I also invited some 'real'
artists to speak at the school; an unprecedented event. One was
an academic old duffer, Max Meldrum, and another was Noel
Counihan, a notorious communist whose scurrilous caricatures

of the prime minister, Mr Robert Menzies, appeared regularly in the *Guardian*, Melbourne's only communist newspaper.

Senator McCarthy's witchhunts in the United States had distant reverberations in Australia, and the Melbourne *Herald* was gleefully publishing the shameful confessions of an ex-party member under the unimaginative banner 'I Chose Freedom'. For years the *Guardian*, full of old-fashioned anti-capitalist cant and naïve pro-Soviet propaganda, had been sold on newsstands and by 'workers' on the steps of Flinders Street Railway Station without anyone taking much notice. Now there was talk of banning this anodyne little rag. The very idea of communism, rarely thought of before, sent a shudder down every respectable back.

I decided to become a communist. Furtively I bought a copy of *The Communist Manifesto* in a back-street bookshop in the industrial suburb of Brunswick, but I found it practically unreadable. The next best thing, so I thought, was to *appear* to be a communist, and this was a path down which I was sure Mr Sutcliffe would not follow me. My political period – the only one in my life – was short-lived, since the *Manifesto* left ostentatiously on my desk so that it could be seen by the most fanatically right-wing schoolmaster in Australia was swiftly confiscated and I never saw it again. However I had discovered that there was a very special pleasure and excitement to be derived from shocking people. I suppose it gave a schoolboy, who was in fact completely powerless, the illusion of power.

In spite of some of the freedoms that I was claiming for myself at school, there was one principle that was ruthlessly enforced: it was something called *School Spirit*, or the compulsory attendance at games. Precious hours of after-school leisure were wasted in those dangerous and futile exercises upon the playing field. Only the sickliest boys escaped, on medical grounds, the ineluctable twice-weekly 'turnout'. First, one entered the dungeon-like tog-room beneath the Memorial Hall, and in an atmosphere reeking of jockstraps and carbolic acid and thunderous with cold showers, one hastily donned the foolish motley of cricket field or footy pitch. Thereafter one would ascend to the oval's miry brink to have one's name ticked off by a yahoo prefect. Like sheep to the slaughter the boys would then subject themselves to hours of health-impairing sport, often returning to their homes after dark, too ill and exhausted to study. Not I.

Twice a week for several years I dutifully 'turned out'. No sooner was my name ticked off on the roll than I would furtively skirt the playing fields and vanish into a cubicle of the school lavatories. Minutes later, in response to a tapped signal on the door, I would open it, and my accomplice, now an advertising tycoon, for whom I performed a similar service on *his* turnout nights, thrust into my grasp a Gladstone bag containing my school uniform. A quick change, an all-clear whistle, and I was outside the school gates, off on a tram – to freedom!

Amazing, really, that this ruse should have succeeded as long as it did; and inevitable, as I now apprehend, that the day should come when, emboldened by habit, I should hear the familiar knock, open the door, and behold a glowering Neanderthal figure. 'The game's up, Humphries,' said Peter Beer, the Captain of the School, for it was he. I was led away to his study, if a room without books may be so called, where I received six strokes of the cane.

Shithouse Spaghetti

I NOW HAD TWO younger brothers, Christopher and Michael, who were enrolled at the junior school, but I saw very little of them during their childhood, except on school holidays which we spent in the new house in Mornington. With an army of workmen, my father had built it in two weeks and I remember our first Christmas there, when the paint was still wet. It was in the bay at Mornington that we all had our swimming lessons from a deeply suntanned, wiry German called Willi Fritsch.

Willi had been a champion at the Berlin Olympic Games in 1936 but had somehow been stranded in Australia, where he spent the war in custody. If swimming could be called a sport, it was the only one that ever gave me any enjoyment, as it still does. Willi lived quite close to us in Camberwell and I once had to call at his house for some reason, perhaps to pay swimming fees. I was admitted by his attractive blonde wife, and whilst waiting for Willi, I noticed an interesting framed photograph of my swimming teacher taken some years before, being presented with a silver cup by Hitler. It was not the sort of snapshot one was used to seeing on a surburban mantelpiece.

My parents expressed concern when I began to form closer friendships with Jewish boys at school. 'Robert seems a very nice type of boy,' my mother would say, unconvincingly, 'but can't you spend more time with people of your own kind?' My mother had dark hair and olive skin, and it was by no means certain that if her ancestry were ever traced it would necessarily reveal a purely Anglo-Saxon heritage.

Jews were admitted to Melbourne Grammar on a very discouraging quota system and even then were only grudgingly excused from attending chapel. They had about them an aura of separateness which I identified with. I felt somehow 'different' and they *were* different.

Robert Nathan, my new friend, was obviously a gifted boy and I felt drawn to his circle. It may have been my parents' suburban anti-Semitism that made these classmates seem somehow brighter, funnier and more attractive than the rest, but, I reflected, weren't the Marx Brothers Jewish? Nathan, though not a brilliant scholar, had the aura of talent about him, and on Sundays he often held musical evenings at his parents' house. These consisted of record-playing sessions and Robert, whose musical tastes were very advanced for a schoolboy's, liked to play works such as the Brahm's *Requiem* and Walton's *Belshazzar's Feast*. I brought along my 78 recordings of *Façade*, the most thrillingly modern and witty music I had ever heard, with the voice of Constant Lambert, and Edith Sitwell herself declaiming the insouciant verses.

By then my mother and father had been forced to relax their fundamentalist attitude to the Christian Sabbath, and I was sometimes allowed to spend a Sunday evening with my friends. On the one hand they were no doubt relieved to know that these evenings were supervised; indeed occasionally there was even a rabbi present in the same house, as well as my friend John Levi, a rabbi of the future. On the other hand, however, they felt as though the traditional Church of England 'values' which they and Canon Robinson had tried for so long to inculcate were being insidiously eroded. In fact, they were.

Some time before, I had become a Sunday-school teacher at St Mark's Church, Camberwell. Autocratic, sanctimonious old Canon Robinson had conscripted me, and every Sunday I had to teach the New Testament to a small class of bored and restless children in the hideous red-brick hall beside the church. I felt I was a terrible hypocrite, mouthing the teachings of the Church of England to these indifferent brats, and at the same time writing agnostic and frankly anti-clerical verses for the school magazine. The rapture of an authentic spiritual experience had always eluded me. I remember at my Confirmation I had hoped and prayed for such a transcendental moment, when Bishop McKay, the Bishop of Geelong, had placed his hands on my head in blessing. But as I knelt expectantly at the altar rail and the Moment came, I felt nothing. All I could smell was the odour of Brylcreem on the bishop's benedictory palms, and I pictured him in the vestry, just before the service, quickly caressing his dark greasy hair before stepping into the Chancel.

My fellow Sunday-school teachers were either devout and elderly parishioners whom I could see in other corners of the hall droning on to a circle of stupefied children, or young conscripts like me. There was a pretty girl called Rosemary Gair teaching the juniors, whom I sometimes met on the tram. Whenever I spoke to her I always moved my head vigorously, making it impossible for her to focus too intently on my acne. Eyeing her sideways at Sunday school, I secretly wondered if she had as little faith as I, or if, indeed, she ever entertained impious fantasies similar to my own. Probably not.

I befriended a fellow teacher called George Howe, who also played the piano and organ at Sunday school. We shared an interest in music and sometimes we listened to records at his home, where he lived with elderly parents. It was a dark Edwardian house in an old section of the suburb, and the streets were shaded with large elms and plane trees. The oldest streets and parks of Melbourne still have mature plantations of trees which have not yet succumbed to the 'Dutch' disease, so that the city has become, almost, a Museum for Elms. George had a large old-fashioned wind-up gramophone, and a complete collection of pre-war recordings of Delius, conducted by Beecham. It was strange sitting in that dim house on a still night in a city of South-east Asia, as this most English of music floated out the window into the heavy English foliage of Canterbury Road.

At last the day came when, not to be outdone by the Infidel, my parents cautiously agreed to let me hold a reciprocal musical *soirée* at our house. My father bought a large walnut-veneered piece of furniture called a radiogram, with a noisy and sometimes violent automatic record changer. Then the night arrived: a small group of my friends and a few serious-minded and very pretty girls from Merton Hall came to Christowel Street and sat in the sun-room in various attitudes of highbrow concentration, while I played them an opera by Ravel. The music wove its spell of chaste eroticism, a spell which was somewhat broken by my mother's periodic interruptions, 'Do you *have* to have it up this loud, Barry?' or, more archly, 'I hope you've asked your friends if they really want to listen to this,' and finally, at about 9.30: 'Would you all like a little nibble of something *before you go home?*' At which my mother, speaking in that distressingly genteel voice she always employed in the presence of strangers, would invite us all into the dining-room for tea and sandwiches and cakes.

I winced with shame and snobbishness when I thought of Mr and Mrs Spira, my friend Leonard's parents, who had escaped from Poland via Shanghai, arrived in Melbourne, started a small restaurant and helped to found a chamber orchestra. When I had gone to their place a few Sundays before to listen to the gramophone, Mrs Spira had offered the boys a glass of Chartreuse; and although their house was much much smaller than ours there were garlicky cheesy smells coming from the kitchen which my mother could not, and certainly *would not*, ever produce.

In the Spiras' small sitting-room it was somehow warmer too, and the lights were dimmer, and some of the boys rested their arms idly around the girls' shoulders almost as if Prokofiev and Bartók and Stravinsky were not entirely the point of the evening.

*

It is strange to think that I, who now leap around the stage performing nimble corybantics to a musical accompaniment in front of thousands of people, once had an aversion to dancing, and such a conviction of my own inadequacy that I would avoid all social gatherings where dancing took place. To arrive at somebody's house in my new dinner jacket and black tie and hear, even in the street, the ominous thump of Dennis Farrington's orchestra playing such popular hits of the period as 'The Roving Kind' and 'A Kiss to Build a Dream On' always brought me out in a cold, apprehensive sweat.

My mother was particularly anxious for me to attend one such event in the company of a friend's daughter, yet even as I collected this unfortunate girl and pressed upon her the obligatory corsage of gardenias and maidenhair fern in a celluloid box, I pitied her. Later that night as we stood by the bar I prayed that someone else would tap her on one of her bare, blue-mottled shoulders and whisk her on to the dance floor forever. Then, looking slightly past me with eyes that already seemed to well with tears of disappointment, she asked for a glass of punch. Eager for something to do – and say – I proceeded to tilt the large jug of fruit-choked liquid gently into her glass which she held close to her deeply *décolletée* ballerina-length dress. The punch merely trickled into her glass, so I tilted the jug at a sharper angle. The dam of pineapple, orange, strawberry and passionfruit ruptured, sending two pints of chilled cordial directly down her cleavage whence it pursued an invisible path to the carpet beneath.

She gave a sort of whimper, and fled to the bathroom where she remained for the rest of the evening until finally I drove her home in total silence. Strange to say, my pity for her completely disappeared and was replaced by a kind of rage against adolescence itself, and the cruel and pointless rituals of my class.

Another of my new interests, which disappointed my parents, was my enthusiasm for secondhand bookshops; indeed, for anything that had the patina of age. 'Do you have to buy those old bits and pieces?' my mother would say if I came home with some dusty old volume after a visit to Mrs Bird. 'You never know where things like that have been.' Some of my books, like the *Tales of D. H. Lawrence*, disappeared mysteriously from my shelves and when I mentioned this my mother said, passing the buck, 'Your father thought it was quite unsuitable, unnecessary and completely *Uncalled-for!*' I never saw the books again, though I suspect they were consigned to some secret bibliocaust in the incinerator at the back of the garden.

My father was beginning to see that the educational opportunities that he had struggled to give us – and barely a week passed when we were not reminded of his sacrifices – could have their disadvantages; could even introduce us to the seamy and seductive world of the Uncalled-for. On the whole, though, he was proud of the As I got for English, and, to gently discourage me from buying old and dirty books, he opened an account for me at Robertson & Mullens, which only sold new and germ-free editions.

My friend Robert Maclellan and I sometimes dined in town on Friday evenings before a meeting of the school Debating Society. To fill in time we would visit bookshops or art exhibitions, and then have a plate of pasta at a small, cheap Italian restaurant next to His Majesty's Theatre. The Spaghetti à la Bolognese was a total novelty for me, as were the strange twig-like fragments in the sauce that suggested that someone had shaken a dead bush over the plate. It was my first experience of herbs.

One evening at about 6.00, we were twirling our forks when a disturbance broke out at another table. There was the crash of a chair falling backwards and we looked across the small café to see a woman with dishevelled hair and a crimson face swaying slightly before she lurched against the wall. Her husband and a small child sat there looking at her with expressions of horror, and also with a kind of grief, that I can still see to this day. The woman pointed to her plate, and at the top of her voice she screamed, 'THIS SPAGHETTI IS SHITHOUSE!' I had never heard a woman swear. The owner hurried to her table. 'Get to the shithouse!' the woman yelled, while her husband made mute gestures of despair and apology to us all. The family was bundled out into the street. The other diners all looked at each other and grinned sheepishly as we heard cockatoo-like cries of 'shithouse' dwindling down the street. It was my first encounter with alcoholism.

My last year of school was almost amusing. Unfortunately, Mr Sutcliffe, of whom I had become rather fond, resigned under suspicious circumstances. It was said that he had tried to expel a group of hooligans who had disrupted a school dance with fireworks, forgetting that they were the sons of rich and influential parents. Some of the parents were on the school board, so Sutcliffe got the shove. He was replaced by a craggy-faced and hearty new headmaster from Sydney, who quickly instituted reforms. The incompetent 'characters' who had hither-to shuffled across the quad or, rather than teach, loitered before the blackboard, were expelled. Younger schoolmasters replaced them, a few of whom even wore casual clothes; crew-necked sweaters and knitted ties. Some of these, we noticed, even failed to bow to the altar in Chapel.

I no longer tried to be good at mathematics, though for years my father had sent me to a succession of coaches in this incomprehensible subject. It was not as though I got bad marks for maths; I got zero, term after term.

Instead I devoted most of my energy to the Art Club and to my new passion for the Dadaists and Surrealists of the early 1920s. Everything I read about their antics and outrages excited me, and the work of Duchamp and Picabia and Schwitters seemed so much more amusing than the landscapes I had been painting in plodding imitation of Cézanne.

John Levi had a crony called Perry whom I persecuted by bombarding his desk with vicious caricatures. I am sure envy lay behind this behaviour since Perry was clearly an authentic artist, although what kind it was difficult to tell. Slowly I relaxed my mean-spirited vendetta and we became friends. Already he was writing brilliant and anarchic monologues and wild irrational tirades that anticipated Lucky's speech from *Waiting for Godot* by several years.

Sometimes our Dada Group went down to the seaside suburb of St Kilda to Luna Park, a large and tawdry fairground which was entered through a huge neon mouth. Between rides on the Big Dipper and mysterious River Caves, amongst the shrieks of plummeting roller coasters and the smell of sparks and fairy floss, we recorded our subversive improvisations in a tiny recording booth next to the Giggle Palace. The wafer-thin black discs we made there were crude and fragile, though a couple, miraculously, still survive.

After Luna Park we sometimes visited the Galleon Coffee Lounge, a raffish café filled with smoke, where I saw my first 'blue' comic, a man called Frank Rich who wore a suit and a moustache and looked like a successful commercial traveller. Next to the Marx Brothers, he was the funniest thing I'd ever seen, although I could never have guessed then that one day part of me would also be a 'blue' comedian.

A new club had opened in Melbourne called the Society for New Music. It met on Sunday nights in a theatre in the old bayside suburb of Middle Park and there, once a month, flocked the highbrows and *poseurs*, the precious, the pretty and the pretentious. The foyer of the theatre was painted black and was hung with photographs of Melbourne actors and actresses looking intense, all smoking and wearing black polo-neck jumpers. The photographs were by a young German called Helmut Newton. When the New Music Society met, the small theatre was thronged with long-haired youths in suede shoes and corduroy trousers smoking Turkish cigarettes with the wrong fingers. 'Window-dressers!' someone whispered, grinning. There were beards too, and women who, in the age of the perm, wore very long straight hair, sandals and not much makeup. And there was a loud babble of foreign tongues. It all felt, well, continental.

The society was founded by Kevin McBeath to foster an interest in modern music and we would sit solemnly in the stalls listening to recordings of Menotti's new operas and occasionally live performances of advanced chamber music. I had recently, after a long struggle, got my drivers licence, and one sultry Sunday evening I was allowed to drive my mother's car to a special Sunday-night recital devoted to the music of Erik Satie.

The three *Gymnopédies* were not then the slightly hackneyed works they have sadly since become, and as their breathless and limpid beauty unfolded at that arty little gathering, I glanced across the aisle and noticed one of the girls I had met at Leonard's house. She was transfixed by the music. There was coffee after the concert and for the first time in my life I found it possible to say the words, 'May I give you a lift home?' That night in a cream Austin A40 parked beneath an enormous lilac tree in full bloom, I fell in love.

Russian Salad Days

'I HOPE YOU'RE not turning pansy.'

Mr Hone, the craggy-faced headmaster, looked up at me interrogatively. What could he mean? It was impossible to know how to reply to such an unexpected and heartfelt expression of concern.'I hope not too, sir,' was all I could manage.

I had been called to the Head's study to explain why my final term's results had been so unsatisfactory; even in subjects like English and history I had gained disappointing marks, though I had won the poetry prize again — with very little competition, it must be confessed.

Mr Hone — soon to be Sir Brian Hone — was obviously sincere, but it was hard to know the basis for his concern. Throughout my last years at school I was always being told my hair was too long, and since the time when my elaborate ruse for avoiding games was discovered and punished by the School Captain, I had been called 'Queenie' Humphries by a few scurrilous boarders.

'You've got a lot of serious decisions to make over the next few years, my boy,' said the bluff old Head, rising from his chair and extending the five sausages of his right hand, 'and I hope you feel you can call on me for help at any time.' I didn't feel I could in the least, as a matter of fact, nor was I quite sure what the decisions I had to make were all about, but I allowed my hand to be lightly sprained by Mr Hone's rugger-toughened grasp, and sheepishly retreated.

It had been suggested that, like some of my dimmer classmates, I might stay back at school another year and repeat my matriculation. However the public examinations had yet to come when we all traipsed into town to that majestic Victorian folly, the Exhibition Building, and sat for our Finals, adjudicated by impartial examiners.

When, after Christmas, the results were published, it seemed that I had done spectacularly well, and to my father's amazement I even won a valuable scholarship to the University. I had hoped to read Arts, but due to an oversight at Melbourne Grammar, I lacked the prerequisite language. I decided to please my parents and enrol at the Law School. I would spend a year catching up on German at a famous crammer, and commence my Arts course the following year. I later heard that due to this blunder, my old school had been given an enormous rocket by the University, and Mr Hone had been hauled over the coals for failing to spot a star pupil. I was immoderately pleased. Most of my contemporaries at school entered the World of Business, the logical destiny of bores. No more than eight members of the entire sixth form went on to University. I remember that one of our masters proudly collected the names of Old Boys who had 'done well', and these he recorded in a small book. It was a very small book.

There was another interruption to the launch of my academic career; military service. I had vaguely known about this, but like many things in my life, had supposed it couldn't happen to me, or, if it did, I would gesture hypnotically like Mandrake the Magician and make it go away. At the medical examination I tried the Conscientious Objection tactic that had worked so well in the past, but it provoked only a derisory laugh. Then I found a doctor who wrote that I was psychologically unfit for military service, but his letter was ignored. And so soon after, I found myself at four o'clock in the morning doing kitchen duty at Puckapunyal Military Camp, seventy miles from Melbourne. Puckapunyal is an Aboriginal word meaning The Land of the Outer Barbarians.

I had sometimes, though rarely, gone to bed at four a.m. but I had never risen at that hour. Minutes after waking and dressing, I was in the camp kitchen scrubbing 'Dixies' – large aluminium vats to which the greasy and gristly remnants of stew tenaciously clung. I was sure that my attempts to dodge National Service had earmarked me for this brutal assignment. I stood all day at the sink, my hands raw with detergent, while the oafish and grinning kitchen hands from the Regular Army sadistically added to the huge pile of clattering aluminium to which the burnt residue of cabbage, cod and mashed potato seemed inseparably bonded.

The stench was the worst. In the kitchen it was predominantly the fart-like odour of cabbage with a dash of onion and offal, but the whole camp was pervaded by the smell of dust and garbage. The surrounding countryside may have been attractive once, but now it had been wrecked and eroded by military exercises over many years so that it resembled an overheated, antipodian Somme or Passchendaele. The camp was huge and the prospect of having to spend three months' penal servitude there filled me with horror. Some of my school friends were in the same regiment and I would glimpse them through the greasy louvres of my kitchen as they marched past at 8.30 a.m. A few even seemed to be enjoying themselves. Should I too be relishing this healthy military life, or was Mr Hone right, and was I turning pansy after all?

At the end of a long day, around seven p.m., I was sometimes too tired to take off my fat-spattered boots. I lay on my horsehair palliase, in one of the long tents of the Melbourne University Rifles, sobbing with rage and fatigue, while some of the more enthusiastic recruits nearby whistled inanely as they scrubbed their webbing, polished their boots and oiled their rifles.

My parents were very pleased that I was in the army. The

fact that I hated it somehow pleased them even more. I was beginning to realize that this was an aspect of the Puritanism which governed most of my friends' lives as well as mine, so that later, at the University, I saw many men I knew doing courses only to gratify their parents or, as the phrase went, 'to get something solid behind them.' There was a moral virtue in suppressing all real talent; in flying in the face of impulse and vocation and doing something, instead, which was completely repugnant. That made parents happy.

At last released from kitchen duty, I did square bashing with the rest of them, though I quickly found that the more laughs I could win through incompetence, the more chance I would have of getting off punishing drills and manoeuvres.

In the evenings, as it cooled down a bit and the foul-smelling dust settled, it was almost pleasant to sit beside the tent on an upturned box reading, or teaching myself to smoke a pipe. Occasionally a surly officer from the Regular Army would strut past, eye one of us severely and bark, 'On your feet, soldier! What's the matter with your right hand?' At which we would spring to attention and deliver the appropriate salute, even though sometimes it was too dark to see the face of our superior. This gave me an idea which briefly restored my failing self-confidence.

With a false moustache of burnt cork and my hair plastered back, I would visit remote sections of the camp at twilight and catch slovenly privates unawares as I surprised them from the shadows. 'What's the matter with your right hand?' was a phrase which, if enunciated at close range and with sufficient savagery, would bring even the most vigilant corporal to a position of tremulous attention, and I was gone before they could, by squinting through the dusk, observe my lack of stripes or my anomalous uniform. I felt a little reassuring gush of illicit power.

By fraternizing with the Entertainments Officer, I managed to involve myself in the camp concert, which was to be a whimsical view of army life on Mars, with musical items pinched from Gilbert and Sullivan. I contrived to get the job of Scenic Designer, an official task which required more and more leave of absence from arduous military training. Luckily Lieutenant-Colonel Duffy, the commander of the camp, was enthusiastic about the whole project and I was given a disused aircraft hangar on the periphery of the camp in which to supervise the painting and construction of the large sets, which I had also designed. These were mostly backdrops painted on enormous sheets of canvas and hessian, and I arranged for a few of my less martially inclined friends to be seconded to my scene-painting unit.

At reveille, as the others clambered into their gear before shuffling on to the parade ground, my little team and I enjoyed an hour's more sleep before ambling over to our hangar for a leisurely few hours painting, or snoozing on the bales of hessian. It was important military work, though it did not earn us the affection of our foot-slogging counterparts. There was a particularly strong pink colour I needed for a sunset which proved to be unobtainable in the hardware stores of Seymour, our nearest country town. I insisted that it was absolutely necessary and, to my surprise, was given a staff car and a driver to take me seventy miles to Melbourne. It was a tremendous jolt to be in the city after two months' rustication at Puckapunyal and the very dull streets of Melbourne were suddenly glamorous and exciting. Even though I wore the drab, ill-fitting uniform of a private, office girls seemed to give me a little squeeze with their eyes. In an artists'-supply shop I found the pigment I was looking for, and to the surprise of the salesman ordered it in huge quantities, instructing him to invoice the army.

At the dress rehearsal of the concert I was a little disappointed to see how lacklustre this special paint finally looked under the lights, but the general effect of our décor was impressive, the show a hit, and my military training came to an agreeable end with a large programme credit and personal congratulations from Colonel Duffy himself.

The ballet of Jupiterian maidens were well
to the fore with their difficult task of female
impersonation and their vocal efforts brought
many rounds of mirthful appreciation from the
audience. They were ably assisted by the antics
of "momma sans" WO1 H. Pearce, Sgt. J. Liddy
and Sgt. F. P. Pi__

The ___ costumed choirs at ___ ___
mo___ ___ of brilliance, particularly in their ren-
___ of the "Tarantara Chorus" and "We Aint
Got Dames."

The sets designed and executed by Pte. J. B.
Humphries and the technical staff showed
amazing imagination and originality, and lent
an almost three-dimensional effect to the three
scenes; while the stage properties constructed
by Battalion Engineers assisted in this concept
of realism.

The orchestra, conducted in a masterly ___
professional fashion by 2/Lt. C. F. ___ and
A___ Conductor L./Cpl ___ ___ood, with Pte.
Catford as ___, performed the musical ar-
rangement by Cpl. C. J. Brumby in a well-
balanced and cleverly executed manner.

The lighting, which accentuated much of
the dramatic quality of the show, was the work

___ ___ ___
Ballet. In
little of th
the ridicul
that.

Take f
knows that
noon off fc
it's not rea
f our trair
a doing t
here's
Coy regret.
ticu rly ou
the inject
of he effic
e miss t
have, too—
noon. Inst
de deux,"
tumes, and
day's train

But stil
cause we're
because Inc
all working

Later that year, I read in the Melbourne *Age* that there had
been a military inquiry into certain excessive expenditures at
Puckapunyal Camp, and particularly the funding of a theatrical
event authorized by Colonel Duffy. One item was particularly
singled out: a quantity of red pigment made from the pulverized
wings of a rare Korean insect, costing over £700.

At the army camp I had taken up smoking, an addiction which
I only relinquished, with the greatest difficulty, in 1980. I did
not indulge my nicotine habit at home for my mother deplored it
and, when quizzed, I always denied that I had been smoking. At
this she would regard me with an omniscient smile and utter her
favourite admonition: 'Don't bother to tell fibs to your mother,
Barry. *I can read you like a book.*' From a woman who read very
few books indeed, this was, paradoxically, reassuring. But it had
not always been so.

As a child, I believed my mother absolutely when she warned
us that 'the wind might change' if we pulled faces, leaving our
countenances permanently fixed in hideous grimaces.

Once at the university I began attending lectures at the law
school. Here and there, amongst my fellow students, I noticed

with a premonitory shudder those who would later specialize in 'matrimonial law'; stirring up the acrimony and greed of their clients so that they might up-grade their German cars or finance their wineries or their vacations at the Villa D'Este. There were girls too, lips now pursed in concentration which would remain forever pursed; for the wind changed early in the lives of these young professionals.

I recognized, also, a few fellows from Puckapunyal earnestly scribbling their notes. They were the ones who had always been keenest in their pursuit of rank and military prowess; the ones who had most loudly sneered whenever I dropped my rifle on the parade ground. Already at that early age they were priggishly, proudly unimaginative; preparing themselves for that day in the future when they would become Silks, with Mercedes Benzes and Saabs for their wives, and original daubs by Fred Williams, and macadamia farms and wineries and distinguished cellars of Australian reds, and big collections of that safest and dullest of all artistic commodities: Georgian silver. There was something about those conscientious young bores with Irish names furiously taking notes to my left and right that told me they would one day be running Australia.

In the evenings I had to present myself at Taylor's Coaching School in a narrow street of the city in order to catch up on my neglected German, but it was difficult to concentrate and I felt surrounded by dunces and dyslexics. My friends were launched on their University careers but I was lagging behind, forced to show up every day at incomprehensible legal lectures and later dreaming and dozing off in Frau Steinki's classes.

Now that it looked as though I had been successfully diverted from artistic pursuits, my mother thought it was safe to rekindle my interest in painting – on a purely recreational level. Both my parents were fond of saying, 'You've got a wonderful hobby there, Barry, and as long as you keep it like that you'll save yourself and your parents a lot of heartache.' They were pleased with my pictures too, or at least the nice ones that weren't unnecessarily 'futuristic'. There was a well-known private art school in a nearby suburb, run by George Bell, a failed Melbourne Post-Impressionist. Bell had taught a handful of quite famous artists and I began to attend his classes every Saturday morning.

Rather to my surprise, my mother insisted on paying the fees for my art classes, as she had paid for my driving lessons, with the caution, 'Not a word to your father about this.' I sometimes suspected she might even be my secret ally against the strictures of my father; someone with a great love of beauty who might have possessed artistic gifts herself which she had rigorously suppressed in order to be a respectable housewife and mother.

At the back of George Bell's suburban house was a studio, and there I would sit with my sketchbook in a semi-circle of chairs on which several real artists – judging by their beards and berets – drew and painted from a live model.

The studio smelt wonderfully of turpentine, and old George Bell, irascible and owl-like, strolled up and down behind us peering over our shoulders and occasionally making pencilled corrections to our work. The surprise to me, however, was the model; a naked girl. She sat there, right in front of me, next to the black studio stove, so that in winter one half of her blushed red whilst the other was pale blue and goose-pimpled. I found it very difficult to concentrate and manipulate my charcoal as I stared at this creature, and Bell's correcting pencil seemed to disagree with every voluptuous contour I put on paper. Looking at some of the others' drawings, I noticed that I was the only one who seemed to have devoted much care and attention to the rendition of pubic hair, and it was fairly clear that my work was still well out of line with George Bell's austere anatomical precepts.

Sometimes we were set painting assignments, but when I propped my picture up with the others, Mr Bell never commented. Often I had the uncomfortable feeling that I wasn't there at all, though at other times I imagined that I detected a sympathetic glint in the model's eye as she rearranged herself, the soles of her feet black from the charcoal dust on the studio floor.

'What have you been doing today, Barry?' my mother would ask when I got home from art class. 'Nothing much. A bit of still life, as a matter of fact,' I would reply evasively. 'I'd like to see it,' said my mother. 'It's awful,' I said, 'anyway, I left it in the studio. If I do anything good, I'll let you see it.' Although I wasn't particularly enjoying Bell's grumpy tutelage, I knew that my parents would stop paying the fees if they knew what we were drawing every Saturday morning.

My attendances at the art school were, in any case, becoming more infrequent as I started experimenting again in creating 'Dada' objects and events.

Some of my old Dadaist cronies from school were now at the University and after lectures we mounted a series of impractical jokes, that is to say, jokes that had no rationale, or even satiric point, so they defied explanation.

These 'happenings' and examples of street theatre predate *Candid Camera* by many years. Sometimes, I'm afraid, they were deeply misanthropic. For example, we selected a small shopkeeper near the campus called Malouf. He was chosen entirely for the euphony and novelty of his name. He was a typical, modest, corner-of-the-street tradesman who sold a variety of merchandise, and once a day, at a specific time, one of us would enter his shop and buy a cake of Lux toilet soap. For this we would offer money that required change. When Mr Malouf put the change on the counter, we would take it and start to go, leaving the soap behind. The shopkeeper would say, 'Hey, you've forgotten your soap.' To which we would make the standard reply, 'I don't want the soap, *I just want to buy it!*' We would then leave and join our accomplices, convulsed with childish laughter. This simple but radical variation on a fundamental commercial principle was repeated countless times until Mr Malouf ceased, at last, to mention our failure to take the goods we had paid for.

Though by now he knew our faces very well, we occasionally conscripted a total stranger to go and buy the soap. Malouf's face would light up to see a new customer who was bound to accept the purchased item, but when he heard the same phrase, 'I don't want it, I just want to buy it,' Mr Malouf became crestfallen and confused. He had entered the world of nightmare.

By now the shopkeeper, with a sigh of resignation, had begun to put the same grubby package on the counter, and one day having paid for it, we actually took it. A minute later I ran back into the shop with a packet of soap. 'I'm sorry,' I said, 'I forgot to leave the soap.' Placing the shop-soiled item on the counter, I left and never returned.

As an epilogue, I should add that we had cut, to the correct proportions, a slice of cooking lard which we carefully wrapped so that it precisely counterfeited a cake of Lux toilet soap. It was this that we had substituted for the product which I had finally returned to Malouf, and, so we conjectured, it would be this that in the normal course of his business Mr Malouf would ultimately sell. The customer would have discovered under unpleasant circumstances, in bathtub or shower, the inadequacy of his purchase, and would have irately complained to Mr Malouf. He, in turn, relieved to have, at last, an explanation of the strange events in his shop, and assuming *a rational explanation*, would then have unwrapped every cake of soap on his shelves.

We were not surprised to learn soon after that Mr Malouf, severely depressed, had closed his business and moved to another district.

Another 'stunt' calculated to disturb and disorient a deeply conventional social group took place on a suburban train. My friend John Perry entered a non-smoking compartment one morning at a time, between commuters, when the compartment was customarily occupied by middle-aged, female shoppers. Perry's disguise was striking, and if the compartment was full someone always sprang to their feet and offered him a seat. His leg was encased in a plaster cast and a neck brace supported his chin. He was, furthermore, apparently blind, wearing very dark glasses, and after travelling some distance in silence he fumblingly withdrew from his pocket a large rolled up sheet of Braille (which was actually part of an old pianola roll), and proceeded to run his fingers across its surface and quietly mutter to himself. The sympathy and awe that this spectacle engendered in his fellow travellers cannot be overstated and it was into this atmosphere that I stepped at the next station on the line.

My apparel was very different. My longish hair had been combed to make it appear even longer, and my fingers were heavily ringed. I wore garish clothes and although it was a non-smoking compartment I kindled a strong-smelling Turkish cigarette, at the same time producing a German newspaper which I read ostentatiously. Already I could sense the aversion of the whole compartment. From time to time I glared across at Perry, until the train pulled up at its next stop. I rose suddenly to my feet, snatched the Braille from his fingers, ripping it in half. I then delivered a kick to his leg, shattering the plaster, and, seizing the glasses from the sightless eyes, I smashed them to the floor of the train, at the same time shouting imprecations in German interspersed with words like 'blind pig'. The other travellers were always transfixed, immobilized with horror by this demonstration, and I always escaped easily. After my exit Perry travelled the rest of the journey and repeated the words 'forgive him, forgive him' until he could hobble off the train at an appointed station and be whisked away in a car.

Our theory was that events of sufficient strangeness and violence, such as this, would change the lives of those who witnessed them, and provide them, perhaps, with their most indelible, if mysterious, memories.

Disguising myself as a tramp and rummaging in garbage close to a bus queue was another enjoyable example of 'street theatre'. Previously, of course, we had planted a cooked chicken and a bottle of champagne in the bottom of the receptacle so that the large queue of staid travellers were at first repelled and alienated by a filthy scavenger and then astonished by the delicious trophies he fished out of the refuse. Wandering away swigging champagne and gnawing on a drumstick I always noticed that a few people detached themselves from the queue and peeked curiously into the bin searching for treasures for themselves. Wise men amongst them may have thought the chicken and champagne were indeed 'plants' but then they would be lead to the question 'why?' It was a question without an answer.

The firm of H. J. Heinz had an excellent product called Russian Salad. It consisted largely of diced potato in mayonnaise with a few peas and carrot chips. Surreptitiously spilt and splashed in large quantities on the pavement of a city block, it closely resembled human vomit. It was a simple and delightful recreation of mine to approach a recent deposit of salad in the guise, once again, of a tramp. Disgusted pedestrians were already giving it a very wide berth, holding their breaths and looking away with watering eyes. Not I, as I knelt beside one of the larger puddles, curdled and carrot-flecked. Drawing a spoon from my top pocket I devoured several mouthfuls, noticing out of the corner of my eye, and with some satisfaction, several people actually being sick at the spectacle. I have done this in many parts of the world and only in Fleet Street in the 1960s did I come close to being apprehended by a policeman. He, however, was too profoundly nauseated to take my name, and as he stood gagging on the salad-splattered pavement I made my escape.

Even more entertaining by far were the two Dada exhibitions held in the Women Graduates' Lounge in the old Union building, and our lunchtime revue, *Call Me Madman!* These are the highlights of my short University career.

The 'art' exhibitions occurred on consecutive years, but have merged in my memory. One of the most notorious exhibits consisted of a large tub filled with old books, one about Cézanne and another called *The Book of Beauty*. Over these volumes a large industrial-sized can of Heinz Russian Salad had been poured. By consulting their catalogues, curious art lovers could discover that this exhibit bore the title, 'I was reading these books when I felt sick'.

Perhaps it was as a revolt against the worthy, timidly modern academicism of George Bell that I developed the idea of making pictures and sculptures out of highly perishable materials, like cake and meat. There were a series of exhibits simply called 'cakescapes': framed, double sheets of glass, between which were compressed cream cakes, lamingtons, swiss roll and rainbow terrace. For a short time these looked rather pretty, even mysterious objects, until mould slowly and decoratively transformed them. An exhibit entitled 'Creche-bang' was merely a broken pram draped with raw meat, and on a pedestal hung with velvet lay a spoon containing the opaque eye of a sheep. This was called 'Eye and Spoon Race'. Most of the exhibits were deliberately infantile and calculated to test the shock threshold of undergraduates, which was surprisingly low.

My 'shoescapes', for some reason, irritated many people. They were framed panels of wood on which large numbers of old shoes, found on a rubbish dump, had been nailed. One of these leather 'reliefs' was called 'My Foetus Killing Me', but it was 'Pus in Boots' which caused the greatest stir: two old shoes brimming with custard. Throughout the exhibition a recording of 'I'm in Love With a Wonderful Guy' from the current musical comedy *South Pacific* was played on a small but strident gramophone. String had been attached to the pickup arm so that the needle repeatedly jumped, and the voice of Mary Martin could be heard singing the same phrase *ad nauseam:* 'I'm in love click I'm in love click I'm in love click . . .'

The apotheosis of the Melbourne Dada Group was a

1952

FIRST PAN-AUSTRALASIAN

DADA

EXHIBITION

ORIGINAL PAINTINGS by:—

picasso

cezanne

humphries

matisse

levi

laver-tree

perry

gawkgin

luigi-bop

van-goof

lunchtime revue inspired by a current Irving Berlin musical, *Call Me Madman!* The object of this 'entertainment' was to provoke the undergraduate audience into some kind of irrational demonstration, and it succeeded all too well. A small orchestra in the wings (the musicians were too frightened to expose themselves and their instruments in the orchestra pit) played an inane and repetitive tune throughout the performance. One of the most effective 'sketches' was 'The Piano Tuner'. The curtain rose revealing the back of an upright piano, which effectively concealed the player. The invisible pianist sounded the same chords and notes over and over again until the audience could stand it no longer and began stamping, jeering and throwing the vegetables with which I had liberally supplied it. At length the dissonance on stage ceased, and, after a long pause, the Piano Tuner came into view. He was blind, and as he fumbled his way towards the wings he smiled wanly and bowed crookedly to the audience over which, by then, had fallen the deathly silence of shame. Needless to say, once the actor had reached the safety of the proscenium arch he discarded his white stick and dark glasses but then revealed himself once more to the audience with a low bow. Having been duped into an expression of unjustified compassion, the audience went wild, and it took little more to goad it into storming the stage.

I hid in a cupboard in my dressing-room as angry students, many from the faculties of law and commerce, thundered past howling, 'Where's Humphries? *Get Humphries!*'

I began to absent myself from lectures, attaching myself more and more to extracurricular groups like the Film Society. I arranged special screenings of surrealist movies like *Un Chien Andalou* and *La Coquille et le Clergyman*. I also strayed into English literature lectures and special lunchtime events when, for example, the British poet Stephen Spender visited the University and addressed a lively student gathering where he was repeatedly heckled by a group of campus communists.

The Rape, c. 1951

I had been chosen to take part in a play by Emlyn Williams called *The Wind of Heaven*. It was a mystical allegory about the second coming of Christ to a Welsh mining village, and I had the role of Evan Williams, an awe-struck peasant, who at the end of the play intones the Lord's Prayer in Gaelic. I had gone to a great deal of trouble to make this recitation as authentic as possible.

The production was chosen as Melbourne's entry in the Australian Universities Drama Festival that year in Adelaide, and I went off there in the train during the mid-year vacation with the rest of our troupe of student players. Amongst them was Graeme Hughes, a brilliant German student and gifted actor whom I had only recently met. Hughes was a troll-like figure whose most prized possession was a set of recordings of *Ariadne auf Naxos*. Older and more worldly than I, he highly recommended to me the merits of West End lager, the beer of South Australia. My parents were very abstemious and I had barely ever seen them drink alcohol; indeed, my mother used to condemn my father's parents for their open consumption of tawny port in front of children.

In Adelaide I was billeted with a nice suburban family, but to be away from home and beyond parental control for the first time in my life was a heady experience, and I was out every night at riotous student parties with Hughes, my mentor in the novelties of intoxication.

One evening, after the Adelaide Dramatic Society had given us Shelley's *The Cenci*, a production which did much to explain why this work is so rarely performed, we went to a party with a large bottle of the liqueur Parfait d'Amour, a viscid purple beverage scented with violets. The effects of this drink, quaffed by the tumbler, were disastrous, and I was volcanically sick in the middle of the Union lawn. The violet stain was still there several days later and inspired the song 'Mauve Chunder',[1] which Hughes and I sang with great success at parties. Thereafter we drank more conventional beverages, but I had discovered Mandrake's secret; a simple and accessible substance that made everything disappear.

1. **chunder** *n. or vb.* Australian (nautical) interj. Vomit. Like the golfers' warning 'fore!' the word derives from a popular expression on the early convict ships. It is an abbreviation of 'Watch under!' an ominous courtesy shouted from the upper decks for the protection of those below.

Shellac Smashing

ONE EVENING AT dinner my mother said to me rather abruptly, 'Look at your father, Barry.' I glanced up the table to where he sat tackling the large T-bone steak he had cooked himself. 'You're killing that man, Barry,' my mother said in a matter-of-fact voice, as though she were merely commenting on the weather or some other immutable circumstance. The family went on eating, though my sister looked as if she was going to cry. There was nothing more to be said. Who was I to disagree with my mother when I had the uncomfortable, guilty feeling that she might be right?

My undergraduate interlude did seem to be at an end and the future looked bleak. I had had fun during my two years at University but there were dark moments. Half-way through my year as a law student, Robert Nathan had died from a tumour. We used to go to see him in his private room at the Alfred Hospital and he was thinner and weaker on each visit. The last time I saw him he suddenly began to shout abusively at me, bitterly reproaching me for being well and alive.

Even my parents were moved by his death, though my father was horrified when, on the evening of Robert's funeral, a group of his friends and I went to see the Marx Brothers' *A Night at the Opera*. To us, however, it seemed the most appropriate way to mourn him.

When I finally scraped through German at the crammers and was able to abandon my irksome law course, I seemed also to have abandoned the last vestige of my ability to concentrate. I started to read Fine Arts, which I enjoyed, but I found myself drifting more and more into the amateur theatrical life of the campus. The Union Theatre was small but well equipped and I spent most of my time there. We were rehearsing, I think, a production of Hecht's *The Front Page* when a strange and cathartic event occurred. Standing at the stage door and looking across an expanse of lawn towards the medical school, I saw a vaguely familiar figure sitting studiously beneath a gum tree reading. I experienced a painful flashback to Grade One at Camberwell Grammar. It was John Bromley, the boy with the soft slug-like skin who delighted in giving me 'Chinese Burns' and 'Rabbit Choppers', the archetypal bully of my childhood.

How quiet and peaceful he seemed now, poring over his book in the feathery shadow of the foliage! Immediately I descended to that room beneath the stage used for storing scene-painting equipment. Looking quickly around, I saw a large sack of white paint powder and, seizing this, I lugged it upstairs and out the stage door. Bromley still sat there in deep shadow. He hadn't moved. Very quietly, with my heart pounding, I crept stealthily towards him until I was directly behind him, and then raised and tilted the heavy sack. A twig cracked sharply under my foot and Bromley looked around and up. By then the bag was evacuating a dense cascade of pigment over the seated student. Just when I thought the white torrent was petering out, it seemed to renew itself. When the bag was finally empty, I turned and cravenly bolted, only once glancing over my shoulder. Standing now, though seemingly rooted to the spot, stood a totally white figure under a tree. Back in my dressing-room, slightly puffed, I experienced the voluptuous satisfaction of vengeance. I remembered, with intense pleasure also, the victim's face as it turned towards me in that instant before the clown-white avalanche struck. It was *not* Bromley. Not, in fact, much like Bromley at all. But thereafter Bromley was forgiven. That blanched and bewildered figure on the Union lawn had unwittingly performed a noble act of expiation.

At the end of my University days I scarcely went to lectures and it became clear that my scholarship would cease. I was aware of a good deal of headshaking amongst my professors and mutterings about me being, what they suspected all along, a 'flash in the pan'. John Sumner, a young Englishman, had, amidst great scepticism, founded a professional fortnightly repertory company on the campus. Sumner had directed me in *The Front Page* and he now asked me if I would like to play a small part in *The Young Elizabeth* starring Alex Scott and Zoë Caldwell. I was not too busy to accept. The part was indeed small, a scheming courtier called Lord Thyrwhitt. Also in the cast was an Irish-Australian actor called Peter O'Shaughnessy who had just come back to Melbourne after working at the famous English repertory company at Leatherhead. He and his fiancée, Shirley, befriended me at a time when I really needed guidance and encouragement. At coffee breaks he would entertain the company with Kenneth Tynan stories and of all the cast he was the most experienced and urbane. I felt that money must have been rather short, because whenever he felt like a cigarette he would casually stroll some distance away from us, quietly withdraw a Turf cork-tipped from a packet of ten, light it and return to the group. O'Shaughnessy was deeply amused by stories of some of my Dada escapades which were still talked about around the theatre. He seemed to get the point of them and he was the first professional man of the theatre, apart from John Sumner, to suggest that there might just possibly be a future for me on the stage.

I rejected, however, all such warm words of encouragement, since I firmly believed, like my parents, that there was no livelihood to be made, or respectable career to be derived, from anything I was faintly good at. I also knew that my vocational *impasse* was causing my father perpetual anxiety, and I wanted to please him. But it was clear that he was disappointed. 'There's no doubt about you, Barry,' he often prognosticated, shaking his head, 'you're always going to learn the *hard* way.' It was a self-fulfilling prophecy.

When I came down to breakfast in the mornings he was always there in the kitchen, in a nimbus of toast smoke, scraping the black fur off carbonized crumpets, squeezing orange juice and juggling bacon and eggs. Still in his fawn plaid dressing-gown with shaving lather on his lobes, he would trudge up the stairs with my mother's breakfast. Moments later he would be fully dressed and down the stairs, two at a time, and off in his Buick to the office.

My father had taken his younger brother into partnership soon after the war and my mother was constantly expressing her doubts about my Uncle Dick's diligence and suitability. 'Never employ members of your own family,' she would say to us in my father's presence; 'it never works. They use you and want more and more, until in the end you're working for them.' At this my father usually sighed and held his tongue. After some years' experience in business, however, I now see that my mother's counsel, though intended as an oblique rebuke to my father, had some sound basis of sense, although it applies less to members of one's own family than to theatrical managers, lawyers and accountants.

My sister and young brothers were at school and I was at home and out of work. I had never thought of the future and never entertained the idea of a job. I always believed, absurdly and romantically, that 'something would happen'. John Levi, one of my best friends, was already in Cincinnati studying to become a rabbi. My other friends were working seriously at the University. All I did was sit at home like a droopy dilettante, leafing through the Sitwells and playing records of Bartók and Hindemith to myself. I had sent off to a special gramophone shop in London called Collector's Corner for some obscure recordings of Kurt Weill's *Threepenny Opera*, a then-forgotten work of the twenties, and when they arrived I would play them carefully with fibre needles. At that time, serious gramophone enthusiasts always followed a needle-sharpening ritual before playing their fragile 78s.

In desperation I decided to go to the Vocational Guidance Centre in the City, and there I spent a whole day answering elaborate questionnaires and being interrogated by a man who seemed like a defrocked Salvation Army Major. The whole family eagerly awaited the results of these tests, which finally arrived in our letterbox, mucilaginous from the vagrant attentions of the snails. The Vocational Guidance Centre had decided, after much deliberation – in those days before computers – that the job I was best suited to was that of a Vocational Guidance Counsellor. Even my father, eager as he was for me to find conventional employment, looked askance.

Then he had a brainwave. A friend of a friend of his at golf worked for EMI and they had a vacancy for a trainee executive in the wholesale record department. They were prepared to employ me for a small wage to 'teach me the ropes', he said. The idea was that I would ultimately become an 'executive', a word with which I was until then totally unfamilar. This scheme was recommended to me as the perfect solution. It was business – *and it was music!* It was that noisy and inexplicable obsession of mine with the gramophone made respectable, bringing in a wage, and possessed of 'a future'. My father seemed to glow with pleasure and relief at the sudden simplicity of it all; as though this job had been staring us in the face for years and we had failed to recognize it for what it was: The Answer To The Problem of Barry.

Thus it was that I found myself on Willison Railway Station every morning at 7.45 with a folded copy of the *Melbourne Age* under my arm ready to step into a first-class smoking compartment and be borne to the terminus at Flinders Street Station. It was the same route that I had travelled three years before to school, but in a different uniform. Now I wore a new grey bird's-eye double-breasted suit specially made for me by Mr Warner, my father's tailor. My father had also ordered a single-breasted navy-blue worsted, an overcoat and a dark grey fedora to enhance my impersonation of a young businessman. The EMI warehouse was in Flinders Lane behind St Paul's Cathedral and a short walk from the station. Just inside its entrance there was a large time-clock, and at 8.25 I would remove the card bearing my name from its slot, punch the clock and report to the manager, Stan Deverell, for my day's assignment.

This is an idealized version of my morning routine. In fact, always late for breakfast, I would rush out of the house and down the steep hill of Lansell Crescent, lined with the houses my father had built, to the small station, only to see the train, *my train*, pulling out. Then, the interminable wait for the next train as the station began to fill up with a different kind of commuter, better dressed people who didn't need to get to work as early as me. With a knot in my stomach I would arrive in town at 8.30 and run, dodging along crowded pavements, all the way to EMI, with my heart thumping and the faint taste of blood in my mouth. After 8.30 the clock always printed my arrival time in red, and at the end of every week the black numerals on my card were few. No one ticked me off, strange to say, and the others just looked at me and exchanged winks and grins amongst themselves. It occurred to me that my father might well have been paying this company to employ me, and I later learnt that he had performed a number of 'favours' for the Managing Director.

In my first few weeks at EMI I had to wear a grey overall and push boxes of records around the warehouse at the back of the building. There didn't seem much point wearing a good suit into town in order to do such a dirty, sweaty job, and I reflected rather ruefully on the long and boring journey that lay ahead of me from the warehouse to the executive office suite.

I had, of course, met the Managing Director, Mr Dennis Hern, at my first interview. He was short, bald and bespectacled and I wondered at the time if this were the type of person my parents hoped I might come to resemble at the end of my long training period. Mr Hern's office was at the 'presentable' end of the building, just near the entrance and off the main carpeted showroom. Every time I arrived late, which was most mornings, I had to pass the open door of his outer office and Pat, his beautiful blonde secretary, always looked up from her typewriter and smiled.

In due course, having gained valuable experience pushing boxes, I was promoted to the wholesale record department, wandering amongst the aisles of steel shelving with a clipboard of orders, and pulling out the records. It was an historic time in the music industry, since the Long-Playing Record was being introduced, and old-fashioned shellac 78s were being phased out. Most of the small record stores in the City and suburbs of Melbourne were distrustful of the new 'microgrooves' and bought them in token quantities, one or two at a time. They saw them as a 'flash in the pan', a phrase with which I readily identified. Tom Goodridge, my immediate boss in the fledgling LP department, warned me that a lot of the Australian pressings were defective, and to be prepared for a few irate retailers returning warped or flawed copies of *Die Schöne Müllerin*, *The Student Prince*, and *Satchmo at Pasadena*. He explained that the official policy was to accept defective recordings and replace them with another copy. However, the returned disc was put straight back into stock and, to use a word that was unknown in those days, 'recycled'. Thus faulty recordings were constantly passing back and forth between the public, warehouse and distributor until the anonymous music-lovers grew tired of complaining. It was little wonder that the modest suburban retailers were so deeply suspicious of the new recording revolution.

When not searching the shelves for orders or taking a quick puff from a cigarette behind the storage racks, I would stand with Tom waiting for customers. Directly across the showroom from my counter was the door of Mr Hern's office, and there was Pat with jonquils glowing on her desk. I would try to catch her eye as she looked up from her typewriter.

One morning Mr Hern muttered something to Stan Deverell who spoke to Tom Goodridge who, like Hermes, led me to the lower regions; a small windowless room in the basement of the warehouse. There was an important job to be done, said Tom, and I was just the man to do it. 'Better get back into your overall, though, Baz,' he added with a wink. I stood in the room as a couple of storemen trundled in an enormous number of cartons filled with 78 records. They then dragged in a couple of tea-chests.

Mr Deverell entered with a hammer. 'Boy, oh boy, son,' said Stan, 'have you copped it sweet! I wouldn't mind a nice cushy job like this myself.' I didn't quite follow his drift. He plucked a shiny new record off the top of the pile and slipped it out of its paper sleeve. 'You see this, Baz? What is it?'

'It's a yellow label Decca.' I squinted more closely at the label. 'It's the Arnold Bax Nonet,' I added, rather wishing I could hear it.

'Wrong!' said Stan. 'It's *discontinued*!' Holding the record at arm's length over the tea-chest he struck it deftly with his hammer. The sharp black shards fell into the box. Stan warmed to his task and shattered a few sets of Sibelius symphonies as he explained: 'In the next few weeks you'll be seeing thousands more of these bloody deletions and this is all you have to do to them.' He brandished the hammer in front of my nose. 'We're moving into the future now, Old Son. It's the age of micro-grooves and the Powers That Be reckon we can't have too many of these old-fashioned buggers collecting dust and taking up valuable space. Are you with me?'

'But,' I protested, 'do they all have to be destroyed, can't you give them away to hospitals, to old people's homes . . .?' I refrained from recommending universities, suspecting that even Stan knew that recordings of classical music would be a most unwelcome donation there. 'Not on your life, Baz,' said Stan gravely, 'it's a question of copyright. They're deleted so we can't sell 'em and we can't give 'em away. All you have to do is break 'em up nicely so we can send the bits up to Sydney to be melted down.'

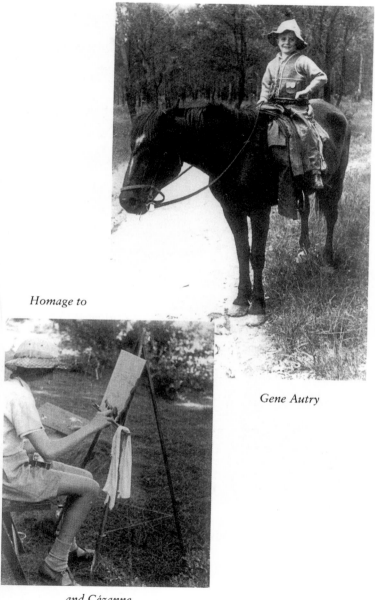

Homage to

Gene Autry

and Cézanne

Barry, Michael and Christopher Humphries

Mrs Pengard in Ambrose Applejohn's Adventure, 1949

Schoolboy surrealist

Rabbi
John Levi

Ratbag
the author

MP
Robert Maclellan, c. 1951

Marriage, 1956

Phillip's Street Revue,
l. to r. Max Oldaker,
the author, Gordon Chater

Sydney by night, 1956

Dr Humphries, 1958

Forkscapes and surgical gloves, 1958

Student actor

The Bunyip

Mrs Everage at Home, 1959

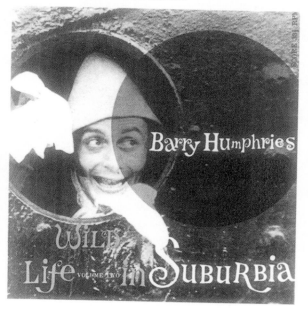

First albums

Venice, 1959

'But if they're not making 78s anymore, why melt them down?'

Stan Deverell looked at me with his head on one side and an expression of long-suffering patience. 'Listen, young fella, you can ask clever questions like that when you're an Executive, but until that far-off day you can do as you're flamin' told!' He looked around the small room which was now filled with teetering skyscrapers of deleted records. 'Sorry there's no windows in here, Baz, but someone will stick their head around the door later and let you know when it's knock-off time. And by the way, Baz,' he handed me back the hammer, 'don't go crazy; you only need to hit 'em once – about two inches *to the right of the hole.*'

After he had gone I sat down on a pile of deleted Diabelli Variations and picked a small record from the top of another box. It was a black label ten-inch Parlophone, and the title was *When the Lighthouse Shines Across the Bay*, featuring Conrad Veidt. There were five boxes of the same recording. I took it out of its sleeve, held it gingerly over the tea-chest and raised the hammer. Only then did I begin to wonder how exactly you located a spot two inches to the right of the hole on a round record.

My former life of freedom at the University already seemed remote and dreamlike as I sat in that small airless basement room all day for weeks on end pulverizing the combined repertoires of Columbia, Decca, Brunswick and His Master's Voice. The irony did not escape me; if there were a Dadaist's hell, this was it.

Sometimes my new life seemed so dismal that my only escape, however brief, lay in books. Perched in a patch of sunshine on the doorstep in Flinders Lane outside EMI, or on a bench in the Fitzroy Gardens, I ate my lunch and read the 'smart' fiction of the 1920s for which I had developed a voracious appetite. *The Madonna of the Sleeping Cars* by Maurice Dekobra, Harold Acton's *Humdrum*, *Peter Whiffle* by Carl

Van Vechten, and the novels of Michael Arlen and William Gerhardie. Immersed in their pages, I could almost forget that I lived in Melbourne in the feeble fifties.

In one of my lunch breaks Tom took pity on me and invited me down to the Cathedral Hotel on the corner of Flinders Lane for a counter lunch. I ordered a beer.

'Is that all you're having?' said Tom, handing me a State Express. 'I thought you'd be a Top-Shelf Man.' I must have looked puzzled.

'You know,' said Tom, indicating the bottles on a shelf of the mahogany back-fitting behind the bar, 'whisky, gin, drop o' rum.' I noticed with a shudder a dusty bottle of Parfait d'Amour, between the advocaat and the crème de menthe. I said I thought a rum might go down rather well after a record-breaking morning. After that I acquired a taste for over-proof Queensland Rum with beer chasers at lunchtime. They got me nicely numb and lightheaded to face the long, iconoclastic afternoon.

I was close to despair when relief came. Friends at the University had invited me back to appear in the annual Student Representatives' Council Revue, so after I clocked out of EMI at night my spirits would rise as I took the tram to Carlton to rehearse songs and sketches with the cast. My mother lent me her Austin A40 on rehearsal nights and these were often very late nights indeed, if there was a party somewhere, or if a few of us went on later to Val's Coffee Lounge. This was a wicked establishment at the top of a narrow staircase in Swanston Street. Here the walls were hung with black fishnet, the lights were dim and the toasted raisin bread more lubriciously buttered than at Gibby's or Raffles or Rumpelmeyers. Val, the proprietrix, was a pretty blonde of about thirty who dressed like a boy; an Australian garçonne. The waiters, as far as one could tell, were men, though they had a tendency to walk in time to the music which was quietly be-boppy.

My father had extended the back of our house to create a large flat for me. I supervised the decorations which, if preserved today and transported to a museum of decorative arts, would perfectly exemplify the avant-garde Melbourne taste of the period. Three sides of the room were pale blue and a fourth was a deep tan 'feature wall'. The curtains were yellow with a dark blue stripe. There were smoked-glass coffee-tables supported by spindly black suction legs, an Italian spun-aluminium anglepoise lamp, and a big yellow 'hammock' chair with a leopard-skin cushion. On the walls hung prints in natural-wood frames by Klee, Miro and Léger, and on the blondwood tablegram revolved microgrooves of music by George Shearing and Khachaturian. More than any other tune, Khachaturian's *Sabre Dance* seemed to dominate the early part of this decade. Whether played by Arthur Fiedler and the Boston Pops Orchestra or sung with silly words by the Norman Luboff Choir, its stabbing, sewing-machine rhythms could constantly be heard on the radio, and, with Auric's sweetly melancholy waltz from the *Moulin Rouge* played by Mantovani, will always evoke the fifties for me.

With such accommodation, it was impossible to explain to my parents, who had done more than their best to make my life exquisitely comfortable, that I would prefer to live in one ill-furnished room. I had made one unsuccessful dash for freedom. An artist's studio above a stable in the older quarter of East Melbourne had become vacant, and without discussion with my parents I rented it and moved in a few possessions. It was only a short walk through the Fitzroy Gardens to the record warehouse and I thought that propinquity might beget punctuality. Having secretly furnished my new 'bohemian' abode, the time came for me to announce my relocation to my parents. Naturally they found the idea wounding and incomprehensible, and I spent no more than two or three delicious nights alone in my studio before my father arrived in his new Buick, silently refilled my case and drove me home. No subsequent reference was ever made to this truancy, but I learned later that other friends of mine had had similar problems escaping from the thraldom of their families. One man, who only felt able to leave home at the age of forty-five, after the death of his mother, is now convinced, with some justification, that she drugged his food, obliging him to return constantly to her steaming, heavily doped, addictive roasts.

I was still trudging off every morning to the record-smashing chamber, on my Executive Training Course, so my parents grimly indulged occasional forays into student theatre. As I had met my mother and father half-way in pursuit of a respectable career and abandoned my loft, they were now more lenient when I sometimes returned home very late indeed, smelling strongly of black Sobranie gold-tipped cigarettes, a ferocious fortified wine called Brandivino and, occasionally, the perfume of one of my more attractive female satellites from the show.

Unfortunately my flat did not have a private entrance and as I tiptoed past my parents' bedroom door, which was always ajar, a light would snap on, I would hear hoarse whispering from their room and my father's voice would croak, 'Is that you, Barry?' Then my mother's voice, more urgent and wakeful, would chime in, 'Do you know what time it is? Do you realize your father has been *worried sick*? I hope you know you have to be at work in three and half hours' time?' Most of these questions were rhetorical since there was nothing to be said, and my parents left no pauses in which to reply. I kept my lips tightly closed so as not to release further incriminating fumes of the night's excesses.

One morning, haggard and hung over from a particularly late rehearsal, I was running out the door already tardy for work when my father stopped me, and gravely led me to the Austin A40, crookedly parked in the driveway as I had left it in the early hours of the morning. He was ashen-faced and trembling slightly as he reached under the driver's seat and produced a small package of contraceptive accoutrements. My heart sank.

'What is this doing in your mother's car?' he said.

I heard a voice, which I recognized as my own, reply: 'I don't know. Perhaps you'd better ask her?' And I turned on my heel and ran for the train. It was one of the most courageous statements of my life yet paradoxically one of which I am least proud. My father made no further reference to this incident, out of embarrassment no doubt, and also perhaps out of a wish to make it un-happen.

Someone had recommended to me a product called Parafeminol, a gelatinous pessary which unfortunately left black and indelible stains on the upholstery of Austin cars. Until I became aware of this drawback I used to buy it from chemist shops in remote suburbs where I was sure nobody could possibly know me. None the less, in ordering this product over the counter, I was consumed with embarrassment, and invariably muttered its name so apologetically that the pharmacist almost always thought I had said 'paraffin'. I never had the courage to correct him, so that consequently, at this painful stage of my life, I acquired large holdings of paraffin oil in all known brands and bottles. They were very hard to hide, dispose of or, when discovered, explain.

The Birth of Edna

'To be a good actor, Barry dear, you must have it here, and you must have it here...' With an expression of Central European sapience, George Pravda pointed first to his head and then to his heart. Then, with a delicate gesture in the direction of his fly buttons, he added '... but most of all, you must have it here!' For a while he regarded me with a whimsical smile. 'You, I'm afraid dear fellow, have only got it ... *here*.' After this gnomic utterance, George tapped his high Slavic forehead quite loudly. It was my first experience of the backhanded compliment; my brains had been praised at the expense of my balls and any hopes I might have had of a theatrical career had been expertly dashed.

George Pravda, who resembled a shifty little concierge in a two-star Prague hotel, had come to Australia after the War and had, in a short time, carved an impressive niche for himself in the semi-professional theatrical life of Melbourne. Most actors I knew revered him as an emissary from the far-off World of Culture. Certainly in the early 1950s culture and foreigners were inseparable. At the Savoy Theatre in Russell Street, Melbourne's intelligentsia flocked to every screening of French, Italian and Scandinavian movies. Anything with a subtitle, however execrable, was received with awe-struck reverence and its merits earnestly debated afterwards over toasted raisin bread and Temple Bar cigarettes in the louche coffee lounges of the city.

One of the most successful continental films of this period was called *One Summer of Happiness*, a tedious Swedish idyll that reached the Melbourne screen only after severe excisions by the Censor, though it still retained a few titillating glimpses of nude silhouettes against a sparkling lake. Undoubtedly this film converted more citizens to a love of culture than the manager of the Savoy Theatre could have dreamt possible. *One Summer of Happiness* was to the Australian cinema of the early fifties what *Peter and the Wolf* was to music, and 'Sunflowers' to art.

The epithet which carried with it the very highest promise of artistic excellence was 'continental'. No more improving evening could be spent than in a continental restaurant eating a continental meal before a continental film followed by a continental supper in a continental coffee lounge preferably inhaling a continental cigarette. Black Balkan Sobranies were very popular with affected youths like myself, and black coffee was still a slightly exotic novelty in a society that either sipped tea or swilled beer. At symphony concerts in the Melbourne Town Hall, it was the visiting continental artistes who attracted the biggest crowds, although Australia's own Bernard Heinz (later Sir Bernard) was a popular conductor, probably because his name sounded foreign *and yet* reassuringly the same as the tomato sauce (Australia's alternative beverage).

In spite of the fact that a tiny percentage of Australians held all Foreigners in superstitious veneration as repositories of Old World Culture, the majority took huge delight in humiliating the new arrivals to our shores. 'Populate or perish' was the catch-phrase of the time, and Australians reluctantly accepted large numbers of 'Balts', not necessarily from the Baltic States. Then the word became a generic term for almost anyone from Overseas who did not speak English, and replaced the pejorative 'reffo'. I once even heard a Chinese restaurateur described as a 'bloody slant-eyed Balt'. For the privilege of dwelling in

Australia, the 'Balts' were obliged to spend their first years in the Land of Sunshine living in concentration camps and doing forced labour. Whatever their European qualifications may have been mattered little to the Australian authorities, and there were gleeful tales of brain surgeons obliged to work as night-soil contractors, and concert pianists conscripted as tram conductors. Thus, while a small minority hankered for the Old World, most of us sought to revenge ourselves against it. Soon, however, the coy euphemism 'New Australian' came into general use, as in: 'make Mine a Steak, that New Australian food gives me the shits!'

Almost a year before Mr Pravda had, with continental charm, given my budding career the thumbs down, I had toured the country towns of Victoria, absurdly miscast as Duke Orsino in a production of *Twelfth Night*. The offer of this role finally emancipated me from my enslavement at the record company. Looking back, I cannot imagine how I managed to tell my parents that I had decided not to be an EMI executive, but an actor instead. I think they still entertained some glimmer of hope that I would fail in the theatre and creep back into my old job, because they persuaded Mr Milligan to give me leave of absence. I never entered that building in Flinders Lane again, and for many years, until they recorded some of my early stage shows, I was unable to read the letters EMI with equanimity.

On the *Twelfth Night* tour we performed for the most part in one-night stands on an assortment of stages; town halls, cinemas and Mechanics Institutes, although in these last mysteriously named auditoriums we never stumbled upon a single mechanic.

I was still secretly unconvinced that I really wanted to be an actor, but touring with this jolly troupe of players was certainly better than smashing records. I envied Stanley Page, who took the part of Andrew Aguecheek, since that was certainly the role I could have played more convincingly than my hobbledehoy impersonation of the lovesick duke. I must be the only actor who ever got a laugh on the line, 'If music be the food of love, play on'. Well, it was not exactly a laugh, but a perceptible titter which rippled through the audience whenever I was on stage, and which was, somehow, worse than open hilarity. For some reason the costumes were vaguely Carolingian and I wore rather loose woollen tights beneath velvet breeches with a dropped crotch. I was convinced that my legs were to blame for the furtive merriment that greeted my every scene, so I kept dodging behind furniture and giving my sagging tights a surreptitious hoist. Three nights into the play the director took me aside: 'Your entrance is awful,' he said. 'You're meant to be a prince and yet you skulk on stage and immediately lurk behind the chairs and tables. What's the matter with you?'

'It's my legs,' I stammered. 'It's these tights. They're laughing at my legs.'

'Bullshit,' retorted the director. 'You've got very good legs as a matter of fact. Don't you realize that you're *naturally* ridiculous?!'

Then there were problems with the wig; an ill-fitting tangle of hennaed ringlets. The actress who played Viola was Zoë Caldwell who later became a star of Broadway and Stratford Ontario, and in all our scenes I could not help but notice how intensely she had to act in order not to burst out laughing. Her eyes blazed, her fingers clawed into my ruffled wrists and she enunciated her lines with such passion that I was almost blinded by saliva. If ever I saw her after the performance, I would invariably mutter the word 'sorry' as she flounced disdainfully past; as though she had been one of my sister's friends at dancing class whom I had almost trodden to death. If only I could have had a shot at Sir Andrew. I knew exactly how I should deliver that wonderful and pathetic line: 'I was adored once too.'

We travelled from town to town in a bus, amusing each other through the long hours of boredom with songs, jokes and little improvised performances by members of the company. Our play was directed by Ray Lawler, who also played Feste. Back at the hotel after the show, he would retire to his room and we would hear his typewriter tapping into the night. We later learnt that he had written a play with an unusual and highly unfashionable Australian setting called *Summer of the Seventeenth Doll*. Within two years this unlikely product of the *Twelfth Night* tour was playing to packed houses in the West End of London. My own creation took another twenty years to get there. I usually sat at the back of the bus improvising, in a flutey falsetto, a speech of gratitude by some fictitious female factotum. Wherever we went there was always a 'bun fight' after the performance provided by the Ladies Auxiliary or a more cultured member of the Country Women's Association. A forlorn affair usually, of trestle tables groaning with asparagus rolls, party pies and lamingtons on which the actors descended ravenously. Our hosts, who had all too recently learnt that great art is *meant* to be boring, stood sheepishly at the other end of the room in their bucolic finery and Sunday best, and there was an inevitable speech by one of the ladies thanking us for bringing culture to their township. Often one felt they were even more thankful when we left in our bus the next morning that we would be taking our art with us – and as far away as possible!

As the tour progressed, my improvised burlesque of these poignant votes-of-thanks grew more elaborate and absurd. Sometimes the *actual* remarks of a headmistress or mayoress at the after-show reception bore an uncanny resemblance to my most fanciful parody and I prattled away on the back seat of the bus, grateful that I could, at least, amuse and entertain by day the actors whom I dismayed by night. My nice, well-meaning lady who was so thrilled that culture had finally come to her town, and who was convinced that Shakespeare's Anne Hathaway was fundamentally just like any ordinary Australian housewife with a growing family of kiddies had, as yet, no name. It was only months later when we were preparing our end-of-season revue and Ray Lawler suggested that I revive the character that I decided to call her after my nanny, Edna.

Except for those jocose interludes in the bus, I cannot say I enjoyed the depressing cavalcade of country towns we visited. This was before the Age of the Motel which revolutionized rural accommodation in Australia. With its *en suite* bathroom, sanitized toilet seat, raw-brick feature wall and foam pillows artfully secreted behind a mustard vinyl lift-out headboard, the motel was still a thing of the near future. Our accommodations belonged to the pioneering past. Bedrooms were gloomy and sparsely furnished with a teetering wardrobe and often an old-fashioned washstand and chamber pot since the bathroom and lavatory were invariably a long walk down the coir-matted corridor. High on the nicotine-lacquered walls there was usually a sepia print in a cheap frame, representing some forlorn and coniferous glen in Scotland or Canada. The iron bedstead supported a sagging horsehair mattress, and the pillows, filled with a porridge of congealed kapok, were deeply impregnated with the beery exhalations of a thousand commercial travellers. In the morning, as your feet hit the cold sticky linoleum, you were greeted by the mingled effluvia of cigarette smoke and curried sausages – an Australian breakfast staple.

The dining-rooms of these establishments were always dominated by huge marble-topped mahogany credenzas loaded with cut-glass cruets, nickel-plated toast racks and domed Britannia-ware cloches. From the high anaglyptic ceiling, amongst the sparsely beaded electroliers, flypapers dangled in sticky convolutions. To the present generation of Australians, flypaper is as unknown and anachronistic as blotting paper or the gramophone needle, but in my youth no restaurant ceiling was without its viscid coil of brown paper palpitating a few feet above one's lunch with an iridescent harvest of trapped and vomiting blowflies.

No meal was ever placed on the table without an encouraging 'There you go' from waiter or waitress, who customarily left a gravy-brown thumb print in the mashed potatoes. I am sorry to say that 'There you go' – the Australian equivalent of *Bon appétit* or *Mahlzeit* – is now uncommon except in the remote provinces of Tasmania and New Zealand, although 'sumthin' t'drink, jellman?' is still current amongst *sommeliers* in those very few restaurants which remain in Australian hands.

Yet it was not the accommodation which made my *Twelfth Night* tour uncomfortable, but the conviction that I had been miscast, not merely as the romantic lead, but as an actor. One of the last towns we visited was Benalla where, as a child, I had been subjected to Great-Uncle Jack's orthodontic experiments. Sure enough, though greatly aged, he attended the performance in a black alpaca blazer, and sat in the middle of the front row watching the whole show through a large pair of racing binoculars, which he occasionally rested on the edge of the stage. The entire cast complained about him and I did not have the courage to admit that he was my relation until, to my embarrassment, he ostentatiously embraced me at the reception after the show. It was my only accolade.

Back in Melbourne, my first and last season in the repertory theatre began auspiciously, and my vocational doubts briefly evaporated when I had a small success as an eccentric cowboy in William Saroyan's *The Time of Your Life*. In Shaw's *You Never Can Tell*, my impersonation of William the waiter actually received critical acclaim, but after that the roles I was offered grew smaller and smaller. Learning my lines was a persistent difficulty and even as I was acting on stage before an audience I mentally turned the leaves of the script dreading that moment, a couple of pages on, where the text became suddenly illegible. Sometimes I could clear this terrible mnemonic thrombosis by letting my arms and legs turn to jelly and erupting in a copious sweat, but more often than not I had to stroll downstage left within earshot of the Prompter, whose voice was frequently more audible in the stalls than it was on the stage.

The nightmare became a reality during our production of Noël Coward's extremely dated three-hander, *Design for Living*. I had been studying my role at home, but in perfunctory fashion due to a distracting romantic entanglement, and even at the final dress rehearsal I was very far from word-perfect. Sure enough, on the first night, in my big scene in the second act, and like some chill, heart-stopping, self-fulfilling prophecy, the worst happened. As I mouthed Coward's brittle lines I mentally flicked through the pages of dialogue that lay ahead. The laughter from the audience grew more distant, the voices of the other two actors fainter as I hit that terrible blank in the script. I went on talking, acting, winning a few laughs, but the blank was getting closer, it was a page and a half away now, then a page, then two speeches. I tried going limp but could only feel my false moustache, undermined by perspiration, beginning to peel off. The blank moment was almost upon me, and once more I tried to visualize the text which lay in my bedside drawer in Camberwell. I was meant to be standing and doing something but instead I sank into a chair. I could see the other two actors staring at me now. Perhaps it was a moment they had dreaded even more than I. A silence fell, and I knew that was when I should have been saying something – *but what*? I could see the Prompter in his shadowy corner wildly gesticulating and uttering hoarse and quite inaudible noises, but I remained frozen in my chair like a man in a nightmare. At length my lips began to form words and I listened to them with a curious detachment.

'You'll find it in the drawer,' I croaked. '*It's in the drawer.*'

June Brunell, my leading lady, looked at me goggle-eyed. How was she to know I meant the script, and that the drawer was locked and the key forever lost. But June was a resourceful young trouper and knew that given time I might accidentally stumble back into the real play. She crossed the stage, opened a drawer in the desk, looked into it and said in a brittle Coward manner, 'It's not in *this* drawer, Ernest. Are you sure you didn't leave it in some *other* drawer?' Noël's comedy began to assume a surrealistic character, and it was many unendurably long minutes before I finally regained an approximation of the text and careered towards the final curtain. The audience, aware that something rather unusual had happened but unable to identify precisely what, applauded politely, but as we bowed June quietly hissed, '*I'm never going to speak to you again.*' And she almost didn't, though I, strange to say, remained a sort of actor thereafter, and she married Helmut Newton, became a famous photographer and changed her name from June Brunell to Alice Springs. True to her word, June never spoke to me again, but thirty-six years later Alice has.

After that, I became *persona nongratissima* in the company. The next offering was Steinbeck's *Of Mice and Men*, in which I played a walk-on, and in the penultimate production, which required the offstage noise of a barking dog, I did the barking. Then in the final show – the world première of *Summer of the Seventeenth Doll* – I had no role at all, human or canine. It was at this point, the nadir of my career, that Mr Pravda, the company's artistic advisor, whose estimation of himself as the incarnation of Stanislavsky was widely shared, proffered me his unsolicited advice, the three requirements of a good actor – cerebral, cardiac and genital.

I had not exactly been fired from the company yet but I received strong intimations that the Christmas show – a revue – would be my last production, perhaps even my last appearance as a professional actor. I knew my parents would be pleased to be proved right. I also knew that some of my friends who had been alarmed that I might be taking 'a nice hobby' seriously would be tickled pink to see me hounded from the theatre and back into the real world of careers and salaries and superannuation. The difficulty was that whenever I thought about a career, or what I might do with my life, my mind went completely blank. At home I had been brainwashed into believing that my few accomplishments were liabilities. The record company wouldn't have me back and I had stopped painting, even Dada was *vieux jeu*. Since I seemed to lack all the qualifications of my more ambitious acquaintances, I wondered if I would ever be given a passport to the adult world or would I end up as a perpetual undergraduate; the type who never really leaves the campus. I knew several grisly examples: former wits and wags and dilettantes now gone to seed. I had seen them, balding and corduroyed caricatures of their younger, more promising selves, rubbing along as part-time tutors or running the University bookshop or still dabbling in student revues. I could see myself being drawn into this grim fellowship of flops.

This may have been why I decided to get married, although it would be wrong to describe this impetuous and dramatic event as a decision since, at the time, I did not feel as though I had had much of a say in it. It was all rather sudden and unfair on both parties, but it did enable me to leave home.

This eventful year had started very badly with my twenty-first birthday. Most of the people I knew had elaborate coming-of-age parties with caterers, marquees in the garden and Dennis Farrington's ubiquitous orchestra, but I wanted none of that. I was still in my last weeks at EMI, sorry for myself and spending much of my time after work at the Swanston Family Hotel, a rendezvous for Melbourne's bohemia. My new mentors, Peter and Shirley O'Shaughnessy, had introduced me to this picturesque public house, which reeked of cigarette smoke, yeast, urine and some unidentifiable disinfectant, and it contained, it seemed to me, between the hours of five and six o'clock, the most interesting people in Australia. In those days pubs closed at six, and when the publican started yelling 'Time, Gentlemen, please! Drink up now, please, Gents!' there was a rush to the bar for last libations and bottles of beer to be consumed at home or in cars, on doorsteps and at improvised parties in nearby studios. This brief period after 5.45 was known as the 'six o'clock swill'.

Amongst the drinkers there were some older faces I knew; I spotted the historian, Brian Fitzpatrick, looking very much like W. C. Fields, sozzled and slobbering over a double Jubilee whisky. Often I bumped into John Eddy, the Financial Editor of the *Herald*, with whose impalpable daughter I had had a long and hopeless infatuation, or the painter Arthur Body, and his brother-in-law John Perceval. On Friday evenings a whole group of painters and potters would appear from the artists' colony at Eltham with their girlfriends, to join the 'Drift', as those relentless evenings of gatecrashing and party-hopping came to be called. The noise was deafening, but the atmosphere was heady and as I stood in that packed throng of artists' models, academics, alkies, radio actors, poofs and ratbags, drinking large quantities of agonizingly cold beer, I felt as though my True Personality was coming into focus.

On the afternoon of my birthday, my parents had arranged a small gathering of aunts, uncles, grandparents and a few respectable old family friends. They had had a special cake made, iced with birthday wishes, and they had prepared an elaborate supper. It was to be a surprise party for me when I came home from work that evening. Unfortunately, it was I who proved to be the surprise.

My mother had not driven her car for several years and although she never actually gave it to me, I could sometimes borrow it freely though at other times it was locked inaccessibly in the garage. On my birthday I had been allowed to take it to work, and it was in this vehicle that I wove homeward later that evening, having drunk some rum and champagne in an artist's studio after the Swanston Family had closed its doors. Half-way to Camberwell I had missed the brake at a set of traffic lights and collided with the back of a truck. The driver had jumped out but, observing no damage to his vehicle, had driven on. The entire radiator of my mother's car, however, was smashed in, and though it still drove, there was a strong smell of oil and burning rubber and a terrible groaning noise so that I had to drive the rest of the way home at a snail's pace. I can only just remember my arrival at the front door and the blank dismay on the faces of all my relations. My father ran out to inspect the smoking wreckage of the car as I was ignominiously bundled off to bed.

I woke much later the next day with a terrible feeling of guilt, shame and impending doom. Thereafter whenever I got drunk I always felt exactly the same, although strange to say it never discouraged me. I always believed it would be different next time; that I would somehow conquer the problem, and eliminate the side-effects. At any rate, nobody ever mentioned my twenty-first birthday again.

The announcement later that year of my intention to get married was a further blow to my already punch-drunk parents. The picture they were forming of their son was bad enough; but worse, what kind of a picture were *other people* beginning to form of *them*! Not only was I a university drop-out – though the word 'failure' was employed in those less equivocal days – but I was already, at the age of twenty-one, an unqualified, promiscuous, chain-smoking tosspot on intimate terms with Jews and Roman Catholics.

I had met my wife, Brenda, during a production of *Love's Labour's Lost*. She was an exquisite little dancer who captivated all the men in the company, and in spite of my parents' profound disquiet we were married within about six months.

My mother refused to come to the service but my father and brother Michael were present, looking rather as though they were attending a funeral. I rented a small flat in the old suburb of Hawthorn, moved in some of my books, pictures and records, and tasted freedom for the first time. Freedom, that is to say, if I ignored the presence of my wife.

Return Fare was the final production of the 1955 season: an intimate revue with an overture that was a crude plagiarism of *That's Entertainment*, and an amiable series of sketches and monologues, delivered by members of the company. Although I was no good at acting, it was generally felt that I had a contribution to make to the more frivolous theatre, so I was invited to write something for the show. Melbourne had been chosen as the site for the 1956 Olympic Games, but unfortunately there were not nearly enough hotels to accommodate the anticipated crowds. Half of Victorian Melbourne – including its grand hotels – had been torn down in the stampede to be modern.

At the time I was racking my brains in search of comic ideas, large advertisements were appearing in the newspapers inviting ordinary folk to billet visiting athletes. Ray Lawler suggested this might be a fruitful subject. 'Why,' he said, 'can't you write a sketch for that woman you used to do in the back of the bus? Edna, wasn't it? Wouldn't she be just the kind of person who would offer her spare bedroom to a Latvian pole-vaulter, provided, of course, that he was spotlessly clean and didn't hang his jockstrap on her rotary clothes-hoist in full view of the neighbours?'

Fired by this idea and encouraged by two of my fellow actors, Peter Batey and Noël Ferrier, I devised a two-handed sketch in which Edna (my average housewife) offered her home as an Olympic billet. I had hoped the role of Edna could have been played by Zoë or one of the other girls, but Lawler thought I should play the part myself like a pantomime dame, and so I did. The dialogue was full of glutinous descriptions of the amenities and appointments of Edna's Moonee Ponds villa, and there were very few conventional jokes. Occasionally Edna broke off to apostrophize her aged mother and her infant son Kenneth on the telephone.

The sketch had a galvanic effect on Melbourne audiences because it described their own homes and their own taste in something closely resembling their own dialect. When the Olympic Games official offered Mrs Edna Everage a cup of tea she beamed at him, and after a long pause exclaimed with a shrill note of ecstasy, 'Look, I'd love one!' The phatic and redundant 'look'[1] preceding a bald statement of fact or opinion had perhaps not previously been brought to the attention of an

---

1. New Zealanders prefer to say 'listen' before almost everything, though it is a completely unconscious locution or verbal tic, like that threadbare word 'basically' in current usage.

Australian audience, and they laughed with a mixture of surprise and empathy, as they did throughout the dialogue, at references to burgundy wall-to-wall carpets, lamington cakes and reindeers frosted on glass dining-room doors. It would be true to say that the audiences who filled that little theatre on the campus of Melbourne University every night positively swooned with pleasure at material which, however childish, required neither subtitles nor that elaborate process of translation and transposition that British and American dialogue always demanded.

I should explain to English readers that in this epoch, the cultural aspirations and vernacular of the Australian middle class rarely, if ever, found their way into 'art', so that Edna's simpering genteelisms and her post-war, house-proud rhapsodies had a kind of thrilling novelty that is hard to believe today.

For my first, and what I supposed to be my last, appearance as Mrs Everage I wore my own shirt under a rather large blue cardigan and a gaudy floral skirt. A clown-like effect was suggested by a pointed yellow felt hat which my mother had bought in a moment of folly, but never worn. Edna wore no glasses, and no makeup except for a line of carmine around the lips, and her legs were bare, hairy, and shod with flat black brogues.

My days in repertory theatre came to an end, but I was lucky. A telegram arrived from Sydney, that big wicked city to the north, which I had only glimpsed years before on a holiday with my parents, inviting me and my young wife to join the Phillip Street Theatre in a new revue. Air tickets would follow and we were to start rehearsals the next week.

My leave of absence from EMI was never mentioned again, and I had heard that the mild, bespectacled Managing Director, Mr Hern, that paragon of Executives, had left under a cloud. My father's brother, Dick, gave us a family post-wedding party and even my parents thawed a little. My mother, surprisingly, even apologized for not being well enough to attend.

But there was, none the less, an atmosphere of goodwill towards me, and relief, too, that I had a new well-paid job — a long way away.

Sinny

'I WOULDN'T TAKE Edna up to Sydney if I were you,' someone said before I caught the plane, 'she's too Melbourne. They've got a funny sense of humour up there.' I had not thought of taking Edna anywhere. In fact, I had no intention of ever getting into that silly frock again.

Brenda and I were met at the Kingsford Smith aerodrome by Eric Duckworth, the business manager of the Phillip Street Theatre and the partner of William Orr, the founder and director. He drove us to our accommodation in the Rembrandt Private Hotel, Kings Cross. We were in the heart of Sydney's most notorious district: the Soho, the Pigalle of the city, and certainly the liveliest, seediest, wickedest, most amusing and most overrated place in all Australia.

Our room, which was a large bedsitter with a kitchenette, was floored with khaki linoleum and we had barely put down our suitcases and inspected the sagging fawn candlewick bedspread when I saw something large, black and glossy dart under the stove. It was my first glimpse of a cockroach, the first of many. Having lived such a protected life all those years in vermin-free Melbourne, I knew so little about cockroaches that I experienced no revulsion whatsoever when I saw them, and thereafter I saw them in their hundreds, scurrying industriously around our small apartment.

Just around the corner and only a few doors from the Rembrandt was the Hasty Tasty, a popular restaurant brilliantly lit with pink, blue and yellow neon tubes, and with miniature jukeboxes on every table. To attract visiting sailors and late revellers, it was open all night and the smell of fried onions from its kitchens seemed to be ducted directly into our bedroom window. On our first night in Sydney we had a hamburger there before catching the tram to the theatre in order to see the latest Phillip Street offering. The show had a few weeks to run, then ours would take over.

Phillip Street was a narrow thoroughfare which ran from St James's church, built in the 1830s by the convict architect, Francis Greenway, down the hill to Circular Quay. It still exists, that is to say there is a street bearing its name, but it is now a draughty chasm between blank, shark-grey office towers and it is impossible to believe that it was once, in the recent past, a street full of such history, charm and character or that the revues performed at its famous theatre were amongst the most fashionable and insouciant events in the Australian theatrical life of the period.

The little theatre which was to be my home for the next eighteen months was really the St James' Church Hall and it had a small stage and a tiny dress circle. For the past two years it had been packed every night with audiences enjoying that sophisticated novelty – intimate revue.

The management showed us to our seats and I saw, with surprise, that the star of the show was Max Oldaker, a musical-comedy figure of the thirties and forties who had been my mother's idol. She had taken me as a child to performances of *The Gondoliers*, *The White Horse Inn*, and *The Desert Song*, that famous production in which Max, disguised as the 'Red Shadow' and mounted on a white charger, had for six evenings and two matinées a week, enraptured the matrons of Melbourne and their wide-eyed offspring. When he sang, even the boxes of Ernest Hillier Chocolates in the stalls were momentarily stilled and the

Black Magic Assortments in the dress circle ceased their susurration.

That evening he appeared in a number of disguises but mostly in top hat, white tie and tails, singing sophisticated and ingenious ditties about champagne and caviare in which he was, from time to time, required to twirl a female partner. His most successful moments were a piquant song about his birthplace, 'I have got a mania to return to Tas-a-mania . . .' and the wildly applauded number 'I'm an Old Red Shadow of My Former Self', in which Max rather courageously mocked his most celebrated role. I noticed from my seat so close to the stage that he rouged his ears – a rejuvenating trick, I later learned, employed by many artistes of his generation.

In the interval, Bill Orr, the director, and Paul Riomfalvy, a charming stage-struck Hungarian and a director of the company, gave us some Australian champagne in their office and told us how the Phillip Street Theatre had helped revive Max's flagging career. 'The audience loves it when he sends himself up rotten,' Bill said. It was my first encounter with this curiously distasteful phrase, but I was to hear it many times over the next months, for it was for this especially that the small, hermetic theatrical world of Phillip Street was famous.

Ten years later, in the mid-sixties, the theatrical slang of the previous decade percolated into the middle-class vernacular, and even housewives were saying, 'Are you sending me up?' Just as America had, in Bernard Shaw's perception, moved from barbarism to decadence without an intervening period of civilization, Australian humour had somehow skipped the ironic and gone from folksy to camp.

The rest of the cast were very young and ebullient and we both felt excited at the thought that in a few weeks we would be on that same stage, 'sending up' similar things and possibly even ourselves. There had been a number of sketches and monologues which I recognized as revamped London revue sketches, and these had been given local colour by the introduction of product names, Sydney radio personalities and social 'identities'. In Sydney, as I later learned, there was a small group of persons who described themselves as 'socialites' and who were accepted by the press, and indeed the public, at their own estimation of themselves. They were always good for a laugh, though it turned out that most of them were on the board of the Phillip Street Theatre and luxuriated in the laughter and applause that the mere mention of their names nightly evoked.

The new revue was called *Mr and Mrs* and had a cast of four married couples, we being the youngest. Somehow the unequivocally heterosexual title of our show was at variance with those naughtier, more epicene tastes which Phillip Street had, in a short while, engendered in its suburban audiences. However the show did give me an opportunity to fly in the face of my Melbourne adviser and introduce Edna to a Sydney public.

The Olympic Games sketch was still very topical and it went down astonishingly well. The character of Edna was not, it seemed, a uniquely Melbourne phenomenon and in this strange, new, raffish city, I began to feel a little more at home. At the party on stage after the first night, suitably primed with Great Western champagne, I even performed one of the most expressionist of all our Dada sketches, 'Tid and the Psychiatrist', in which a cretin and his therapist slowly exchange personalities. In the absence of my old partner, John Perry, I played both roles myself and it was a party turn guaranteed to bring most social gatherings to a premature close. However in Sydney people seemed to sit through my tirades with an amused indulgence. I needed to draw attention to myself, for I was in a strange city, missing my Melbourne friends, scared of my marriage and worried that I might disappear forever.

Finally driven out of the Rembrandt by the roaches, particularly when it was discovered that their favourite refuge was the pop-up toaster, Brenda and I moved to a lodging house in a suburb called Centennial Park on the Bondi tramline. This was a street skirting the swampy, forlorn and, by Melbourne standards, sparsely arborated parkland, named in commemoration of Sydney's 1888 centenary. Its houses all faced across the road towards the elephantine Moreton Bay figs and coral trees of the park, and were formerly the unlovely mansions of book-makers, abortionists and speculative builders. Their style was indeterminate; an inflated yet debased variant of Arts and Crafts, where rusticated stone, stucco, 'tapestry brick', shingle and bottle-green half-timbering gauchely united.

The neighbourhood had been sadly declining since the Depression, so that when we arrived in Lang Road with our suitcases, these rambling villas were mostly subdivided into bed-sitting rooms. (In recent years they have been restored to private residences by people from Advertising and the Gown and Mantle business.)

In spite of the fact that we were working hard as revue artistes the journey 'home' on the tram, past the fumid and raucous taverns of Oxford Street towards the Centennial Park's gloomy portal, was dispiriting. Awaiting us was the small room with its treacly wainscot and curio ledge, a sagging pink chenille bed, and, in the morning, breakfast in the large shared kitchen where I caught glimpses of my fellow tenants; mostly aged and itinerant, and all lonely.

Sometimes I would go for long walks in the desolate park opposite. In those days it was not thronged with jogging bankers and their sun-wizened wives. On one of these walks I came across a cluster of young trees with a plaque stating that they had been planted in memory of somebody's son. The sight of this shivering little plantation in a bleak corner of the reserve increased my feelings of homesickness and alienation. Every day I walked past them I felt my rage and frustration grow, until early one morning I borrowed a small tomahawk from my landlord's toolshed and, skirting the empty park until I arrived at the memorial grove of trees, surreptitiously, angrily and to my eternal shame, I chopped one down.

My parents wrote to say they were off on a trip around the

world. There was a cheque for £500 enclosed. A great deal of money then, and, no doubt, a belated wedding present. Our boarding house had become intolerable and the last straw was the arrival of a couple called Cartwright, who looked very well-mannered and mild in the daytime but at night kept us all awake with bloodcurdling, drunken rows. We decided we could now afford to move to quieter premises and with a sense of relief we rented half of a large bungalow on the cliffs near Bondi Beach.

Mr and Mrs proved to be a short-lived attraction, but my contract was renewed for the subsequent revue called *Around the Loop*. Once more it starred Max Oldaker, a gifted young English comedian, Gordon Chater, and a large cast of pretty girls. Chater had come out to Australia in the touring company of *Seagulls over Sorrento*, liked it and stayed. Rather outrageous and given to scatological jokes, he achieved a great personal success in this revue, giving performances which, as I later realized, were an inspired combination of Max Adrian and Hermione Gingold. The best material had been carved up between Max and Gordon at rehearsal and I, who shared their small subterranean dressing-room, had to content myself with the leftovers.

From our first meeting Max Oldaker was friendly and generous. He put up with a great deal of macabre teasing from Chater and me. 'Isn't it funny, Max,' panted Gordon one night as he dashed down the rickety wooden stairs in a black suspender-belt to execute another lightning costume change, 'in a few years time, Barry will be thirty, I'll be forty and you'll be dead.' Max took such brutal sallies with an amused stoicism, seated at his cramped dressing-table rouging his lobes and patting his bald spot affectionately with a brown cosmetic.

I had written an old-fashioned recitation for Mrs Everage called 'Maroan', about a congenital Australian pronunciation difficulty, which I delivered in the same dowdy and rudimentary costume that I had worn as the Olympic hostess. I vowed it would be positively the last time I would ever impersonate this character.

MAROAN

You've read in all the magazines
About the Colour Question:
Should we be black, off-white, or beige?
May I make a suggestion:
Maroan's my favourite colour,
It's a lovely shade I think –
It's a real hard colour to describe,
Not purple – and not pink.

All our family loves it and
You ought to see our home,
From the bedroom to the laundry –
Every room's maroan!
When we bought our home in Moonee Ponds
It didn't have a phone,
But it had one thing to offer:
The toilet was maroan.

Look, I fell in love with it at once,
I felt the place was mine.
You see the day I married Norm
My bridesmaids were in wine.
Our wedding cake was iced to match
And glowed in splendour lonely,
And they drank our toast in burgundy
Which sparkled so maroanly.

The day my mother had her turn
We heard an awful groan,
I dropped young Ken, dashed to her room
And there she was – maroan.
And now she's in the twilight home,

> We're going to England soon,
> But one English custom gets my goat:
> They call maroan, 'maroon'.

This, my only real moment in *Around the Loop*, was always politely received, but there was a feeling in the audience, none the less, that snobbish jokes about Australians getting it wrong were in poor taste. Years later the only person who ever seemed to remember this squib was the author Patrick White, who had just returned from Europe and was living in an outer suburb of Sydney.

In the evenings in our dressing-room, as we applied our makeup, I would sometimes improvise new characters for the amusement of Max and Gordon. There was someone called Basil Clissold, a youth who was so paralysed with inhibition that he could barely complete a sentence. Then there was Sandy Stone, an elderly and childless Australian who talked affectionately about his wife, Beryl, who was obviously a battle-axe. On one of my disconsolate walks, this time on Bondi Beach, I had met an old man whose voice was at odds with his rather sturdy appearance. It was high and scratchy with a sibilance caused by ill-fitting teeth. I had asked him the time and he had replied, 'Approximately in the vicinity of 5.30.' Sandy Stone's scratchy and pedantic utterances became quite successful in the dressing-room where my most memorable performances took place. My nostalgia for vermin-free Melbourne inspired a musical parody which Max Oldaker enjoyed singing before he went on stage. It began:

> Deep in the Wheaties something stirred
> Lo, twas a cockroach the size of a bird. . .

'How do you manage, Max,' I once asked him, 'to smile with such sincerity at the curtain call on a thin Wednesday matinée?'

'Dear Barry, it's an old trick Noël taught me and it never fails.'

He demonstrated, standing in the middle of the dressing-room in his Turkish towelling gown, eyes sparkling, teeth bared in a dazzling smile. 'Sillycunts,' beamed Max through clenched teeth, bowing to the imaginary stalls. 'Sillycunts,' again, to the circle, the gods and the Royal Box.

'It looks far more genuine than "cheese", dear boy,' said Max, 'and you've just got to hope that no one in the stalls can lip-read.' I couldn't help thinking of all my mother's friends at those Melbourne soirées, their palms moist and their hearts palpitating, as Max Oldaker, the Last of the Australian Matinée Idols, flashed them all his valedictory smile.

Yet, despite the convivial atmosphere at Phillip Street, I still felt like an exile in Sydney. I was stranded amongst people who could not even muster the glottal energy to pronounce the 'd' in the name of their own city. They looked so different from their Melbourne counterparts. They wore beach clothes in town, they were shorter and taller and flasher and poorer, and their faces told a story in which beer, cigarettes and strong sunlight played a dominant role. At the time, they seemed to me like parodies of people; like the Toby jugs on the curio ledge at the Wattle Tea Rooms. William Dobell, perhaps the greatest Australian artist, has painted the Sydney face a thousand times, and at the time he was vilified for being a mere caricaturist. At the Granville Returned Servicemen's Club, at 11.30 on Sunday morning, the faces looking up at me as I stood on the small stage were all Dobell creations.

One afternoon a week before, I had been in the back bar of the Criterion Hotel in Park Street where Jim Gussey and the ABC Dance Band used to drink. Someone introduced me to an agent called Ted James, a pushy little man in a shabby fawn suit worn over a maroon cardigan. He had that authentic aura of seedy vainglory which typifies all agents great and small. Ted was a small-time agent, but since I had never met an agent before I was impressed. A measure of his lowly standing amongst agents was that he, in turn, was impressed by me.

Several freezing 'schooners' later, and this little fox-terrier of a man was singing the praises of the Phillip Street Theatre, and all who performed therein. He had never, it emerged, seen a production there, but if I was one of the stars – here I feebly demurred – then he, Ted, would get me a club booking for a top fee, like *that!* He snapped a pair of Craven A-lacquered fingers.

I vaguely knew that the suburbs of Sydney were full of licensed establishments run by Football Clubs and Returned Servicemen's Leagues, and it was to one of the latter that Ted James directed me the following Sunday morning.

'But what exactly will I do, Ted?' I plaintively inquired after we had been drinking in that echoing lavatorial bar for about three hours. Ted ruptured the cellophane on another packet of Cravens, tapped one into his mouth and extended towards me the cork-tipped pan-pipes with his freckled marsupial paw.

'Yiz Act, Brian, jus do yiz Act!'

I wondered why so many people preferred to call me Brian. I later learned that getting people's names *almost* right was an Australian – and particularly a Sydney – courtesy. It was enough to call people something.

When Laurence Olivier and his wife Vivien Leigh were touring Australia in 1948 the Lord Mayor of Sydney, at an official reception, introduced them as 'Sir Oliver and Lady Leigh'. When told the actors had been slightly miffed by this imaginative transposition of their names, the Mayor had merely shrugged affably and said, 'Shit, you can't win 'em all.'

'But I don't think I've got an act, Ted,' I ventured lamely.

''Course you've got an act, Bri,' said Ted, calling for more schooners. 'They wouldn't book you for the Phyllis Theatre if you didn't have a flamin' act! You'll kill 'em out at Granville next Sunny, and look out for Les Foxcroft, he's the other comic on the bill. He knows his stuff, and he'll show you the ropes if you get the wind up.'

*

The train trip to Granville took an eternity, the area was treeless and dismal and the Club, an insalubrious weatherboard structure, was thronged with men at eleven a.m., all drinking and noisily operating one-armed bandits at the rear of the hall. Backstage, Les Foxcroft introduced himself. He was a courteous man, and he offered to go on first and 'warm them up'.

'You'll find they're a hard nut to crack here in Granville,' he warned me. 'Do you work blue?' I had no idea what he meant. 'You'll find that they go for a bit of blue material out here.'

I looked down at my best navy-blue double-breasted suit made by my father's tailor, and I felt reassured. At least I had the blue material.

'How long is your act?'

'Oh,' I replied evasively, 'depends on the laughs!'

Les gave me an odd look, and went on stage. I could hear bursts of laughter during Les's act, but I couldn't concentrate. *What was my act?* Had I been drunk when I agreed to do this? Of course I had. Extremely drunk. As full as a Catholic School. In a minute it would be my turn to step on to that bleak platform, and at 11.55, when most people were still in church, I would be 'doing my act' in broad daylight in front of about one hundred and fifty rough, tough, well-oiled veterans. I thought of the 'top fee' – £5. I needed it. The back bar of the Criterion was an expensive habit. I decided I would go on and give them my old Dada party turn, 'Tid and the Psychiatrist'. It would be the first time that the expressionist theatre had ever come to Granville.

When Les left the stage to warm applause and a few stentorian 'Good on yiz!' he winked at me. On I went.

'We take you to a psychiatric clinic somewhere near the top of Collins Street. Dr Scott, brilliant graduate in Cretinology, is examining a new patient, called, for the moment, Tid. A rather big youth. The doctor is speaking . . . '

The Dobell faces looked up in silence. I had jammed a homburg hat over my lank hair, whitened my face and blackened

my eyes so that I resembled a personage in a Fritz Lang movie –
a resemblance that was probably lost on this audience.

'Well, Tid, my boy, what's the trouble old chap? By the way,
how old are you?'

Changing character to that of the imbecile, I took off the hat
and crossed the stage. Then, in a keening voice, 'Nearly sixty.'

A restlessness seemed to be spreading through the audience.
Quickly I became the doctor again. 'Well, Tid, I'm afraid I'm
going to have to take the dimensions of you.'

There was no doubt about it, my audience were beginning to
mutter amongst themselves.

'Your waist . . . one mile fat. Your height . . . six inches! Tid,
I'm afraid we're going to have to give you some special therapy
exercises for fear you'll grow up different from other boys.'

The members of the Granville Returned Servicemen's Club
were not merely talking amongst themselves now; they were
leaving their seats. They were actually turning their backs on
my performance – on my Act! I decided to talk louder, and
slower, in an attempt to regain their attention, but it was too
late. Soon all those backs, those cardigans and singlets and
little-boy shirts, were turned as they ambled to the rear of the
hall and resumed their assault on machines. One by one the
handles slammed down, the coins jangled, the talk and laughter
grew louder and the bar was back in business. It was as though
I wasn't there, and Dr Scott's final, eldritch scream as he
capitulates to cretindom was drowned in a cacophony of indifference.

Silently the club manager thrust a beer-soaked fiver into my
hand and, with a sour sideways nod, indicated the door.
Groaning inwardly, I wondered what he would tell Ted James
about my cabaret debut. Probably give him a real earful,
I imagined. Les Foxcroft travelled back with me in the train
and I sat in shame and silence as we rattled towards Wynyard
Station.

'Don't let them get you down, Brian,' Les condoled. 'There
are plenty of jobs better than this, son.' He offered me a

a nove called

Aid

bewildering—

exasperating—

insidious—

exciting—

*Tid, by Barry Humphries, from the title page of the exceedingly
rare first edition*

compensatory City Club, and a light. 'Being a comedian is a mug's game anyway.'

He was right. But what else could I do?

I was still uncertain of my artistic vocation; drawn to music and painting as well as to the theatre. Uncertain, too, of my choice between connubial life and creative solitude and between Australia and beckoning England. I vaguely knew I had to forge something original out of these contradictions and irresolutions.

The Assembly Hotel was Sydney's 'bohemian' pub. It was conveniently located one block from the theatre, and I took to calling in there every evening before the show. Very different from the Swanston Family Hotel in Melbourne, where amongst the boozers and hangers-on real artists could sometimes be found, the Assembly was patronized by actors from the radio studios next door. Here, propped up at the bar, and already the worse for too many gins and tonics, were the heroines of all the soap operas I had listened to as a child. Many of the old serials were still on air, and these permed and sozzled harridans who practically lived at the Assembly would, from time to time, fall off their stools and totter to the adjacent Macquarie Studios to impersonate yet another sexy ingenue, pert minx or warm-hearted wife and mother. Their male counterparts were equally unappetizing, with faces the colour of condemned veal. They possessed, none the less, voices that were famous throughout Australia, and on the wireless these burned-out old hacks became handsome doctors, benevolent family solicitors and likeable cads – whatever the script required. They took great pains to suppress their natural accents, since in the limbo of soap opera they were never asked to impersonate Australians. Hence they all adopted a fruity and adenoidal singsong which they supposed to be 'international', and can still sometimes be heard from older radio announcers. Today, Australian actors have gone to the opposite extreme. Convinced that they don't sound faintly Australian when speaking naturally, they assume a grotesque parodic accent unknown outside the Australian film industry. Consequently, the dialogue in most Australian movies is incomprehensible.

There were even a couple of child actors who drank copiously at the Assembly. That is to say, actors who *sounded* like children of both sexes on the air. One was a middle-aged catamite with a puffy, puckered face, like a balloon two weeks after the party, and the other, a stunted eunuch with a nicotine-stained forelip. Over this small troupe of men and women whose miraculously unravaged voices still thrilled the nation's housewives, hung a terrible Sword of Damocles – television. Few of them survived the new invention.

In the ladies' lounge, that is to say, in a cheerless tiled room off the saloon bar where rudimentary seating was provided, met another hermetic Order. It called itself 'The Push', a fraternity of middle-class desperates, journalists, drop-out academics, gamblers and poets *manqués*, and their doxies. These latter were mostly surburban girls; primary-school teachers and art students, who each night after working hours exchanged their irksome respectability for a little liberating profanity, drunkenness and sex. I belonged to neither group at the Assembly. The radio actors ignored me; I was too young and green for them. The Push shunned me as well because I was actually doing something vaguely and peripherally artistic. If they had any unifying credo which was endemically Australian, it was a snobbish philistinism and a distrust of success. In the Assembly, for the first time I heard a commercial artist bad-mouthing the painter Sidney Nolan, who was in the early flush of his European fame. ''Course he's pulling the wool over the Poms' eyes,' he was saying to a rapt and convinced circle. 'The only reason he's doing well is he's hired a big public-relations firm. Trust old Sid, the cunning bastard!' Few of those talentless tosspots who snarled their endorsement of this theory in 1957 had the faintest idea what public-relations firms were, though by the sixties they were probably working for one.

The radio actors also excoriated those of their number who

had 'got away'. Peter Finch, Coral Browne and Leo McKern had gone to London and quickly got 'too big for their boots'. They were called expatriates, a word I heard for the first time in the Assembly Hotel. Success was less threatening when it happened to a 'fuckin' ex-pat'.

'Finchie's back in town for a few days,' someone said. 'Jeez, that's nice of him,' said another. 'He won't be coming in here for a beer, that's for sure. Talking to his old mates would be a real come-down after all that hobnobbing with Larry and Viv.' But 'Finchie' did rashly look up his old mates. There was a party in his honour at our theatre after the show, and he arrived very drunk indeed, his face cancelled by a diagonal smear of vermilion lipstick. Someone, clearly, had been very pleased to see him.

The difficulty about a theatre job is that it interferes with party-going. By the time the curtain falls and you fly out the stage door and into a taxi, armed with a remote address, scrawled hours before on a sodden beer coaster, the party is either over or has moved elsewhere. Usually, however, the revellers have attained an alcoholic frequency you can never quite tune into. A concupiscent smile and a scribbled address from some girl in a bar at five p.m. can lead to many a wild-goose chase at 11.30 as you arrive, comparatively sober, at some reverberating bungalow in a distant suburb. Sometimes my poor wife would be woken in the early hours of the morning by a taxi-driver requesting her aid in waking me up or lugging me from the back seat of his cab to a convenient sofa, or the floor. Meanwhile Joe, the stage manager, was adopting the tiresome habit of confiscating flasks of St Agnes 'Hospital' Brandy discovered behind the mirror of my dressing-table.

I had taken to 'nibbling' between appearances on the stage. I was getting awful hangovers as well, until a barmaid recommended the Grappling Hook. 'Ever tried a Grappling Hook, luv?' It is equal parts Australian brandy and port wine and should be drunk very fast and as early in the morning as possible. If it stayed down, the hangover evaporated, and normal drinking could be resumed. To me, then, this seemed as pragmatic as it was civilized. Certainly it had to be imbibed in a hurry, because it was the most nauseating cocktail imaginable, and one to which the floor of the stomach rose in protest like a trampoline. The guilt of early-morning drinking was simply assuaged: I was not drinking alcohol at all – I was taking medicine. It was inevitable, of course, that with these health priorities, I saw less and less of my wife Brenda, and spent more and more time trawling for some obscure consolation in the bars and clubs of Sydney. Late one night at the Journalists' Club, a Scottish poet and drinking companion called Alan Ridell pointed out Kenneth Slessor. Slessor was Australia's greatest poet, whose work would fit quite snugly into any respectable anthology of later Georgian verse. He had written little in later years, when he toiled as a tame literary hack for Sir Frank Packer on the *Telegraph*. At the time I saw him, the great man was stooped over a snooker table, concentrating on a plant with a lot of right-hand screw. I introduced myself and mumbled something about my long-time admiration for his work. Slessor looked me up and down, took a long pull on his drink and said, 'Why don't you get your fucking hair cut?' I was always a reluctant lion-hunter after that.

Inevitably, at some noisy party, very late, I found myself locked in a bathroom with an exciting older woman. Not much older, however. After that there were the deceptions, assignations and all the dangerous stratagems of grown-up turpitude. The solvent and the catalyst was alcohol, my seductive new friend, which always kept its promise. I felt that I had successfully smuggled myself into the adult world on a forged pass.

Bunyip

O N M Y R A M B L E S around the secondhand bookshops of
Sydney, I had come across a copy of *More Pricks Than
Kicks* by Samuel Beckett, published in the year of my birth. It
contained a memorable phrase, 'No gardener has died, comma,
within rosaceous memory.' Poetry or hokum, one could never
be sure with this author. The volume, which I recently saw
listed in the catalogue of an American rare-book dealer at
$2,000, cost me 4s. 9d., a tidy sum, none the less, in those far-off
days. Searching for more works by the same author, I had also
read the novel *Watt*, so I was already a Beckett enthusiast,
when my early mentor, Peter O'Shaughnessy, wrote from
Melbourne to say he was planning to produce the first Australian performance of *Waiting for Godot*, and would I play
Estragon?

The long run of *Around the Loop* was drawing to a close, so
I accepted Peter's offer and hastened back to my hometown at
the first opportunity for rehearsals. Brenda and I were now
living apart, although I knew, with a heavy heart, that I would
have to return to Sydney and discuss our affairs, and mine in
particular. It was a desolate prospect. Fortunately my parents
were still abroad, quietly reconciling themselves to the idea of a
married son, who was meanwhile conspiring to unmarry himself. Their postcards kept arriving from Italy, France, Japan,

Canada and Switzerland, where my father had won a small prize in some tourist competition for his coloured slide of Lake Geneva.

This was a time when Australians were leaving for Europe by the boatload. Nice young physiotherapists, primary-school teachers and mothercraft nurses, all off on the Big Trip in order to make up their minds about some local beau to whom, after brief and catastrophic experiments with Italian ship's stewards and Austrian ski instructors, they would inevitably return and marry. The older couples, like my parents, usually had some Royal objective; a glimpse of the Queen perhaps, or several hundred Kodachromes of an English phenomenon known as 'pageantry'. They never returned to Australia without first purchasing several copies of the *My Fair Lady* album for culture-starved friends and relations. They also preferred to visit only what they commonly described as 'the clean countries', i.e., Holland, Switzerland, the Lake District and Scandinavia. And in handbags and hip pockets they carried, neatly folded, yards of toilet paper with which to upholster the lavatory seats of Europe.

While rehearsing for *Godot*, my friend Margaret and I shared a small flat in St Kilda with an obese British actor called Philip Stainton, who played Pozzo in the play. On his mantelpiece was an enormous glass jar containing a prescribed appetite-suppressant called Dexedrine. On the way to the theatre every night he helped himself to these by the handful and crunched them like Floral Cachous. Our eyes fell eagerly upon these innocent-looking tablets which, combined with beer, gin or fine wines, dispelled hangovers far more effectively than the traditional Grappling Hook, and Philip was only too happy to share his abundant supply of 'little yellow friends'. It may be that this generous self-medication has blurred some of my recollections of this period but, perhaps in spite of it, *Waiting for Godot* was a modest success. It was, however, almost too much for Melbourne audiences, who had only just acquired a taste for the last fashionable dramatist, Christopher Fry, and, had they but known it, were soon to be assailed by the turgid didactics of Brecht and his disciples. Yet after my fragmentary appearances in the Phillip Street Revues, it was wonderful to be on stage all night without a break. Gratifying, too, to hold those pauses, carefully indicated in the script, for as long as one dared. As I sat there in my filthy tramp's attire looking into my boot during one of these meaningful caesuras, I often wondered what I would say to Brenda when I saw her next.

Soon after the play closed, my wife and I formally separated. A Court of Law had ordered that I pay her what seemed to me then the extortionate sum of £4 a week in maintenance. I was therefore relieved to hear of more work on the horizon. O'Shaughnessy was planning a Christmas attraction; *Pygmalion*, starring him and his wife, and a new children's play called *The Bunyip and the Satellite*. It was proposed that I play Colonel Pickering and the 'Bunyip', for which Arthur Boyd had painted a ravishing backdrop. Since bunyips existed only in Aboriginal mythology, I felt free to create a prancing, bird-like clown, with a falsetto that inevitably got huskier after twelve performances a week in the stifling Christmas heat. With so much capering and singing before packed audiences of cachinnating kiddies, I was so exhausted when my time came to be Pickering that, during some of Professor Higgins' longer speeches, I literally fell asleep on stage. But I developed, with practice, a cunning method of leaning on the mantelpiece, chin in hand and half-turned upstage, so that my narcolepsy went largely unnoticed. I modelled my characterization of Pickering on the dean of Ormond College, Professor Newton-John, who had kindly lent us his house for rehearsals. His beautiful daughter Rona played Clara Eynsford-Hill and sometimes his wide-eyed youngest daughter, Olivia, would watch rehearsals.

The children's play, for which I had written several songs, was a hit and I must say I enjoyed the local celebrity the *Bunyip* brought me as I immersed myself enthusiastically in the wild bohemian life of Melbourne. Not far from the city was Eltham, a picturesque riverside hamlet, where, in adobe houses amongst the eucalypts, dwelt painters, potters and artistically minded and free-thinking academics and civil servants. On Friday and Saturday evenings, after the pubs had closed, the road to Eltham was thronged with a cavalcade of dusty vehicles, party bound.

Until the small hours the blaring gramophones filled the bush with the voices of Dylan Thomas, Lotte Lenya, Harry Belafonte and Bill Haley and his Comets; frightening the wallabies and traumatizing the kookaburras. Within the houses, the flagon claret flowed, as beard, sandals and sheepskin vest discussed Arthur Koestler, Jackson Pollock, Stan Frieberg, Saul Bellow and himself, with a long-haired, chain-smoking, breast-feeding, unmarried ceramicist. Improbably, a favourite author of the 1958 Melbourne intelligentsia was C. P. Snow, whose stupendously boring *oeuvre* was, I am now convinced, introduced to this circle as a joke. Beneath Brueghel prints depicting the bucolic revels of yesteryear, dancing to 'Island in the Sun' and 'The Alabama Song' from *Mahagony*, pissed architects made whispered arrangements with the barefooted wives of rustic abstractionists. Needless to say, I danced there in the midst of them all, feeling alive for the first time.

On the crest of a wave, O'Shaughnessy and I set about devising an intimate revue in Melbourne. He had strenuously opposed my efforts to drop Mrs Everage from my repertoire. Even in Sydney, Peter had urged me to develop this character with a monologue about the new Opera House and its lack of child-minding facilities and nice non-cultural amenities for those who disliked opera. The piece we wrote together was too overtly satirical for Phillip Street and was dropped after one trial performance. It was also thought to be too wildly improbable. In the following decade, however, all of Edna's prophecies came true. Sydney had something it could put on a stamp or a travel brochure and what happened inside it mattered little. The original plans for the Opera House were so drastically modified by the bureaucrats that the building can now only accommodate the most limited repertoire. When Benjamin

Britten visited Sydney soon after the building was completed, he unwisely remarked on the smallness of the pit. 'Pig's arse, it's small!' replied an indignant official. 'You could fit an entire orchestra of musicians in there.' 'Only,' said Britten drily, 'if they were all Japanese and playing piccolos.' More recently a senior member of the Opera Board was asked where their audiences came from. He might have been speaking for every opera house in the Western World when he replied, 'We'd be up Shit Creek if it wasn't for the Jews and the poofters.'

In the new revue Edna was encouraged to do what she had never done before; chat intimately to the audience. There in her twin set and pearls, frumpy blue floral skirt, hairy legs and flat shoes and with a rudimentary maquillage beneath her yellow felt hat, she expatiated on her favourite obsessions: her family, Royalty, culinary matters and interior decoration. For the first time, perhaps, audiences laughed at the mention of duck-egg-blue venetian blinds. An umber and more-ish yeast derivative called Vegemite that had anointed the toast and sandwiches of a generation of Australians here made its theatrical debut. Mrs Everage also reflected the fear and resentment that most Australians felt towards the new and, unfortunately, necessary arrivals to their shores; Italians, Greeks, Yugoslavians and 'Balts'.

Able to talk fluently on any subject whatsoever without drawing a breath, Edna became the living, glittering incarnation of Tristan Tzara's famous Dadaist dictum, 'Thought is born in the mouth.'

Shortly before our revue opened at the New Theatre in Flinders Street, I had made a 45 recording called *Wildlife in Suburbia* for a small Melbourne company. On one side was Mrs Everage's Olympic Hostess sketch, now updated as the Migrant Hostess, and on the other, Sandy Stone made his first appearance, enthusiastically describing a whole week in his vapid life. When Sandy 'had a bit of strife parking the vehicle' he was articulating a very new Australian problem, and one that has not gone away. My producer felt that this character would work on stage, and so, in a frayed checked dressing-gown and clutching a clammy hot-water bottle, I delivered my first Sandy monologue, with plenty of long, Beckett-like pauses during which the piano tinkled nostalgic and evocative airs such as 'When You Grow Too Old to Dream' and 'Little Man You've Had a Busy Day' and 'It's a Lovely Day Tomorrow'.

In the small cast of the revue was a former member of a New Zealand ballet company, Rosalind Tong. I had met her at a New Year's party of nostalgic Kiwis, and soon after we began living together in a flat which I decorated with some of the pictures I had started to collect. A portrait by Tom Roberts, a Fragonard print and a small chalk drawing by Whistler of a French model who, in her old age, had come to live in Melbourne. My parents had returned from their trip, and, sadly, refused to acknowledge my new arrangements, believing that I had succumbed to the bad influence of older friends, which was roughly true. My father dolefully reiterated his favourite augury, 'There's no doubt about you, Barry, you'll learn *the hard way*.'

One of the most successful of the Eltham group was the painter Clifton Pugh. Dour and pipe-smoking, Pugh was a kind of outback academician who lived in a rambling mud-brick house on a large estate of native bush evocatively called Dunmoochin'. Rosalind and I often went up there to stay amongst the wallabies, bellbirds and the flies, and Cliff painted my portrait looking haunted, angular and aesthetic. My interest in art revived and I decided to have another 'exhibition'. Pugh offered to help and used his influence to secure the staid premises of the Victorian Artists Society. It was a large gallery to fill and I recruited a small team of helpers to realize some of the exhibits. One of my assistants was a beautiful undergraduate in a cobalt-blue shift and provocatively laddered black stockings; her name was Germaine Greer. A young sculptor called Clement Meadmore helped create a display of Platytox boxes, a new 'product' designed to eradicate the platypus, and most other beloved marsupials. There was small print on the box hinting that a liberal sprinkling of this toxin might also conveniently reduce the Aboriginal population. Needless to say, these boxes were filled with sawdust, but the effect of this display on the public was gratifyingly subversive, particularly on those who were embarrassed by the anthropological wildlife of Australia.

Pugh and I collaborated on some parodies of Aboriginal art, which was then just beginning to be taken seriously. On to the earth-coloured and patterned surfaces of these pictures we glued trashy modern objects like soup tins and photographs of the Royal Family. Back at our bed-sitting room, Rosalind helped me create some dangerous 'sharp reliefs', or pictures entirely constructed of broken glass or mirror. From some, the glass tusks and shards projected as far as three feet from the wall, like the Helictites which grow on the walls of caverns, and visitors to the gallery had to approach these works with extreme caution, and could be seen sidling warily past them. Unfortunately, in slicing up large sheets of glass there were inevitable depredations to a mushroom wall-to-wall.

Besides overtly satirical exhibits, I continued making pictures and sculptures out of rubbish, especially bent forks, which I discovered in large quantities in wasteland used for the dumping of hospital refuse. From this contorted cutlery 'forkscapes' were constructed, and although some of these possessed a certain lyricism, they deeply disturbed high-minded Melbourne art-lovers who had only just come to terms with the duller manifestations of Modern Art. Large numbers of people visited this show which, in the guise of 'Dr Humphries', I opened at twenty-minute intervals throughout the day.

Surprisingly, I also sold several exhibits, including a large 'shoescape' consisting of about thirty rotting and disintegrating boots, salvaged from the local tip and crudely nailed to a wooden panel. These had been sprayed white and upon this intricate 'texture' I had painted a conventional landscape. The whole picture was rather sportingly framed by my father who, it seemed, was slowly becoming resigned to the presence of

INSTRUCTIONS.

Platy-Tox is a new, scientifically prepared KILLER guaranteed to rid your district of —

PLATYPUSES   KOALAS
KANGAROOS   WALLABIES
EMUS   KOOKABURRAS
LYRE BIRDS   WOMBATS etc.
BROLGAS

Just sprinkle a small quantity of Platy-Tox in creeks and around trees known to be infested by these vermin, and you will be thrilled by the amazingly lethal powers of Platy-Tox. Platy-Tox is approved by the Dept. of Agriculture and is available to 'The man on the land' in bulk, powder, or spray form at specially reduced prices.

GUARANTEED HARMLESS TO WHITES

Made by Australian Platy-Tox Laboratories Inc. Melbourne — Sydney — Brisbane — Darwin.

KEEP
YOUR
COUNTRY
CLEAN!

PLATY·TOX

FOR ALL BUSHLAND PESTS

A surviving Platytox box

insanity in the family. He regarded me at this time, I believe, more with pity than anger. To his surprise and mine, the 'shoescape' was sold to John Reed, a Melbourne lawyer and collector who was an early patron of Sidney Nolan, but unfortunately the work is now lost – or has shuffled back to the midden whence it came.

This exhibition, which was more like a theatrical event than an art show, attracted a great deal of publicity and I received many interesting offers. Channel Seven, one of Melbourne's first television stations, approached me to make a weekly appearance on a children's programme as the Bunyip. For the rather large sum of £9 a week I was to sit on a log on the studio floor and tell my juvenile audience a little story lasting for about fifteen minutes. Most television in those days was live, which lent a certain precarious intensity to these monologues. Every Monday morning I would have to dream up a new Bunyip story, often with Rosalind's help, and then arrive at the studio in plenty of time to apply the elaborate makeup, which included a long beak-like nose, modelled from nose-putty. My hair, always rather lank, had to be interwoven with leaves, another time-consuming procedure, and then, of course, I had to don the costume.

As the weeks passed, however, I began to devote less and less time to conscientious preparation. Sometimes it was even: 'Christ, I have to be in the studio in half an hour. What the hell will I tell the kids this week?'

One week I was especially late, and ill-prepared. My mind was a complete blank. *En route* to the studio I scanned the roadside for a suitable bush or peppercorn tree from which to pluck enough leaves to pin in my hair and, double-parking the old and slightly smoking Austin A40, which had been relinquished by my mother, I rushed into the dressing-room and furiously tweaked a lump of nose-putty into a vaguely recognizable beak, while someone pinned a few fronds and twigs to my scalp. By then, an anxious floor manager had appeared at the door, pointing imperatively at his watch, so that I had barely pulled up my tights and sat on my studio log when the red light on the camera announced that I was on the air. 'Hello, boys and girls!' I squeaked breathlessly. 'Have I got a funny story for you today . . .!' My brain whirred as a large clump of gum leaves detached itself from my hair and fell into my lap. The floor manager seemed to be gesturing at me, and pointing insistently at his nose. Improvising wildly, I allowed my fingers to stray casually to the place in the middle of my face where my beak ought to be. It was not there. I glanced down. It was on the studio floor. Applied far too hastily, it had refused to bond with my nose.

My Bunyip story that week got me into real hot water. Fables about leprosy in the Australian bush were not thought to be suitable or tasteful entertainment for children, even though, as an ex-Sunday-school pupil and teacher, I recalled that references to this malady cropped up rather often in the Bible. There were complaints, too, from parents about the Bunyip's free use of Australian slang, which large numbers of small, uncritical children were beginning to emulate. The following week a contrite Bunyip, with a restored proboscis, ritually washed out his mouth with soap and water, live on camera. But by then the damage was done. The producer had words to say; and, disgraced, I retired from children's television for ever.

I decided that the time had come at last to go to England, although I had not the faintest idea where I would find the boat fare. Peter, who was also contemplating a trip abroad, suggested we jointly give two farewell performances in Melbourne at the Assembly Hall.

My divorce had come through and, since Rosalind and I were seriously considering marriage, we flew to Auckland so that I could meet her parents and also perhaps write some new material for my valedictory concert. Alas, I had no sooner been introduced to my future parents-in-law than I was struck down with agonizing toothache, and I spent every day for the rest of my time in New Zealand in a dentist's chair having critical root-canal surgery on the very teeth which, many years before, had withstood Great-Uncle Jack's innovative experiments.

This orthodontal catastrophe cost me most of my savings and I realized that if the two farewell shows were not a complete sell-out we would have to remain in Melbourne for another year. The Australian Broadcasting Commission came to my rescue and invited me to do two half-hour television 'specials' of my own material. These were, again, live, so that no record of them survives, but they provided Mrs Everage with her television debut.

In one sketch, she exchanged beauty and fashion secrets with the famous Melbourne model, 'Bambi' Shmith, who is now, perhaps thanks to Edna's homespun advice, the Countess of Harewood.

I had had some experience of the world of fashion before this. A girlfriend of mine worked at the Greta Meirs School of Charm, which ran a special course for housewives. Twice a week, wearing my slightly threadbare EMI navy-blue suit, I conducted elocution classes for a group of eager young matrons and aspiring models bent on self-improvement. I cannot imagine what I could possibly have communicated to these comely and trusting souls. My own diction has always been slurred and scratchy, but I bought a book on voice production and spent most of the classes drawing diagrams of the throat and larynx on a blackboard and encouraging my young married pupils, some of whom I imagined to be of a libidinous inclination, to open their mouths as wide as possible and glossaly explore their soft and hard palates, whilst I peered between their lips and made knowledgeable noises. From time to time Greta Meirs herself would look in on one of my 'lessons' and listen sceptically for a few minutes as her ladies, dressed to the nines, with tight chignons and faces tangerine from their previous makeup class, performed their guttural and sibilant exercises. The money had been good, but the engagement, alas, was short-lived.

The Testimonial Performance, as our two-man show was

pretentiously called, attracted large crowds. Peter and I did several 'duets', including a very funny scene from Ionesco's *The Chairs*, but my Sandy Stone and Edna pieces appealed more strongly, it seemed, to the mood of the audience.

I also impersonated a park derelict in the uniform of army greatcoat and sandshoes which these 'deros' seemed always to wear. The performance was a lugubrious parody of Marty Robbins' popular air, 'In My White Sports Coat and a Pink Carnation', which I sang unaccompanied and *adagio misterioso*: 'In my white sandshoes and my army greatcoat I'm all dressed up for the park.'

At the end of the show, I'm afraid I may have rejoiced a little too overtly in the applause of the audience, for my colleague Peter rebuked me quite sharply for 'hogging the limelight', and his dressing-room door closed rather loudly. Although I have always had a reluctance to appear on stage which amounts almost to a phobia, I have found that once this has been conquered, the virtues of self-effacement and modesty quickly elude me.

Rosalind and I bought two third-class tickets on the Lloyd Triestino vessel *Toscana*, and in the beautiful garden of an artist friend we were married in the Melbourne suburb of Brighton. The ceremony was performed by the Reverend Douglas Tasker whom I had met in the saloon bar of the Swanston Family Hotel, and in gratitude for his services I presented him with a large and important Forkscape.

Our meagre savings were unexpectedly supplemented by the sum of £40; the proceeds from the sale of my Whistler drawing. About a year before, when I was very broke, a business-man friend told me that if I ever wanted to sell my picture he knew of a rich buyer. Morrie Bardas was an interesting character, who had established a thriving sportswear company since his arrival in Australia from Poland before the war. He had a great love for music and for books, especially the work of D. H. Lawrence, and an almost prurient fascination with

Melbourne's artists and writers. In his dapper suit and tie he was one of the many unlikely people who frequented the saloon bar of the Swanston Family Hotel. He told me that his wealthy acquaintance wished to borrow my pastel and would almost certainly give a good price for it after having lived with it for a couple of weeks. As a schoolboy I had paid the huge sum of £14 for this drawing over a period of many weeks so I plucked up the courage to ask £40 for it now. Morrie raised his eyebrows a little sadly, but took the picture. For the next year I kept asking him when his friend was going to cough up, at which he looked most uncomfortable and apologetic and explained that the buyer had gone 'overseas', but would *definitely* pay up when she returned to Melbourne.

When I got the cheque for my farewell show, I suddenly realized I wanted my Whistler back. What was forty quid? I asked myself. Morrie looked very ill-at-ease when I announced my decision. The lady, he said, had taken the drawing to London, had it verified at Christie's, and agreed to pay the money. He pressed the miserable sum into my hand, which, after twelve months, had not accumulated interest. Where is my picture now, I wonder. No doubt over-framed, under sticky non-reflective glass, with a gilded picture-light glaring above it, on the rag-rubbed wall of some hideous Melbourne mansion. I told this sad tale, with suitable embellishments, at a Sydney dinner party some years ago, and one young woman took a keener interest than the rest in my story. 'I know the picture well,' she said, 'but I never knew how my mother came by it.'

All our friends came to see us off at Port Melbourne, including my father, who, as a belated wedding present, had bought Rosalind and me two new suitcases. A photographer friend persuaded me to put on Edna's hat and look through the porthole waving a hanky. It was my next record sleeve.

Raspberry Ripple

I ALWAYS LONGED to live in a city where you couldn't drink the water. Here at last it was; a far cry from Melbourne, so prim and proper and *potable*. I had been woken soon after midnight by the sounds of running footsteps and excited cries outside my porthole, and I had rushed up on deck in time to see the amethyst lights of Venice, and the Doges' Palace, pink and nacreous, sliding past, as the *Toscana* nudged its way into the Canal San Marco. It was my first glimpse of Europe and of a city that actually smelt of something. In Venice, and in Vicenza, I hunted out everything I could find by the Tiepolos, father and son. In an old church on the Giudecca, late one afternoon, I peered up at a fresco on the ceiling which seemed to be in an appalling state. One could almost see the particles of paint exfoliating from the surface of the picture and joining the other bright motes in the gold slanting sunshine. I felt that if I stood there long enough, arm outstretched, I might, a year hence, discover a cherub's rosy kneecap in my open palm. We spent the next few weeks there, then travelled through northern Italy, living cheaply, visiting museums and climbing every campanile in sight. In Rome we dossed down in the studio of my artist friend, Lawrence Daws, and met the old and ailing Martin Boyd, Australia's greatest novelist, whose nephew, Arthur, I knew. By then we were almost out of money, so that by the time we reached London, after an endless journey in third-class railway carriages, I had only 4d. left in the world.

The 1st of June 1959 was a hot day in Mayfair when I presented myself at the ormolu reception desk of the English Speaking Union in Charles Street. I had joined this highly respectable club in Melbourne years before, since they regularly held dances and 'socials' attended by very pretty girls, and I hoped that reciprocity with the London Branch might help me secure comfortable accommodation in the West End. However the lady behind the desk regarded me with not a little distaste. My hair was lank, and after nearly two months' rough travel through Europe in the same clothes, I must have presented a striking contrast to the neatly groomed middle-aged Americans and decorous English ladies who frequented the club. I was told firstly that they had *no accommodation*, not even for students, and a commissionaire escorted me, rather roughly, back into Berkeley Square. I looked at my 4d. It was enough for a phone call to my sister, Barbara, who was already living in Paddington. She lent me £20 and my European career began.

In Elgin Crescent, Ladbroke Grove, a Polish couple let us a tiny bed-sitting room in their attic for £4 10s. a week. Although the street was quite respectable, we were not far from the scene of the recent race riots, and only a few streets away from Rillington Place, where Christie had murdered and immured his pathetic victims. Notting Hill still had about it an agreeably seedy pre-war atmosphere, so well described in the novels of Patrick Hamilton. In winter the yellow smog, smelling slightly of brimstone, curled around the houses, and the air in the pubs was thick with Old Holborn tobacco smoke. The Portobello Market was only two blocks away and, in those days, surprising treasures could be had there. I remember one stall groaning with the unfashionable and unsaleable cameo glass vases of Émile Gallé, one of which I purchased for a pound.

I had been given the names and addresses of a few people who might help me; one was Charles Osborne, a hospitable fellow Australian who was the co-editor of the *London Magazine*. Another was Peter Myers who, with his partner Ronnie Cass, had written a celebrated revue called *For Amusement Only*. Myers and Cass had visited me backstage in Melbourne and urged me to look them up if I ever came to England. At his house in Bishop's Bridge Road, Myers gave us a very good lunch. Another person I had an introduction to was Eric Maschwitz, who was head of light entertainment at the BBC. He was a famous song-writer who had written the lyrics of 'These Foolish Things' and 'A Nightingale Sang in Berkeley Square'. He was very kind and helpful and told me to let him know when I was doing something.

My sister's £20 was running out fast and I decided to take a night job, so that I could attend some of the auditions advertised in *The Stage*. Lawrence Daws and his girlfriend, Heather, had come to live in a basement flat nearby. Lawrence needed a night job as well, and together we found one at Wall's Ice-cream Factory, Acton, a very depressing neighbourhood which could be reached by bus from Holland Park Avenue. Every night at about 6.30, Laurie and I would meet in the pub at the corner of Addison Road, have a pint of bitter and a Weights cigarette, and then catch the Acton bus for the night shift in the Raspberry Ripple section of the ice-cream factory. The clamorous interior, with its steel gantries, galleries and cat's-cradle of intersecting conveyer belts, was like something from the imagination of Piranesi.

There were no nitpicking hygiene regulations then; no inspections of fingernails or latex gloves. My task was to stand at a conveyer belt all night long, watching the swiftly flowing procession of Raspberry Ripple packets and ensuring their smooth passage. If there was a blockage, chaos very quickly ensued and before I could fumblingly wrench a squashed packet off the belt, or staunch the sticky leakage, a siren would sound, lights flash, and the entire plant grind to a throbbing halt. A foreman would then rush to my side and, after cursing me, he would restore order and set the machinery in motion once again.

Something seemed to go wrong in my part of the factory every night. At about 3.30 in the morning I had only to doze for a second on my feet or think about something else and the works would become instantly constipated. There would be a horrible pile-up and a massive loss of Raspberry Ripple from the ruptured cartons.

Finally I was relieved of this exacting work and placed in a bare room, not unlike the room in which, only three years before, I had broken gramophone records. It was, I soon apprehended, a sort of kindergarten for the terminally incompetent. This chamber contained a large galvanized-iron drum, surrounded by a circle of chairs on which sat a group of overalled and impassive West Indians. Every few seconds tins full of deformed ice-cream packets were thumped down beside us and these we had to unwrap, flicking the glutinous contents into the central receptacle. In Dante's description of the Torments of Hell, there is, to my knowledge, no scene depicting an ice-cream factory, though there should be. Glancing at my co-workers, I saw no real evidence of boredom, though by about five a.m. the fistfuls of Raspberry Ripple sometimes fell short of their destination or occasionally overshot it, leading to a playful exchange of creamy missiles (amongst my dark-skinned colleagues). The smell was all-pervasive and even after the hottest, deepest bath and the most lavish application of cologne I was convinced, as I performed my audition pieces by day, that my tenacious nocturnal aroma could be detected in the stalls. Bleary-eyed and somnambulistic after the sleepless torments of the night, I recited my monologues and sang my songs, imagining those anonymous producers in the darkened auditorium finding themselves inexplicably hankering for a Wall's Raspberry Ripple. I had become a subliminal human advertisement for ice-cream.

But I did get a job in the end. It was a brief appearance on a Rediffusion television talk-show hosted by Godfrey Winn, the novelist and journalist. One of my letters of introduction was from an Englishman who had worked in Melbourne for the Australian Broadcasting Commission. He was a fan of my new character, Sandy Stone, the boring old man with the hot-water bottle, and he had warmly recommended me to Winn who put me on the show, which was live, without ever having seen the act. My spot was preceded by a long and obsequious interview with the former Governor of Cyprus, and then I was perfunctorily introduced as a hilarious Australian comedian.

The camera found me seated in a chair with my dressing-gown and clutching my hottie, and I launched into an abridged version of one of Sandy's grindingly banal monologues about Melbourne suburban life. There was no studio audience but over on the interview set I could see Winn twitching and blinking in my direction, shrugging apologetically towards the Governor of Cyprus and running a fastidious finger around his cutaway collar. I had barely got into my stride before a floor manager started giving me a vigorous wind-up signal, and my first appearance in Britain petered out apologetically.

No one approached me at the end of the show, least of all Godfrey Winn, and I skulked out of the studio just in time to catch the tube and the bus to my night shift in Acton. In the *Evening News* that day there was a small paragraph about me on the entertainments page; the headline read,

A STAR HERE?

The piece had been written by Julian Holland, an English journalist who had been in Australia to cover the Test Match, and who had stumbled upon one of my performances. With not a little courage, he had given my debut on the telly a generous plug. I could not help feeling that I had let my champion down badly, and as the interminable night wore on I angrily shied dollops of ice-cream at an imaginary effigy of Godfrey Winn.

In Oxford Street in those days there were, for some reason, a number of near-tramps who sold plastic raincoats to tourists.

For such a character I had written a macabre little song with a sexually perverse undertone. Somehow I had contrived to rhyme 'plastic rainwear' with 'Mr Norris changes train-wear' – a reference to the fetishist personage in Isherwood's Berlin novella. It was a song that sounded sophisticated if you did not listen too carefully – which is probably true of most sophisticated songs.

I was called back to one of my auditions twice to sing this decadent ditty and it got me a job. Colin Graham and his friend Disley Jones were planning a musical version of Sweeney Todd, the Demon Barber of Fleet Street, at the Lyric Theatre, Hammersmith with music by Anthony Bowles. They offered me the part of Jonas Fogg, a madhouse-keeper, with two very good songs to sing. With Jones' brilliant Pollock's Toy Theatre sets and Graham's witty direction as well as Tony's ingenious tunes we looked all set for a big hit. But the critics were lukewarm and to our dismay this elaborate little operetta which had taken so long to rehearse closed a few days before Christmas 1959.

The stage door was right beside a small market, and after the last matinée the street traders were so sorry for us they sold us our Christmas geese and turkeys at outrageous discounts. I did, however, have a few memorable weeks in a beautiful theatre which has since, inexplicably, been torn down, reconstituted and embedded in a concrete office tower. The old Lyric had a curious and convenient feature. Opposite the prompt corner in the proscenium arch was a small door and a spiral staircase. This led to a tiny cubicle or 'snug' attached to the dress-circle bar but hidden from the theatre patrons by a screen of frosted and engraved glass. Here the artistes, and especially I, could enjoy a quick drink between appearances on stage. It was a quaint amenity which may have depended too trustingly on the temperance of actors, and I have never encountered it elsewhere.

So, when the sixties dawned, I was out of work again. We had moved from our attic to a basement; this time a few doors from Notting Hill Gate's underground station and the rumble of the Central line was periodically audible in the cheerless flat, which we heated to a stifling temperature with an Aladdin paraffin stove. I resumed auditions and Rosalind, between ballet classes, got a part-time job in the local fruit shop. We also took in a lodger, a boy from the Royal Ballet, who lived in the dark back bedroom with a view of the light well. This fuliginous cavity resounded with clattering noises from the kitchens of an adjacent Lyons Corner House. It seems to me now outrageous that we should have charged rent for this dismal accommodation, but we did.

Occasionally we held dinner parties at which I provided Algerian red wine from Del Monico's in Soho costing 4s. 9d. a bottle. Special guests like the painter Sidney Nolan, the dancer Lynn Seymour and John Dexter, a young theatre director, were all offered this noxious beverage which could not be sipped without a violent shudder. In the end I took to mulling it with lemon, cloves and brown sugar, spiked with cheap brandy, and people rather liked it, especially those who did not mind having black teeth for several days afterwards.

Black was the colour of the early sixties, and everybody under thirty seemed to wear a black duffle-coat. The Campaign for Nuclear Disarmament was a popular cause and with friends from Oxford, I joined that long, black and rather inspiring procession which shuffled to Trafalgar Square from Aldermaston. I had found a theatrical agent in Regent Street called Myrette Morven, who had once understudied Cecily Courtneidge, and I had my photograph taken for the Spotlight Casting Directory by a famous theatrical photographer called Angus McBean, who looked as though *he* were understudying the role of Augustus John, with his Burlington House beard and carpet slippers. The photographs made me look rather soppy and unemployable.

The first stage show I ever saw in London was at the Metropolitan Music Hall where the Westway now hideously passes over the Edgware Road. To stand with a pint of

Guinness at the back of the circle and watch the show was exactly like being in a painting by Sickert. There was a wonderful bill of old-time players that night including Hetty King, the male impersonator, G. H. Elliot, 'The Chocolate-Coloured Coon', who sang his famous song 'Lily of Laguna', and Randolph Sutton who brought the house down when he sang, with tremendous poetic feeling, 'On Mother Kelly's Doorstep'. I felt that this night in the theatre alone had made that 13,000-mile journey to London worthwhile. Soon after this performance shamrocks were painted on the fire curtain and after a brief Hibernian interlude, the theatre was given over to bingo and within a year it had been demolished. Thereafter, except for the Palace of Varieties in Leeds and some small theatres in seaside resorts, the Music Hall died.

One day Miss Morvan put me up for a new musical comedy which no one thought stood a chance, though it had been written by Lionel Bart, who already had two big successes in the West End. I must say the thought of *Oliver Twist* set to music sounded unpromising to me as well, but I went to the audition and sang my Demon Barber's arias bravely into the darkened stalls. It was depressing to pour so much energy into what seemed like an empty theatre, and I was relieved to see the occasional flare of a match and the glow of a managerial cigar. They called me back three times and then Miss Morvan telephoned to say they wanted me to play the part of Mr Sowerberry, the undertaker, one of the smallest parts in the show, and to understudy Mr Ron Moody, who was to play Fagin. For this and some chorus work, I was offered £15 per week.

We started rehearsing at a hall in Bloomsbury and I met the director, Peter Coe, and the composer and librettist, Lionel Bart. It was then that Lionel Bart announced that he had enjoyed my audition so much that he had actually written a new song for the undertaker, called 'That's Your Funeral'. Thus I was to rehearse a number which, had I but known it, I would sing on at least seven hundred future occasions. *Oliver!*

soon became the musical success of the decade and I had suddenly become a West End actor without ever having set foot in the provinces or served my apprenticeship in 'weekly repertory', a discipline in which I knew, from grim Melbourne experience, that I would certainly fail. I had found my way on to the West End stage by a most agreeable shortcut.

It was exhilarating to be up there on stage every night in my assortment of Dickensian guises with an orchestra in the pit and a rapturous audience crying for more, even if it wasn't for more of me. Ron Moody looked discouragingly robust and I wondered if I would ever get a chance to take the leading role, even for a night. I didn't. The catch to being an understudy is that you have to rehearse with any new additions to the cast and in *Oliver!* the small army of pickpockets was constantly changing. Thus, I found myself in the theatre for several days a week, rehearsing with Oliver Twist's understudy and a succession of Artful Dodgers and precocious brats. During these endless rehearsals the wings were thronged with ambitious stage-struck mothers. I soon got to know the role of Fagin so well that I could leap on to the stage and perform it now; but then it was to no avail.

Working in the West End at night and often during the day gave me an ideal opportunity to explore London. Now that I was earning money I could venture into secondhand bookshops, and sometimes, for very little, I could pick up a treasure like William Beckford's first book, *Extraordinary Painters*, written at the age of sixteen, and in orange wrappers a rare copy of *Zang Tuum Tuum*, Marinetti's Futurist Manifesto on 1913, belligerently inscribed by the author. Then there were the pubs. In Australia they were no more than licensed urinals, but in London they were often more comfortable and congenial than the basement flat in Notting Hill Gate. Right next to the theatre was the Salisbury, which had an Edwardian gin-palace glitter and a camp theatrical clientele, but I preferred the Lamb and Flag in Rose Court and I persuaded the more convivial members of the company to drink there between the matinée and evening performance on Wednesdays and Saturdays. The jovial publican began to greet me like a long-lost friend. On one occasion I found myself without enough money for an expensive round of drinks and he, at once, offered me something which to a dedicated drinker is more precious than love: namely, credit. I had only been in the West End for a few months, and I had a slate. At last I was beginning to feel like an adult human being.

Alan, our ballet-dancer boarder, sometimes drove us into the countryside in his small car, when it had not been borrowed by an opportunistic artist *manqué* from Sydney called Robert who had come to London in the hope of becoming a critic. Why were people from Sydney always so pushy? Probably the convict background, I reflected.

Around north Soho there were the beatnik pubs where my long hair was less noticeable in the throng of black-duffle-coated men and the barefoot hoydens with their lewd mascaraed glances. In a bar near the Portobello Road I met John Gawsworth, a sub-Drinkwater poet and self-styled King of Rodonda, a title he had inherited from M. P. Shiel, the 1890s writer of fantasy whose books I avidly collected. Shiel's ashes were in a biscuit tin on the mantelpiece in Gawsworth's olid Westbourne Grove bed-sitting room. There he once made me, from cabbage leaves literally picked up off the vegetable end of Portobello Road and some cartilaginous scraps, a dubious stew, seasoned with a generous pinch of Shiel's incinerated residue. Gawsworth, charming and erudite in his rare moments of sobriety, was always on the cadge. Sliding deeper into alcoholism, he was rarely, as they say, 'in showroom condition'. But he had known so many of the authors I liked that we spent hours together in one pub or another talking about Havelock Ellis, Anna Wickham and Arthur Machen until he lapsed into total incoherence.

After about eighteen months, rumours circulated that Ron

Rosalind, Emily, Tessa and the author at Little Venice

Christmas, 1965

Tessa and Emily, 1969

By Cecil Beaton, 1967

The author in Little Venice with his Conder collection

The Surfie

The bride's father

The author with Small Bigscape, 1968

Drunk: with and by David Bailey, 1969

Sober

Edna Everage with Barry McKenzie

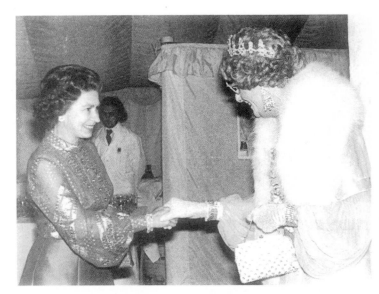

An historic encounter

The Republican (Sir Leslie Colin Patterson)

Moody planned to retire from the role of Fagin and I immediately wrote to Donald Albery offering my services should the leading role be vacated. I knew the part backwards and I felt sure that my case would be sympathetically considered. However, I did not realize that I had become indispensable at the boys' rehearsals. As an understudy, I was *too good* to be wasted in the lead! The director began auditioning for the new Fagin, and I, with shattered hopes, had to go through the ignominy of priming and rehearsing the orphans, so that the new star could take over. It need hardly be said that I looked on the other contenders for my role with a jaundiced eye. The final insult came when the part was given to a recently arrived Australian actor *whom I knew*! As a matter of fact he was very good, but that was completely beside the point and I decided that I had had enough of this theatre and its managerial treachery and ingratitude. Mr Albery, soon to become Sir Donald Albery, had assured me that after eighteen months' service at my original salary, a release from my contract might be considered, *if I were offered something extraordinarily promising elsewhere*.

But nothing seemed promising or extraordinary enough. *Beyond the Fringe* at the Fortune Theatre had been a sensational success and I knew Peter Cook slightly and had met Dudley Moore at the Lamb and Flag. As the show was going to Broadway, auditions were being held for a replacement cast. I auditioned and they immediately offered me a job replacing Peter Cook when the cast changed, but *Oliver!* would not release me. The same thing happened with an offer to join the Aldwych Theatre Company, and a new revue by Steven Vinaver called *Twists* with music by Carl Davis for which I auditioned in the basement of the Cambridge Theatre. Apparently I almost scared Oscar Lewenstein to death with an expressionist monologue.

I was feeling trapped in my undertaker's shop, as night after night, and with growing resentment, I capered about on Sean Kenny's creaking and relentlessly revolving set.

An impresario from Melbourne proposed that I put together a one-man show of monologues for an Australian tour, and going back home to do something creative for a while suddenly seemed an attractive idea after the hack work which my West End job had become.

I was due for my first brief holiday from *Oliver!* and, at the suggestion of my Oxford friend, Ian Donaldson, we decided to take this vacation in Cornwall, at a cottage he knew near Zennor. There I hoped I could write my one-man show, even though I knew I would never be released from my contract to perform it. Loosemoore's Farm was only just across the fields from the house in which D. H. Lawrence had lived with his German wife, Frieda, during the First World War. Their persecutions there are described in Lawrence's curious novel *Kangaroo*, although reading it I tended to side with the locals. I took with me a suitcase full of Australian newspapers and magazines which I had got from a friend in Fleet Street. There were copies of the *Women's Weekly*, filled with tips for the fashion-conscious Australian housewife and illustrated recipes, mostly in colours of brown and orange with splashes of yellow, since every Australian dish of this period was garnished with pineapple chunks. The *Women's Weekly* also contained an interesting illustrated fashion section called 'What people are wearing Overseas', candid snaps of movie stars in their first-night finery with a sprinkling of bedizened Sydney 'socialites' photographed on the way to a Royal Garden Party in London. There was a strong bias towards Thai silk, which was *the* textile of the period.

Leafing through those pages, as we huddled beside a wood stove in a Cornish farm cottage in February, I felt instantly transported back home to a world of cosy certainties; a land of sponge cakes and pavlovas and curried Hawaiian spag hoops and gingham, seersucker and Thai silk. It was hard to believe that I was actually living in that mysterious unattainable place, which Australians call 'Overseas'. The *Australian Home Beautiful* was also a valuable inspiration with its decorating hints and strong emphasis on the 'latest trends from Overseas'. There was that word again, that mythological, paradisiacal place where every self-respecting middle-class person in Australia would rather be. It was Utopia, it was Serendip, it was the Land of Oz and the Isle of Cythera.

At night, dead on eight, as I tapped away at my typewriter, I was interrupted by a curious humming noise. It was me singing, under my breath, the overture to *Oliver!*, a tune which has never been completely flushed from the uttermost ventricle of my memory. Today, every time I do a new show it returns to me just before the curtain rises, like a virus. It is in my system like herpes. It is the first few bars of Lionel Bart's 'Food, Glorious Food', and I thank him for it.

In the evenings we would put on our coats and mufflers and walk the windswept mile to the Tinners Arms for a drink before dinner. I was getting on quite well with my script until one morning in late February, my wife and I decided to go for a walk along the cliffs. Patches of snow still lay on some of the fields like scattered laundry and as I crossed a small fast-flowing stream of melted snow, I put the heel of my Wellington boot very carefully on a central stone before swinging my right leg across to the opposite bank. But the stone was icy, my boot slipped and I sat rather absurdly, but with a freezing shock, in the shallow rushing water. Rosalind was close behind me and in reaching out to help, tripped and also fell. It was ridiculous, but there for an instant we sat. It was only when I tried to get up and slipped again that I realized how close to the precipice we were and how steeply inclined the stream. Unable to clutch at any vegetation on the bank, we had started to move, first slowly and comically, and then very fast, as the stream became a stone chute that abruptly turned a corner and jettisoned us over the cliff's edge.

I came to, sitting on a narrow rock ledge, my legs dangling over an abyss of some two hundred feet. Below were jagged black rocks around which the sea frothed and crashed. Over my left knee splashed the icy cataract which had deposited me on this precarious shelf. But where was my wife? I looked over my shoulder and saw her higher up the cliff, clinging to some gorse. I tried waving until I realized that my right arm was lifeless and there was a tingling sensation in my right shoulder. I only managed to call out and tell her to scramble to the top somehow and get help.

I was alone on the face of the cliff for many hours. I watched the light on the rocks below change, the sea grow calmer; I saw the shadow of my own cliff fall across the water and still no help came. It was a very unfrequented coastline and I began to entertain the idea of jumping. If I missed the rocks and landed on my feet perhaps I could walk to safety. The pebbles, two hundred feet below, began to look soft and inviting. I desperately tried to make my past life flash before my eyes, but nothing happened. Was this an omen? It had become bitterly cold on the cliff face and I was trembling; moreover my water-logged jeans began to slip, centimetre by centimetre, and with a minute squeaking noise, on the glassy rock. I must have dozed off, for I awoke suddenly to the sound of calling voices and there was a great wind ruffling my hair. Straight ahead on a bright patch of sea I saw another shadow hovering. Then there were cries of 'Hang on there, man!' 'Hang on, for God's sake!' As I became aware of the roaring helicopter above and the profile of the cliff's shadow on the sea bristling with other shadows, I heard cries growing louder and remember very little more, except for a tilted view of Cornwall in the late afternoon, as I shivered in a cocoon of blankets.

I heard later that Rosalind, badly concussed, had wandered aimlessly for several miles, finally appearing at the door of a cottage and saying blankly, 'There is a man on the cliff.' Armed with this slender information, the rescuers mounted my deliverance. Friends drove us back to London but the pain of my dislocated shoulder and fractured arm was so bad I was put in the Royal Free Hospital. The climax to our Cornish holiday had made the front page of every newspaper in Britain, and

Joan Littlewood sent me a telegram, 'GET WELL SOON, BIRDMAN'. Painfully, I had fallen off England, but I had also, it seemed, dropped out of the cast of *Oliver!*

A Nice Night's
Entertainment

S OME MONTHS BEFORE this successful struggle with the
forces of gravity, Rosalind and I had been the beneficiaries
of another rescue. We had been rescued from our subterranean
flat in Notting Hill Gate by a saintly couple. Bill and Deborah
Kellaway were two Australian friends who lived with their
young family in Grove Terrace, Highgate Road, one of the
architectural treasures of North London. In exchange for little
more than a modicum of household help, they offered us a
small flat at the top of their house with views of tousled tree-
tops and Parliament Hill.

Here we lived until we returned to Australia to present my
first one-man show, which I had decided to call, rather flatly, *A
Nice Night's Entertainment*. This was always Sandy Stone's
assessment of an evening out, however dull, although in recent
times this has been displaced by the encomium 'thoroughly
enjoyable', usually with a strong emphasis on the adjective.

'How did you like *The Silence of the Lambs*?'

'Look, it was *thoroughly* enjoyable. In fact we all *thoroughly*
enjoyed it!'

Then London was a Mecca for Antipodean painters, and
Australian art was 'hot', largely due to the perfervid advocacy

of Bryan Robertson, the director of the Whitechapel Gallery. Arthur Boyd, perhaps one of the greatest and certainly the most 'European' Australian painter, had set up his studio in Highgate and other artists had followed.

One weekend Arthur, the painter Charles Blackman and I decided we would go to Paris to see major exhibitions of works by Goya and Braque. Leaving our wives in London we set off on that wonderful train which used to leave Victoria Station at dinnertime, enter the bowels of a boat at bedtime, and whisk its passengers through the landscape between Calais and Paris the next morning. As we enjoyed our breakfast I recognized at the next table Sir Herbert Read, the art historian, but I could not pluck up the courage to separate him from his newspaper in order to boast that I knew most of his pre-war surrealist poetry off by heart and that I thought his novel, *The Green Child*, was a masterpiece. I suppose I still remembered the brutal rebuff I had received from Kenneth Slessor in the Sydney Journalists' Club years before. Still, it felt odd watching that grey-haired stranger whose innermost reflections I felt I knew so well reading his paper across the aisle.

In Paris after a day of pictures, museums and a few cocktails here and there, Arthur Boyd seemed to become apprehensive. Charles and I certainly had delinquent tendencies, and Arthur keenly felt his responsibility for getting me back to London in one piece, so to speak. That evening, after a convivial dinner, Charles and I 'escaped' and went on an extended tour of the bars and clubs of Montmartre. Yet finally, even Charlie announced that it was time to go back to our Left Bank hotel or poor old Arthur would be calling the police. On hearing this I managed to give him the slip, and disappeared into the Paris night for several hours which are, alas, forever lost to my memory. I do, however, remember as dawn broke, creeping back into the room in which we all slept like the three bears. Just as I fell asleep I was aware of Arthur Boyd fumbling in the pockets of my jacket. Feigning slumber, I saw him in the dawn light carefully counting what little money remained in my pockets, and then retiring to his own bed with an audible sigh of relief. Like the dear man and conscientious chaperone that he was, he knew exactly how much cash I had had, and he had been checking to see if I had lavished any of it on nocturnal pleasures more expensive and dangerous than Calvados.

Meanwhile my Australian impresario, Clifford Hocking, wrote with renewed confidence that I could manage a whole evening alone on stage, although I was far from convinced. However, the tour was postponed when we fell off the cliff and it was two months later and much physiotherapy on my fractured arm before we could set sail.

John Betjeman and Elizabeth Cavendish came to see us off. John had recently visited Australia for the British Council and someone had given him my Sandy Stone gramophone records, which had reminded him of *The Diary of a Nobody*. We became instant friends and I would visit him at his small house in Cloth Fair near the Smithfield meat markets and in the shadow of St Bartholomew the Great. He described himself, not as a poet but as a 'senior journalist', and in his book-cluttered sitting-room lined with green Morris wallpaper and hung with pictures by Conder, Laura Knight and Max Beerbohm, he dispensed generous late-morning drinks to friends like Osbert Lancaster, Philip Larkin, Kingsley Amis and, very often, an Anglican priest or two. Then, in an exalted mood, we would all repair to Coleman's Chophouse in Aldersgate Street, where the atmosphere and appointments were immutably pre-war, and remained so until the enlightened sixties, when the entire eastern side of that old thoroughfare was razed to the ground and replaced by council houses in the Brutalist style.

At Coleman's we would tuck into roast beef and Brussels sprouts, and drink champagne from pewter tankards. John always insisted on paying, which was just as well. His *Collected Poems* was a bestseller and he was fond of exclaiming, with huge merriment, 'I'm as rich as Croesus!' The poacher's pockets in his jacket bulged with books and round canisters of Players cigarettes which he liked to smoke because the art-work on the tins hadn't changed in thirty years.

We shared several interests, especially in the Music Hall and the writers and artists of the 1890s, and he gave me many slim volumes of the period with wide margins and precious verses by dim and half-forgotten poets. 'Dimness' was his favourite term of approbation, and he knew I admired the rather dim, but once brightly hued, paintings on silk of Charles Conder, the English-Australian friend of Wilde and Lautrec, who had died of syphilis in 1909.

'There must be a few chaps who knew Conder who are still with us,' said John one morning, picking up the phone. 'I say, let's give Maresco Pearce and Augustus John a tinkle and ask them over for some bubbly!' Alas, neither of these octogenarian painters were in the reminiscent mood that day, and died soon after. Like me, John Betjeman relished such mysterious links with the past.

My pursuit of Conder, whose turn-of-the-century vogue had been brief, and who was now almost totally forgotten, led to a couple of curious incidents. Once, in the Crown, a pub near Leicester Square, which, in the early sixties remained unchanged since the 1890s when it was a poets' pub, I was accosted by a very old man with rheumy eyes, a greasy woollen muffler and mittened fingers around the handle of his pint of mild. He said he had been a doorman at the Leicester Galleries in the early years of the century, and that I reminded him of one of the artists who used to exhibit there. 'Who was that?' I asked. 'Well, Guv'ner, you wouldn't know him, and he's been gone these many years, but he was called Conder.' The hairs on the back of my neck twitched. 'Not *Charles* Conder?' I said, in astonishment. 'Can you remember what he was like?' 'Well, I've told you, sir, and it was over fifty years ago, but he was an *e-ffeminine* type of a chappie, very like yourself!' Later I was to befriend John Rothenstein, the author of a brilliant and evocative life of the artist, who remembered meeting Conder, then mortally ill, on his parents' doorstep in 1906.

I had noticed in a contemporary book on this artist that many of the illustrations were reproduced by courtesy of their owner, a Miss Amy Halford. I looked in the telephone book and discovered to my amazement that there was one Amy Halford listed with a Kensington telephone number. Impulsively I dialled it and a very old lady answered the telephone. Slowly and quite loudly I explained the purpose of my call, but she had got hold of the wrong end of the stick. 'Darling Charles!' came the Edwardian voice through my cream plastic receiver. 'I haven't heard from you for weeks. How are you? The fan you painted for me looks glorious and Edmund Gosse was here with Ricketts for tea yesterday and thinks it is one of your best. When are you coming to see me?' Our conversation was rudely interrupted by a brisk modern voice, 'This is Miss Halford's nurse. Miss Halford is not strong enough to speak on the telephone, I'm afraid. She should be having her rest. Good day.'

Although I had made some progress on my script in Cornwall before the accident, I had still a long way to go; so it was probably just as well that our voyage to Melbourne, via Rotterdam, Lisbon, Genoa and Auckland, lasted six weeks, and I could finish writing the show. We travelled on a Norwegian cargo ship with only twelve other passengers, and it was rather like being in a play by Agatha Christie. There were two nuns, an Australian honeymoon couple, and the Gillespies, a middle-aged pair migrating to Australia; a destination that we all knew they would detest. They actually began to complain about their anticipated social hardships when we were three hours out of Lisbon, and since everyone sat at the same table, the troll-like Norwegian captain had to exert great self-control in listening to this lady's ceaseless whinging. We were rather pleased therefore, when somewhere in the Indian Ocean during rough weather, poor Mrs Gillespie's chair capsized, throwing her legs over her shoulders, and she was seen by all, on that tropical evening at least, to have abandoned the humid confinements of her panties. From that undignified moment until we berthed at Auckland, Enid Gillespie never emerged from her cabin.

Also on board was an elderly German widow and her blond nephew; the son, we gathered, of a German industrialist in New Zealand. His urbane and smiling scepticism about the Holocaust was not the least of his charming attributes, though we were only privy to his political and racial views on those few occasions when he graced us with his presence. Most of his time was spent below decks providing amusement for rougher members of the Norwegian crew, who, given certain inducements, were prepared to overlook the German invasion of their country and had their own quaint methods of burying the hatchet.

In Auckland my wife was reunited with her parents, and with some success I tested my new material at a lunch-hour performance at the University. We got to know a few Kiwi poets and writers, especially Karl Stead and his beautiful wife, Kay, who to this day, remember more about my visit to New Zealand than I do. (See Asides.)

When we finally reached Melbourne, my parents were there to greet us and there was even a family dinner party to which we were *both* invited! My sister, now living in Melbourne, had married Robert, an engineer, and already had a daughter, Penelope; my brother Michael was in his final year at school and Christopher was studying architecture at the University. They were much changed since I had seen them last and seemed to regard me with a shy diffidence. I sadly regretted that my early marriage and expatriation and the inevitable age difference had created a gulf in my relationship with them.

Although I was nervous about my opening night at the Assembly Hall, my father, it seemed, was even more apprehensive. On the day of the final dress rehearsal, the box-office lady called me over. 'Had your dad in here this morning, Barry,' she said. 'What a nice man, and thinks the world of you too.'

'What did he want?' I asked.

'Look, it was funny really, and I reckon I shouldn't be telling you this, but he wanted to buy all the seats in the house to give to his friends in the Rotary Club.'

'*All* the seats?' I asked stupefied.

'Every blessed seat,' said Joan. 'He has to be your number one fan.'

'What . . . what did you tell him?'

'Well, I more or less told him I would if I could but I can't. You're *sold out*, aren't you?'

I told her I hadn't known that and I asked her what he had said.

'He didn't say anything really, just looked amazed. But I found him a single for himself right up at the back on the side, and he wouldn't take a comp either.'

A Nice Night's Entertainment was successful. Thanks, really, to Cliff Hocking, who had thought of the idea in the first place and John Betjeman, who had written a laudatory blurb for the programme. (See Asides.)

We extended the season, and then we did the show in Sydney in the Macquarie Radio Theatre, right next door to the old Assembly Hotel where I used to drink with the radio actors in the Phillip Street days.

Apart from Edna Everage and Sandy Stone, one of the most popular characters in my show was an Australian beatnik; a black-clad, suburban rebel in that period garment, the duffle-coat. These feckless hobbledehoys were to be found in the coffee lounges of most Australian cities, where they strove to resemble minor characters in the romances of Jack Kerouac. My beatnik carried a cheap guitar, which I had bought in Lisbon, and with exiguous skill I accompanied myself in a self-pitying ballad, which I whined and bleated in the manner of Bob Dylan. Such being the fate of satirists, this item was particularly popular with beatniks.

We took the show to Newcastle and also to Adelaide, which I had not visited since the days of Mauve Chunder. Hospitality, as usual in that most *gemütlich* of Australian cities, was lavish and although I was not unaccustomed to performing on stage with a hangover I usually found a 'hair of the dog' a helpful form of self-medication.

Then an imperious summons arrived from Broadway. *Oliver!* was to be presented there, and Mr David Merrick, the impresario, wished to reinforce the New York cast with as many members of the original London production as possible. The show was already touring; it was, in fact, about to open in Toronto and I was offered a tempting financial inducement to resume my old part as the undertaker and once more understudy the leading role of Fagin. On the one hand it would be exciting to live and work in New York but on the other I had little appetite for another long captivity in a show that I could sing in my sleep and to experience once again the demeaning and frustrating life of the understudy who never goes on. But when Merrick agreed to pay me even more money and limit the engagement to three months, I accepted. Moreover, Rosalind was expecting our first child, so it all fitted in rather well, and we could be back in London from New York in comfortable time for the birth.

It was agreed that my wife would join me in New York and I flew alone to Toronto. But I was not, in fact, entirely alone. I had been asked to be the unlikely chaperone to 'the Artful Dodger', a small boy called Davey Jones, who was later to become a celebrated member of the sixties band, the Monkees. He had been a star of the West End production of *Oliver!* and, like me, was another of David Merrick's last-minute replacements. What Davey and I did *not* know was that the two American actors whose roles we were usurping had no idea that they were about to be sacked. They had happily toured America, and Toronto was their last stop before Broadway.

We were met at the aerodrome by one of Mr Merrick's henchmen who smuggled us off to an hotel and invited us to see the show that night, but with a caution not to go backstage in case the cast smelt a rat. We realized that the management had, with despicable ingenuity, made us somehow to blame for the dismissal of two fellow actors. Since then I have often pondered on the anomalies of 'show business', which is not really a business but a game played with all the petty deceits, subterfuges and bitcheries one would expect to find in a provincial amateur dramatic society.

But an hour after I stepped off the plane there was another shock in store for me. Clive Revill, the actor playing Fagin, had laryngitis. Since I was the new understudy, I had to go on – *that night*. Except for rehearsals, I had never appeared on stage as Fagin before and had not studied the role for more than twelve months. As far as I was concerned, *Oliver!* was a past interlude, over and done with. Now, after a long flight, I had less than two hours in which to prepare myself for the leading role in a major musical.

The theatre, named after a munificent Canadian brewer, was new and enormous and that evening, as in a dream, I somehow pulled it off. I also, in a frenzy of compensatory over-acting, pulled off my false beard, although it is unlikely that the audience noticed this, since they seemed miles away; so far away, in fact, that the performance must have resembled a puppet show. I could, however, see the front row, and to add to my distractions I could see one man in particular, in the middle of the front row, leaning forward and staring at me balefully. His face was pale and cadaverous, and his lips seemed to move in time with mine. He was, of course, my unhappy predecessor, and he was there every night until Mr Revill's larynx revived. How could I complain and have him removed, if only to a less conspicuous seat in that vast auditorium? He had been ignominiously removed once already, so that every night I had to watch him down there, miming and muttering his way through all my scenes and songs. He was there at the stage door after every performance too, being stroked and embraced by commiserating chorus girls, whilst I, like a pariah, skulked into my dressing-room.

New York in the early sixties was an attractive place to be, even in the dead of winter. Like jetlag, mugging had not been invented, though neither phenomenon was unknown. There were no aerosol spray cans, so there was no graffiti except the decorous old-fashioned kind, and the tallest skyscrapers were still the venerable Empire State and the Chrysler Buildings, both pre-war. Harlem was visitable on foot, even at night, and Greenwich Village, where we rented an apartment, felt village-like and residential. From the women's penitentiary which loomed over Seventh Avenue the inmates screamed down their friendly obscenities to passing pedestrians, and at the nearby Village Vanguard you could hear Louis Armstrong, Sarah Vaughan and Art Blakely and his Jazz Messengers or Count Basie at Birdland on Broadway.

We lived in what was called 'a walk-up, cold-water' apartment on West 10th Street. This meant it had no lift and no heating. The latter inconvenience I failed to grasp, but on our first night there, as the icy wind off the Hudson rattled the windows and soughed under the door, I soon became aware of its disadvantages. Subjacent were two colourful establishments, Alex's Borscht Bowl and Ruth's Poodle Parlour and the co-mingled aromas of stewed beetroot and canine shampoo filtered up through our bare floorboards.

Directly above us dwelt Mrs Lyles, the Haitian supervisor of the small brownstone building, and wafting from her premises came an unidentifiable stench; the effluvium, we surmised, of certain arcane and unneighbourly rituals. Why else would I have surprised her on the staircase late one evening conveying to her apartment a caged and apprehensive chicken? Mrs Lyles and I disliked each other intensely, for it was to her that I had always to address my complaints about the discomforts and inadequacies, not to say the gelid conditions, of our accommodation. She was exasperatingly unhelpful, so that I was obliged to carry my grievances to the owner, a Wall Street business man and amateur artist, who kept our flat as a bohemian pad for the summer months. When I told him that I was almost certain, judging by Mrs Lyles' dusky and credulous visitors, and by the midnight incantations and aromas which filtered through my ceiling, that she was a fervid practitioner of Voodoo, he replied sententiously:

'It must be a difficult period of adjustment for you, Mr Humphries, being so fortunate as to have once lived in a homogenous society.'

Oliver! was a hit, but it was not the only successful British show on Broadway. Anthony Newley was appearing up the road in *Stop the World, I Want to Get Off* and Peter Cook, Dudley Moore, Alan Bennett and Jonathan Miller were starring elsewhere in their London success *Beyond the Fringe*. Rosalind and I began to see something of Peter Cook and his wife Wendy at their comparatively luxurious apartment which was not just full of Tiffany lamps but something far more precious – Central Heating. On Sunday nights Peter and I used to go to the Apollo Theatre in Harlem to see a new black singing group called the Supremes.

The cast of *Oliver!*, thanks to Mr Merrick's indefatigable battles with Actors Equity, swarmed with English actors, and since we were all being paid a great deal more than we were used to, and were in a constant mood of celebration, our dressers, like bewildered Ganymedes, were sent scuttling back and forth to nearby liquor stores during each evening's performance. A stranger glancing into one of our dressing-rooms might have supposed we were all throwing cocktail parties. One of the British actresses failed to appear on stage one evening and a duet became abruptly transformed into a solo, punctuated by anxious glances into the wings. The woman was found asleep on the dressing-room floor in her Dickensian finery with a gin bottle in her hand, like a figure in an engraving by Hogarth. The rest of us stumbled uproariously through our scenes, impatient to return to the Bacchanalia that reigned in our dressing-rooms. It was little wonder that the hard-working Americans in the cast, who earned a great deal less than we, looked on these boozy revels with the disdain of the Pilgrim Fathers.

After the show I did not always proceed directly home but

loitered in some of the more picturesque taverns of Greenwich Village. My favourite was the Ninth Circle, on West 10th Street, only a few doors from Ruth's Poodle Parlour and Alex's Borscht Bowl. The propinquity of my apartment enabled me to spend a few guiltless hours at the Circle every night, and I felt, as I stood at the dim bar of my 'local', ankle-deep in peanut shells, that I was as close to the threshold of my own home as any man need be. There was nobody I knew at the Ninth Circle and nobody who knew me, except for one drinker who always addressed me as 'the English Poet', probably because of my hair, which was unusually long for those days. I gathered he was some kind of minor academic because he told me he had been invited to Oxford University and earnestly besought my advice, as an 'English Poet', as to whether or not he should accept.

Although we drank together every night, I never quite caught his name, and one evening he insisted that I come with him to a party. With the aid of another drink, I suppressed a brief qualm about my wife sitting at home alone watching television, and accepted. But it was a difficult party to leave early. It was snowing heavily, and there, parked right outside the bar, was a large furniture van into which the other guests – and my friend had invited all our fellow drinkers – scrambled. Within the vehicle fitful candlelight revealed more people, sprawled and huddled, smoking and drinking, while a tape-recorder transmitted the music of John Coltrane and Miles Davis. The doors were slammed and slowly and silently the van glided off into the night. I have no idea how long this 'mobile' party continued, or at what hour it at last came to rest outside the Ninth Circle and we tumbled out into the snow, but I had, at least, overheard the name of my host. It was Jack Kerouac.

Rosalind and I attended many of the big uptown art shows in smart East Side galleries: Rothko, Rosenquist, Rivers and Rauschenberg. At one of these shindigs I was jostled against a picture which was still very wet, and I later found that I had one of the finest passages from Hans Hofmann's best period imprinted on the sleeve of my beige corduroy jacket. At the Gotham Book Mart I met Salvador and Gala Dali, who invited me back for afternoon tea at the St Regis Hotel when they promised to visit Australia, and there were many big parties thrown by society hostesses for the *Oliver!* Company. At one of these, in the Waldorf Towers, where the champagne and caviare omelettes flowed and the walls dripped with Sisleys and near-Monets the colour of boiled sweets, I wandered off into a small study where a fat, ill-favoured woman in surgical hose sat alone watching *I'll Cry Tomorrow* on a small screen.

'Wouldn't you like to join us all at the party?' I urged her affably.

'There are more int-er-esting people on television,' barked Elsa Maxwell grumpily, as her eyes swivelled back to the screen, which at that moment showed a group of derelicts on Skid Row.

As the evening wore on the theatricals grew rowdier, until our hostess struck several loud blows with her Tiffany-topped cane on a Boule table. 'Would y'all hush your voices, ladies and gentlemen, *please!*' She pointed a Van Cleef'd finger at the ceiling. 'Mr Cole Porter is trying to get some sleep!'

Our time in New York was drawing to a close and I had not the faintest idea what I would do on my return to London. Very soon there would be three mouths to feed. Peter Cook told me he had started a nightclub in London called the Establishment. It followed the success of his fortnightly *Private Eye* and Peter felt I should present some extracts from my one-man show at this already highly fashionable venue. I was not at all certain that my vignettes of Melbourne suburban life were really attuned to the taste of a sophisticated late-night London audience. But Peter had listened to my Australian gramophone records and was sure I would be a hit. He even offered to pay me £100 a week. A fortune in that far-off epoch!

Rosalind and I sailed back across the Atlantic with our

baggage stuffed with gramophone records, books, glass, sheets and baby clothes. Since the *Sylvania* docked at Greenock in Scotland, we had to pack all our loot into a hire car and drive down to London. We had only parked the car outside Charlie Blackman's house in Highgate for about fifteen minutes, but it was long enough for thieves to break in and steal the entire proceeds of my New York engagement. Fortunately the police were able to retrieve from a vacant allotment in Muswell Hill the sleeve of one corduroy suit. It was my original Hans Hofmann!

Between rehearsals at the Establishment I was attending Professor Norman Morris's special classes for fathers-to-be at the Charing Cross Hospital. Although I heard myself asking clever questions at the end of the Professor's talk, I felt more woefully ignorant of the awesome events that lay ahead than I ever dared let on.

The Establishment club was a long room in Greek Street which had been redecorated by Sean Kenny, the designer of *Oliver!*, in a kind of heavily timbered, Tudor–Constructivist style. There was a bar at the front at which young satire groupies loitered; pale-faced girls with fringes, pearlized lips and eyes like black darns. They said 'Yah' and 'Soopah' a great deal and they all seemed to know Dudley Moore quite well. Would these crack a smile at Edna Everage or Sandy Stone I wondered, as the cold hand of fear entered my breast and gave my heart a little squeeze. Late at night when the club was packed I watched a typical Establishment show. Eleanor Bron and John Fortune did a very funny sketch about middle-class pretentiousness, like a sort of Hampstead Nichols and May, and John Bird impersonated Harold Macmillan to a convulsed audience. There seemed to be a lot of jokes about upper-class politicians and once again my flesh crawled with misgivings about my own folksy act. I remembered the warning of those well-meaning Melbourne friends back in the fifties. 'I hope you won't be doing Edna in Sydney. *She's far too Melbourne.*

They'll never get the point.' I had got away with it in Sydney, but Soho in the sixties was another matter altogether. I sat at the bar morosely drinking until the Late, Late Show when they tried out new acts, usually wags from the Great Universities. One unprepossessing fellow seemed to get a lot of laughs with a none-too-hilarious monologue about the Royal Barge accidentally sinking in the Thames.

'He looks like a Methodist minister's son,' I thought uncharitably, as the birds around me hooted and soopahed. How was I to know then that David Frost *was* a Methodist minister's son?

As opening night grew nearer my portrait was specially taken by Lewis Morley, a Chinese photographer who later became one of the most celebrated photographers of the sixties with his famous image of a naked Christine Keeler straddling a chair. I was surprised therefore when an extremely truculent young man called Jeffrey Bernard attacked me in the French Pub in Soho for sitting for Morley and not him! Bernard apparently thought he was the Establishment's official photographer, though it was hard to understand how the fault could possibly have been mine.

On my first night on the pocket-handkerchief stage, I bravely launched into Mrs Everage's opening song. The pianist was an Australian girl who had failed to warn me that acute anxiety sometimes caused her to strike so many wrong notes that a tune could become unrecognizable. To this dissonant accompaniment I trilled Edna's hymn to 'The Old Country' as courageously as I could, but it was disquietening to look down and see, through the clouds of cigarette smoke, and at a round table only a few feet away, the critics busily scribbling in their notebooks. One in particular I recognized to be Bamber Gascoigne, the theatre critic of the *Spectator*, looking rather trapped, whilst others could be seen crawling out half-way through the performance. It felt horribly like the Granville Returned Servicemen's Club all over again, as the murmur of talk grew louder and the exodus to the bar more rowdily overt.

Backstage, after my performance had finished to the most perfunctory smattering of applause, I bitterly cursed myself for ever having agreed to trot out these whimsical provincial marionettes, who never made so much as a single reference to the Rt Hon. Harold Macmillan. The reviews confirmed my fears.

Bamber Gascoigne in the *Spectator* called my turn 'distinctly soporific' and Julian Holland, an erstwhile champion, said I lacked 'anger'. The worst part about it all was that I had to do the whole thing again the following night and the night after that and the night after that. Three weeks of public failure and rejection.

I was almost relieved when Nick Luard, the business manager, politely told me that they would have to cut my season short. I felt I had let my friend Peter Cook down badly, though I was pleased that he was still in New York and not in London to witness the disaster in person. However, there was another positive event in my life which alleviated all the pain and ignominy of failure. On the 14th of May 1963 my daughter Tessa was born at the Charing Cross Hospital.

By coincidence, on the same day Spike Milligan sent me a telegram asking me to play the lead in his new play, *The Bedsitting Room*, if I were free to start rehearsals immediately. I was wonderfully free.

Ruth

[faint mirrored text at top of page, illegible]

THE ARRIVAL OF Tessa dispelled most of my feelings of gloom and self-reproach after the Establishment débâcle. Overnight I became a doting father and, as I held my daughter in my arms and felt her exquisite mauvely-mottled fingers patting my face and plucking at my tie, I little thought that, many years later, those same fingers might be playfully reaching for my credit card.

Tessa, Rosalind and I lived in a rented house in Highgate, not far from the Archway Road. We inherited it from Leonard French, an artist friend from Australia who had just gone back to Melbourne. I had never wished to live permanently in England, much as I loved it. Always, at the back of my mind, I had a picture of some idyllic abode in a garden by the sea. Portugal perhaps, or Tasmania? Sometimes, in my imagination, this prefiguration of my fantasy residence was more vivid than at others. There was a terrace, azaleas and a colonnade hung with wistaria. Once in the early seventies at the Paris flea-market I came across a painting of my dream house by a forgotten French artist. It matched my vision in every detail, my 'coign of true felicity'. The terraces, the gardens and the shining sea. The dealer asked far too much, of course, and I walked away with the intention of returning an hour later to haggle, but when I came back the picture was gone.

The Bedsitting Room, a post-nuclear farce by John Antrobus and Spike Milligan, had already opened at the Mermaid Theatre but just as the play was about to transfer to the West End there was some dispute involving firearms between Spike and his leading actor, Graham Stark. That, apparently, was when I was summoned, Spike having seen my show in Sydney. As if the job and the money were not enough, I even had an understudy, a young actor called Michael Gambon.

In the lunch break after the first day of rehearsal, I was taken quietly to one side by one of the actors. It was Valentine Dyall, a tall, haunted-looking man with a glass eye. Before the war he had been a classical actor of great gifts of whom much was expected, but he had, in later years, failed to live up to his early promise. Yet there was always a trace of hopefulness, of jaunty vanity – sometimes winning and sometimes merely ridiculous – attached to his decline. His voice was his most famous attribute; sepulchral, supercilious, aristocratic, it had become known throughout Britain on BBC Radio in Dyall's celebrated impersonation of *The Man in Black*. Spike Milligan often used him in *The Goon Shows*, usually in the role of an effete and crazed Englishman, but he was especially funny on stage in *The Bedsitting Room*, in a role which he hoped might re-establish his reputation in the West End.

It seemed that Valentine had drawn me to one side in the saloon bar of the Round Table to warn me about another member of the cast. Discreetly rolling his good eye in the direction of a balding and mild-looking man in a navy-blue blazer, quietly sipping a half of bitter, he hissed:

'Never lend money to that man over there, dear boy. He looks nice, and he is nice, but you'll never see your money again.'

Oddly enough, in the next few hours at least two other members of the cast drew me aside and confided the same warning, so that I began to feel slightly sorry for poor old Vernon, as he was called. He certainly didn't look like a sponger, but I tensed up a little at the end of the day when he sidled up to me in the bar, looked cautiously over his shoulder, and asked me casually how I was 'fixed' for cash. I was forewarned.

'I'm terribly sorry, Vernon,' I said, quite truthfully. 'I'm afraid I don't even have the price of a round of drinks tonight.' Vernon beamed. 'Just as I thought, dear fellow,' he said. Then, with another furtive glance over his shoulder, he pressed £10 into my hand and whispered, 'The ghost doesn't walk until Friday (this was theatre slang meaning that we did not get paid until the end of the week), and I had a feeling you might be a bit short. Pay me back any time you like.' He gave me a conspiratorial wink and patted my shoulder. 'I have a feeling we're going to become good friends on this show.'

I was too astonished to do any more than croak, 'Thanks, Vern,' and I pocketed the tenner very gratefully as a matter of fact, vowing to pay him back as soon as the ghost walked. 'What sneaky bastards actors are,' I thought. 'Why would they gang up and bad-mouth a sweet and generous chap like that? Envy, probably. Never underestimate the power of envy!' I paid Vernon back on the nail, though he was terribly reluctant to take my money, and there was lots of 'Are you sure, old chap? Are you really absolutely sure you can spare it?'

Once we had opened at the Comedy Theatre in Panton Street, with the cash flowing and the laughter from full houses rolling over the footlights, I realized with a sense of elation that I could still be funny. After the Establishment I had begun to fear that I might have lost the knack. Spike Milligan, though marvellously risible, was sometimes unpredictable; he once went home at intermission without any warning, so that the ill-prepared understudy was obliged to take over his role in the second half, to the confusion and bewilderment of the audience, and cast.

In the second act I had to spend a long time in bed on stage with a very pretty actress called Jacqui Ellis. We just lay there in the half-darkness for about forty minutes whilst Spike performed the most astonishing and hilarious improvisations. I was aware that Miss Ellis was married, but estranged from her husband who, she informed me, was an extremely jealous and violent man. Indeed, he had been seen lurking in the vicinity of the stage door on several occasions and had even made attempts to enter the theatre. I was especially alarmed when I learnt that her husband was none other than Jeffrey Bernard, that chippy photographer whom I had quite inadvertently miffed. I was fairly sure that his bark was worse than his bite, but I none the less dreaded the possibility that one night Bernard, after a few large ones, might overpower the stage door keeper, storm on to the stage and alter the course of the play in a manner transcending the surreal imagination of the author.

One Saturday morning in Highgate, Rosalind and I had had a leisurely breakfast and Tessa was rattling the bars of her play-pen when the doorbell rang. It was Vernon. I asked him in for a cup of coffee and he explained that, although he lived in south London, it just so happened he was in Highgate on business and so thought he would drop in. My wife suggested that he might like to stay for lunch and we could both journey into the West End for the matinée. Vernon, however, looked ill at ease.

'The silliest thing has happened, old boy,' he said. 'I've got a little deal going through up in this neck of the woods and I've come all this way and completely forgotten my bloody chequebook.' My hand had gone to my own chequebook almost before he had finished speaking.

'How much do you need?' I asked. Vernon was blushing, and was he perspiring slightly?

'Well, £75 would get me out of a terrible hole,' he said, 'but don't worry, I'll go back to Wimbledon and come up again next week, if the deal hasn't fallen through.'

I wrote him a cheque for £100 and stuffed it in the top pocket of his blazer. It felt rather good to help such an atrociously maligned fellow actor, and a man who had also been a Spitfire pilot in the War. 'Pay me back when the ghost walks,' I said magnanimously.

Later that week Vernon proudly gave me a cheque and I thought no more about it until the bank suggested that I re-present it. I did this a couple of times before confronting Vernon, who went very red and fulminated against his bank manager. At once he wrote me another cheque, which bounced as well. Terry, the publican at the Round Table, showed me a large pint glass filled with cheques. Vernon had written all of them. 'But how can he do it?' I protested. 'How does he *feel*? We're on stage with him every night.'

'There's not a pub in the West End where he dares show his face,' said Terry. 'Did he give you all that old moody about being a Spitfire pilot?' I nodded forlornly.

'He's a master!' said Terry, with something almost like admiration. 'But mark my words, he'll put the bite on you again one day.'

Weeks later, and incrementally, Vernon did cough up. But on the very last night of the show, and with exquisite timing, he touched me for a fiver. I never saw him or the money again, but only the other day I heard that he was still alive, well and working. No doubt living on borrowed time.

I drove a turquoise Mini Minor to the theatre every night, in those days before double yellow lines, and on some evenings, if a friend had come backstage, we might stop in Soho for a nightcap. Colin MacInnes told me about a wonderful club called the Colony Room which everyone went to after the pubs had closed. Colin had written books about Soho, although he had spent his childhood in Melbourne. His mother, Angela Thirkell, the granddaughter of Burne-Jones and the cousin of Rudyard Kipling, was a popular novelist of English upper-class manners who had improbably exiled herself in Melbourne between the wars. Colin told me that as a little boy she had sent him off to Scotch College in white lacy frocks, and when he had suffered the inevitable derision of his jeering classmates she had turned up and embarrassed him still further by castigating the schoolmaster in her loftiest Kensington accent.

When I knew him, Colin affected a manner of careless truculence. He wore his grey hair very short, dressed always in jeans, and seemed to prefer the society of 'spades', as London's West Indians were called. He was the most charming and generous of men until he had had a few drinks, and then he underwent a dramatic personality change, and he could turn very nasty if he didn't like the look of you.

Upstairs in Dean Street, amongst the membership of the Colony Room, there were about fifty personality changes every night. I had become quite adept at picking people with an allergy to alcohol, or those unfortunates without will-power who were obliged to construct their personal lives uncomfortably around their thirst. For example Terry, the publican at the Round Table, often allowed a select few of us to go on drinking after closing time as his personal guests. There was a childish, illicit pleasure in sipping away in a closed bar. And yet, around one a.m. I began to worry. *Should he be there?* I wondered. What about Terry's wife and kids upstairs? Was it entirely fair to keep this charming fellow up drinking large scotches, when his domestic responsibilities lay elsewhere? I completely forgot that my *own* wife and child were miles away in Highgate, and asleep, one hoped.

Sometimes I entertained fantasies of abstinence. What would it be like? I knew one or two people who did not drink, but *had*. Why on earth did they stop? 'Couldn't handle it,' was my invariable answer to myself. Perhaps, one day, I might cut down. I decided I would – one day – if it started to cost me more than money. Meanwhile I reflected how lucky I was to be able to take it or leave it. It just so happened that I preferred to take it. Such was freedom of choice.

The Colony Room was one narrow flight up, small and dimly lit, with a mirrored wall which duplicated the lucifugous drinkers. On a stool at the bar, just inside the door, sat the proprietrix, Muriel Belcher, a bawdy *jolie laide* with an air of successfully repressed refinement. A piano tinkled in a dark corner and Colin introduced me to the pianist, another Australian, called Malcolm Williamson, who later quitted the club and became the Master of the Queen's Musick.

There was no one in the club that I knew, but a few I recognized. Tom Driberg, the MP and old friend of John Betjeman, was talking about E. M. Forster to a very drunk and uncomprehending guardsman. Francis Bacon, the Vorticist artist, stood at the bar ordering champagne for everybody. He was the first man I ever saw wearing black leather from head to foot. There also seemed to be an assortment of ambiguous-looking businessmen around him; perhaps they were naval Commanders in mufti, doing a little cruising on dry land, or were they just some of Francis' placenta-coloured models, whom he depicted coupling smudgily on billiard tables?

A beautiful Canadian girl, whose lion-coloured hair hung down like a curtain over one eye and kept getting in her gin, took a fancy to me. She was called Elizabeth Smart, and she worked on a fashion magazine. A few words from her to Muriel, and I was a member! To what privileges I wondered, if any, would membership of this wicked little den entitle me? Perhaps only the dubious luxury of paying double, and sometimes treble saloon-bar prices for large and highly intoxicating drinks and, of course, the titillating propinquity of some high-class riff-raff.

Muriel took a liking to me too, or so I thought; in her fashion she was generally polite to all male members, unless they failed to settle their extortionate 'slates'. At the Colony one was always encouraged to buy large rounds of drinks without a demand for immediate payment, and this highly civilized procedure found extraordinary favour with the clientele until the time came, weeks later, for them to get out their chequebooks and pay the price of pleasure. Muriel lost her suaveté only when someone behaved very badly indeed; though the Colony's rules of bad behaviour were, to say the least, flexible. The girls who used the club, however, unless they were Liz Smart, or inebriates with titles, fared less favourably. 'Hello, cunty!' Miss Belcher would frequently greet wide-eyed debutantes on their first visit, as they stumbled in the door on the arm of some black-tied debauchee, and 'Fuck off, cunty!' as they left, generally alone.

I must say that I found this a most congenial and amusing haunt, and, perversely, the fact that it was so expensive lent it an added allure. As I mounted the stairs and heard the voices and the music floating down to greet me, with Muriel's psittacine laughter rising high above them all, I felt a curious anticipatory excitement. 'What was going to happen tonight?' I wondered. 'Where will it all end?'

It ended, of course, with a hangover, and a guilty apology to Rosalind. I always vowed 'never again' after an evening at the Colony, and, oddly enough, I always meant it.

I had arranged for some of my possessions, especially books and pictures, to be sent over from Australia to furnish the flat in Highgate. Tessa was growing fast and when *The Bedsitting Room* closed we went to Lisbon for a family holiday, for me the first of many visits to that beautiful Lusitanian land. At Highgate we entertained many of the Australian painters who had set up their studios nearby, and my closest neighbour was John Perceval, Arthur Boyd's brother-in-law, an old friend from Melbourne. John was a brilliant painter and ceramic sculptor, but he had started drinking heavily and developed an alcoholic *folie de grandeur*, disdaining all drinks except Johnny Walker Black Label, and I became very worried about him. He missed the Australian sunshine but contrived, in his flickering paintings, to make Highgate Wood resemble the bush.

A visitor of this period was Patrick White, whose early novels I hugely admired. Patrick and his companion, Manoly Lascaris, had loyally come to see *The Bedsitting Room* but were politely non-committal in the dressing-room afterwards. Patrick's aged mother still lived somewhere in Kensington, perhaps in a mansion flat next door to Miss Amy Halford. He was very censorious, indeed toffee-nosed, about Australians living abroad, however temporarily, even though he had lived in London and Greece for large chunks of the thirties and forties. After one of these chauvinistic outbursts, Manoly interjected: 'But Patrick, you know you hate Australia!' Patrick shot him his cold dowager's stare.

He had dedicated a short story to me and we invited him to lunch with Sidney Nolan. Sidney's wife Cynthia, a complex and saturnine woman, was excessively protective of her husband's privacy and their unlisted number was always being changed.

Later on the day of White's visit, after several bottles of Madeira, Nolan suggested that I telephone Cynthia and invite her to join us for dinner in the West End, but I had no sooner announced myself than she barked: 'How did you get this number? You can't speak to Siddy anyway, he's busy in his studio and doesn't want to be disturbed!' The phone slammed down. Poor Cynthia never knew her busy husband was standing right beside me, or that Patrick White, the great Australian novelist, was anxious to dine with her. She would have been mortified had she known, avid lion-hunter that she was.

In 1960 the wardrobe of Heather Firbank, sister of the novelist Ronald Firbank, was sold and dispersed. Gowns by Worth, Mme Vionnet and Patou, some never worn, others worn no more than once and all in storage, were snapped up by the Victoria and Albert Museum, and the remnant knocked down to the public. From this, on some absurd caprice, I bought a pair of fine cambric bloomers trimmed with lace and blue ribbon, and bearing Miss Firbank's embroidered monogram.

Once, as Patrick White and I talked about our mutual attraction to the author of *Valmouth* and *The Flower Beneath the Foot*, I showed him the Firbankian knickers. Never before or since have I seen him so excited, but as he tremulously fingered the fabric, his delight changed to an expression of regret. At the evanescence of this flimsy textile? Or perhaps also at the size of the garment – impossibly slighter than his own substantial loins.

Later I asked Patrick, who found the author's mantle an

intolerable burden, what he would prefer to do. 'Look after a few goats on a Greek hillside,' he said. 'I'd like to be a goatherd.' Years later, though in Sydney, surrounded by a small and bleating herd of caprine disciples who munched and swallowed everything he said, his dream came true.

Peter Cook, it seemed, was still a fan of mine, even after my ill-starred appearance at his club. He was back from New York, and he asked me if I felt like writing something for *Private Eye*.

A comic strip. When I lived in the Notting Hill basement I had made a gramophone record which included the plaintive monologue of an Earl's Court Australian; a youth called Buster Thompson who huddled together with his mates in an Anglophobic ghetto, drinking Foster's Lager, a Melbourne-brewed beer, which in those days could be obtained only at one pub in London. Cook thought that a character like this, an Australian innocent abroad, would make a diverting comic-strip hero, and he introduced me to a New Zealand artist called Nicholas Garland.

Humphries by Garland   *Garland by Humphries*

228

The origin of the name Barry McKenzie has been amiably disputed. I think Peter Cook came up with it, though my own name must have obviously inspired it. Nick certainly created the 'look' of the character: tall, gangling and lantern-jawed. I felt he should seem rather old-fashioned in a double-breasted suit and tie, like the former Australian Prime Minister Sir Robert Menzies, and we decided he would always wear a broad-brimmed hat, like the rural Australians sported when they came to town for the Royal Agricultural Show. It went without saying that Barry, like Buster Thompson, would have to be a *thirsty* person, with an idiosyncratic taste for the most obscure lager in the world: Foster's.

After a few script conferences Garland started drawing up the first strip, which showed Barry's arrival in England (by boat):

''Streuth, this trip isn't the full two bob, I can't even see the flamin' White Cliffs!'

'This is Southampton, not Dover,' says a snooty British stereotype in a bowler hat, who is standing next to Barry at the rail.

Peter Cook wanted as much of the colourful Australian idiom as possible in the dialogue, although I realized that a great deal of it would be obscure to a British audience. It was necessary, therefore, in order to initiate readers into the mysteries of Australian colloquial speech, for Barry to repeat certain actions and forms of behaviour. For example, Australians had an enormous vocabulary celebrating incontinence in all its infinite variety. Thus Barry was always 'shaking hands with the wife's best friend', 'pointing Percy at the porcelain', 'going where the big nobs hang out', 'shaking hands with the unemployed', and 'draining the dragon'.

Since he mostly subsisted on a liquid diet, he was invariably 'chundering', a term I had first heard at Melbourne University, and which was not in general currency. If he wasn't 'chundering', Barry might be 'laughing at the ground', 'playing the whale', 'parking the tiger', enjoying a 'liquid laugh' or a

To Barry the hump 'going the Knok'

Barry Humphries in the sixties, as drawn by Gerald Scarfe

'technicolour yawn' or, simply, 'calling'. One could, depending on the regurgitative pressure of the last few drinks, 'call' for Bert, Herb, Charles or Ruth. Generally speaking, the most painful form of projectile vomiting would be to call 'Rooooooth!' After a good party, healthy young Australians of this generation would casually inquire of each other: 'What did you call last night?'

Although the adventures of Barry McKenzie, when they first appeared in *Private Eye*, met with the same stunned indifference as my nightclub act, Peter Cook and his editor Richard Ingrams nursed the strip along. Ingrams was an unkempt and acne-flecked young man, rather like a neglected grammar-school boarder, with dried shaving lather on his lobes and a demeanour that suggested cricket and Best Bitter. As a National Serviceman in the Korean War, he had made a brief excursion into adult life and then wisely retreated to the more congenial milieu of the sixth-form common-room, which the offices of *Private Eye* resembled. In these raffish premises in Greek Street one could usually find the jovial actor and artist William Rushton, the poet Christopher Logue, who contributed a regular column, and often that guru of the *Eye*, the amiable Irish rogue Claude Cockburn. He was what used to be called a 'card', and had been married to Jean Ross, Isherwood's 'Sally Bowles'. Claude was that anachronism, a Communist with a sense of humour, who liked nothing better than to dish up propaganda as truth.

Also drifting through the office were sympathetic people like John Wells, the Eton Schoolmaster and wag, caricaturist Gerald Scarfe, the crusader Paul Foot, the pedagogue Christopher Booker and the gifted cartoonist Barry Fantoni. Unkindly nicknamed 'Sycophantoni' behind his back, he was the only member of Ingrams' circle from the wrong side of the tracks. However he made up for this solecism by laughing immoderately at all the Editor's jokes. Ingrams had a gruff and diffident charm, but also, as I later discovered, a strongly puritanical streak; so that whilst he and his cronies freely indulged, on the pages of the *Eye*, a scatological vein of schoolboy humour, he looked rather askance at jokes about sex. Luckily there was enough childish and excremental ribaldry in Barry McKenzie to satisfy the editorial policy.

After a few months Garland and I got into our stride, the drawings became surer and my balloons bigger. Our hero had started soliloquizing rather in the manner of one of my long-winded stage characters, yet whereas in the theatre I tried to get the dialect and vocabulary of a class or profession exactly right, 'Bazza' spoke in an invented idiom; a synthetic Australian compounded of schoolboy, Service, old-fashioned proletarian and even made-up slang. The comic strip ran, with a few interruptions, almost until the end of the decade and spanned that period of the sixties to which the Press attached the epithet 'swinging'.

Whenever I was on tour in Australia, I had to keep Nick Garland well supplied with material so that the strip could continue uninterrupted during my absence, but sometimes the

text dried up and I received urgent telegrams and entreaties from artist and editor. It was rather like the old Bunyip days, when I perilously left the writing of the script to the eleventh hour. On one occasion Garland had only enough dialogue left for half a strip so, rather wittily, he drew Barry McKenzie with empty balloons and a vignette of me lying unconcerned on a tropical beach with a can of something in my hand.

Richard Ingrams was extremely tolerant of these lapses and lacunae, although once or twice I was politely warned that the strip would have to be axed if I kept failing my deadlines. It may also be true to say that editorial goodwill and our very occasional raises in salary could have been due to Barry McKenzie's growing popularity; it might even have sold a few more *Private Eyes*! Although I had signally failed to make any impression on English audiences with my Australian stage act, it looked as though I might be reaching another audience through this comic-strip character who bore my name.

Only recently have I perceived the autobiographical elements in Barry McKenzie's adventures. Like Barry, as he wanders through the moral quicksands of the sixties, I felt I was always on the periphery of 'the action', waiting for something to happen. Like McKenzie also, I seemed to drink too much in those very situations when it would have been more prudent had I not drunk at all. It was a therapeutic release for me, at the time, to write scornfully about the affectations and excesses

Cartoon rough by Barry Humphries: 'Barry McKenzie,
dental practitioner'

of the 'poor old Poms', with whom I, Barry Humphries the artist, had failed to ingratiate myself.

Barry McKenzie's amorous ambitions were another matter. Always in a state of heightened sexual erethism, he invariably failed to make contact with the desired object or completely misread any signs of encouragement. In one episode Barry, confronted with an open invitation from a young woman, suddenly discovers that she is a fellow Australian. His desire turns to ashes and he showers upon her a vituperative diatribe, reminding her of her family back home, the fragility of her mother's varicose veins, her disabled brother Craig, her Sunday-school precepts and, even more obscurely, the threat of modern promiscuity to Australia's unblemished War Record. Here it is difficult to see exact resemblances between Barry's conduct and my own. There is no doubt, however, that I did from time to time, and after too many 'tubes' or 'cold ones' or when I may have been as full as a fairy's Filofax, put my hand on the wrong knee.

As the sixties progressed and my own life became more unmanageable, so did Barry McKenzie's. My first encounters with pyschotherapists are echoed in the comic as Barry, confined by a strait-jacket and interrogated by a slightly crazed, womanizing and Jewish doctor (Meyer de Lamphrey), rails against the injustice of the Brits. In a later episode the doctor himself is seen to have a drinking problem and there is an unpleasant accident, later transferred spectacularly to the cinema screen and much emulated thereafter, when Barry calls copiously for Ruth on the head of his therapist.

Spiked

J OAN LITTLEWOOD'S PRODUCTIONS, and Miss Littlewood
herself, had been for so many seasons a feature of the
London West End theatre, that any wonder at the extent of her
vogue would have seemed ignorant or provincial. I had known
her for some years and while I was still appearing in *The
Bedsitting Room* had even 'moonlighted' in a pantomime by
Peter Shaffer which she directed at Wyndhams Theatre. The
pantomime, which only played matinées, came down just in
time for me to sprint across Leicester Square to my evening job
at the Comedy.

Joan always wore the same clothes; a long pleated grey skirt
and a short grey jacket nipped in at the waist, like the already
very old-fashioned 'New Look'. White sockettes, flat shoes and
a knitted hat completed her habitual ensemble and spared her
from any accusations of being over-dressed for the rigours of
rehearsal. One of her early successes had been *Fings Ain't What
They Used to Be*, a musical by Frank Norman and Lionel Bart,
and Frank had just written another play with a Soho theme,
called *A Kayf Up West*, which Joan was to direct at a theatre
she had resurrected: the Theatre Royal at Stratford, in the East
End of London.

Frank Norman was an *habitué* of the Colony Room and the
French Pub and I had always been rather scared of him, since

his good-looking but fleshy face bore the scar of a razor slash, and he affected a surly manner, liking to 'put the mockers' on people he distrusted, or perhaps even feared. He had written several vivid and original books about his childhood and youth in boys' homes and Borstals, and had been taken up by the literary Establishment as a sort of home-grown, and anodyne, Genet. Frank usually wore a cashmere overcoat – a symbol of his success – and he was fond of flexing his shoulders like a pugilist under the fabric, but all of this belied a good-natured and sensitive man.

Joan invited me to join the company and play about four roles. She could coax remarkable performances out of very unlikely people and she was not over-fond of 'professional' actors. I suited her well; I was unlikely, and not too professional, but an even more unlikely member of the company was Jeffrey Bernard, who to everybody's surprise, including his own, gave one of the best performances in the show. I played, amongst other things, a Greek café proprietor, an old lag, a sinister toff called Lord Sexkilling and a nun. Bamber Gascoigne, who had found me 'soporific' at the Establishment, redeemed himself in his review of *A Kayf Up West* by calling my performance 'the main pleasure' of the evening.

On the tube journey home from Stratford East, Jeffrey and I enjoyed asking commuting Cockneys if they would kindly direct us to the buffet car. One needs to have had quite a few drinks to find this as hilarious as we did.

We did not, as we had fervently hoped, transfer to the West End, though Jeff and I spent a great deal of time there all the same, especially in dives like the Kismet; a dark basement in Cranbourne Street, which had once been an Indian restaurant and retained the old, curry-impregnated flock wallpaper. The Kismet was open during that inconvenient hiatus between three p.m., when the pubs closed, and 5.30, when they re-opened. Whenever I called in there for a quick drink on my own, I would notice several solitary drinkers whom life seemed to have passed by. It was distressing to see them still there several hours later.

A publisher called Paul Elek got in touch with me out of the blue to edit a volume of literary bad taste. It was to be called *Bizarre*, since much of the material was to be culled from a French periodical of that name, but ultimately I drew most of the book's elements from my own collection of oddities and curiosa. It was a vulgar and dissonant gallimaufry of *fin de siècle* decadence, kitsch, blasphemy, teratology and silliness, beautifully published. Most critics who reviewed it hated it. W. H. Smith refused to sell it and Philip Toynbee accused me of 'vile whimsicality'. It is not to my credit that as the sixties wore on many more books even viler and more whimsical were published in imitation of *Bizarre*.

I found myself, almost to my own surprise, in another Lionel Bart musical; a kind of industrial operetta with a fashionable Liverpool setting, called *Maggie May*. In the midst of this entertainment there was a scene in a club where a rock 'n' roll group performed a Beatles pastiche. But as well as a dash of the Beatles, there was also a dollop of Brecht in the person of myself as a sardonic tramp, with a drum on my back, cymbals between my knees and a harmonica wired to my lips. At intervals during the show, which was set in the docks, I would interrupt the action with an alienating chorus or two of the Weill-like 'Ballad of the Liverbird'. The money was wonderful, and the billing was not far below that of Miss Rachel Roberts, the star. I had, furthermore, taken special lessons to perfect my Scouse accent.

But when we opened in Manchester for the try-out, the play ran for over three hours. Ted Kotcheff, the director, had to make some drastic cuts and one of them was me. Thereafter, instead of materializing spookily in a spotlight throughout the evening, I now opened the show, and closed it. As Kenneth Haigh, the hero, lay on the stage fatally electrocuted, Miss Roberts sobbed and the dockers stood in a grieving semicircle around him, the ominous thump of my drum sounded in the wings, my cymbals whispered, and I shuffled to the centre of the stage to keen my valedictory lament. It was an affecting *coup de théâtre*, but the audience had to wait a long time for it. In fact, I had exactly two and a half hours in my dressing-room between appearances. If a member of the public was slightly late, they would miss my first entrance, and if they had a train to catch, they would miss my second.

Once we were installed at the Adelphi Theatre in the Strand, and the carefully pruned production was one of the hits of the season, I began to find my prolonged incarceration backstage irksome. I shared a dressing-room with three other actors who had lots of scenes and songs, and they darted in and out all night. Once I had sung my opening number I would slip the heavy drum off my shoulders, unbuckle my cymbals and slump at my dressing-table with a cigarette and a book. After a few weeks of this I decided it was probably healthier to go for a walk, but my walk was usually quite a short one, from the stage door to Yates's Wine Lodge next door to the theatre. Yates's was a darkly timbered Tudor-style corridor between Maiden Lane and the Strand. Its clientele was mostly old and Irish, and it served an inexpensive port in half-pint glasses which always seemed to contain a quarter of an inch of gritty brown sediment. Propping up the bar in this gloomy establishment soon palled, and I began to amuse myself by visiting the cinema opposite, where vaguely indecent Continental films were exhibited. I would always keep one eye on the luminous dial of my watch so as to be back in the theatre in plenty of time to re-apply my tramp's makeup, and to be harnessed with my heavy musical accoutrements.

After a few months, I began going to the theatre, and occasionally to parties. Often I would miss little more than the first fifteen minutes of the play, and, leaving immediately the curtain fell, I could make it comfortably back to the Adelphi. The parties were riskier. One was in Hampstead at Olivia Manning's, so I was obliged to keep a taxi waiting while I had a few drinks before retracing my journey. Another party was in Putney.

A close friend of mine at this period was Georgina Barker,

the daughter of George Barker the poet. Her mother was Elizabeth Smart, my sponsor at the Colony Room. Georgina was an acquaintance of Augustus John's family and, when she told me they were throwing a big party at their Putney home, I airily agreed to call in for a drink. I did not bargain for the fog. That night I had not retained my taxi and when, after an hour or so of dancing and drinking, I asked my hostess if we could call a cab she laughed; 'Have you seen the weather out there?' she said, pointing through the leadlights at the swirling Thames-side mists. 'You must be joking!' I rushed out into the night and by a sheer miracle discovered a taxi, which after much haggling agreed to convey me, at a snail's pace, to the West End. Thanking a God whom I had rarely addressed in recent years for my deliverance, I reached the theatre with barely enough time to transform myself into the Balladeer. When the curtain fell, the company manager warned me that I had caused some anxiety to himself and to Cuthbert, my dresser, and that I was not to leave the theatre ever again under any circumstances.

My old friend Spike Milligan was about to open at the Comedy in *Son of Oblomov*, an eccentric version of a Russian classic. 'Come to the opening night,' he urged me. 'We don't go up until 8.15, and when we come down you'll still have a quarter of an hour to get to the Adelphi.' I shook my head, but Spike was wearing his hurt look. 'Come and see me in my dressing-room tomorrow night and I'll give you a ticket near the exit, and don't be late, old cobbler.'

I knew I could probably sneak out of my show one more time and Cuthbert, if suitably recompensed, would cover for me. After all, I reasoned, I wasn't going to Putney, or drinking. And if I left Spike's exit door dead on 10.30, I would be almost over-prepared for my final dirge.

When Spike handed me my ticket, he gave me a glass of *vin rosé* as well, and a vitamin tablet. 'I don't take pills,' I said with the prudery of all drinkers. 'It's not a pill, mate,' said

Spike, 'it's a food. These are great for the liver.' My liver had been aching slightly, or the part of my body where I imagined my liver to be, so I swallowed the damn thing, washed it down with wine and wished my friend good luck.

Trust Spike to turn everything upside down, I reflected from my seat in the stalls. On stage the actors, with Milligan in the middle, were bowing to the audience and the curtain was rising and falling. The public, joining in the joke of a finale at the beginning, were applauding wildly. But something was wrong. People near me were getting up, looking for their coats and . . . *leaving*. The curtain remained down, and the house-lights came up. A chill seemed to grip my heart. 'Was this the end of the show?' I thought. 'Have I been asleep?' My mouth felt furry. That tablet . . . ? I had left my watch on my dressing-table back at the Adelphi to heighten the illusion of my presence thereabouts, but now I desperately needed to know the time. Clutching the wrist of a startled theatre-goer on my right, I stared at the face of his watch; *it was 10.55!* In five minutes I was due to appear, elaborately disguised as an old man wearing a drum on his back, cymbals on his knees and a harmonica, before an expectant audience and the full cast of a West End show, on the stage of a theatre on the other side of town!

I hurtled out of the exit into the street. Amazingly, at that moment a vacant cab rounded the corner. Pressing a salad of money into the driver's hand I leapt into the car and we careened in the direction of the Adelphi Theatre. I was drenched with sweat as we turned the corner into Maiden Lane on a couple of wheels and I saw the company manager standing in the street, beside him my poor little dresser holding a drum and a cymbal. I fell out of the taxi and bolted in the stage door to the concrete steps which led down two flights to the stage level, and, as I ran, Cuthbert hitched various instruments over my flailing limbs. The enormous drum, only tenuously attached to my back, crashed against the stairwell, as with a free hand I slapped some blackish greasepaint arbitrarily across my face until at last I stood, panting in the wings.

On stage all was silent. Uncannily silent. Kenneth Haigh lay prone, the dockers stood in a grieving tableau and Miss Roberts sobbed. How long they had kept their vigil I knew not; but the thump and crash of my descent to the stage must surely have transmitted itself to the audience. I took a deep breath and shuffled to the centre of the stage, trailing my abridged equipment. I glanced into the orchestra pit where Marcus, the musical director, gaped up at me. I realized, only then, that I was wearing modern dress; a figure who bore no resemblance whatever to the ragged old Liverbird who had opened the show two and a half long hours before. 'Perhaps they will read something allegorical into this,' I reflected, as I croaked my closing lines.

The company, who held me in a kind of amused contempt, let me off rather lightly, but I was hauled over the coals by Mr Bernard Delfont, and rightly so.

The next day Spike phoned and asked me how I had enjoyed the show. 'It was great,' I lied. 'Did you make the Adelphi in plenty of time?' he probed. 'With time to spare,' I said. Did I imagine it, or was there a little silence on the other end of the phone? And was it just a vitamin tablet, and an innocent glass of wine? Who will ever know?

The author with Sacheverell Sitwell

The author with Mischa Spoliansky, 1986

Sir Leslie Colin Patterson

Alexander Horace 'Sandy' Stone

Dame Edna, a recent Hollywood study by Roddy McDowall

The author and John Betjeman c. 1974 Chelsea

Oscar and Rupert Humphries, 1992

By Cecil Beaton

With David Hockney in California, 1992

Lizzie Spender

The author at dinner in Los Angeles

Lizzie, Barry and Stanley, 1992 by David Hockney

Boudoir Fingers

THE MEMORY OF this incident had barely faded when I found myself travelling a very great distance indeed every night after the show. I was no longer living at home, but in a large hospital. Several doctors had conferred together over my 'case' and it had been decided that I should spend my days and nights in 'treatment' at Halliwick Hospital in remote Winchmore Hill, with special permission to commute every evening to the theatre to perform my job. There was a strict curfew governing the time of my nightly return to the institution. I had been given a course of capsules, and the doctors had told me to drink very little alcohol with them or, preferably, none at all. Since it was absurd and impractical to adopt the latter recommendation, I settled for a loose interpretation of the former.

This dramatic change in my circumstances had sprung from an unfortunate confrontation between Rosalind and my friend Georgina, whom I had hoped might never meet. A psychiatrist, who was called in to adjudicate in this delicate matter, decided that I had gone mad, and that I would benefit greatly from a sojourn in neutral territory; a lunatic asylum. I had had no previous experience of psychotherapy, or anti-depressive drugs, and had only once been in hospital, with a fractured arm, so the novelty of my new predicament kept me toeing the line – for the time being.

Although I was managing to give a good performance on stage every night – or thought I was – the rest of my life seemed to have slipped away into the realm of fiction, so that the things that were now happening to me seemed almost to be happening to someone else. The theatre was reality; reality was theatre. Above all, I felt it was prudent to do as I was told; and it was strangely comforting to slide back into a kind of acquiescent second childhood.

I have no memory whatsoever of what I told my therapists during many interviews. Monstrous self-justifications, probably, and grotesque alibis. If my increasingly abnormal drinking was ever mentioned, I was only too happy to chat about it, and it was almost with relief that I heard one doctor say he thought it might be interesting to investigate, over a long period of time, the causes of my growing obsession. It was the *long period of time* that appealed to me. I knew I was in good, sound medical hands when nobody told me to stop.

Although none of the doctors was explicit, I felt very strongly that they wanted me to give up one, or all, of my pleasures. God-given pleasures to which I was surely entitled, even if they did not give me very much pleasure.

I was not in Halliwick for long; in fact, after a month I was expelled as incorrigible, because, with my busy life and my many nocturnal preoccupations, I found it impossible to abide by the curfew. Some nights I would appear like a phantom on Georgina's doorstep, and at others I would implore Rosalind to let me come home. A kind and thoughtful friend of mine, seeking to cheer me up, would sometimes drive me back to the hospital in his car; and to sustain us for the long journey north we would stop for a nightcap or two at various bars, clubs and discothèques. I felt that the assortment of tablets that I had been given may have been mis-prescribed, since they seemed to interfere with the pleasant effects of alcohol. In the interests of my health, therefore, I stopped taking them.

By the time I was expelled from hospital we had moved house to Little Venice in Maida Vale, one of London's prettiest neighbourhoods. In my absence, the move had been arranged by Rosalind since we had slowly, and almost with relief, assumed the roles of efficient Organizer/Nurse and helpless Artist/Invalid. No sooner were we established in this charming maisonette than Clifford Hocking arrived from Australia and suggested another tour, this time in big theatres. I wondered if this was part of a conspiracy to get me as far away from Georgina's flat in Westbourne Terrace as possible.

It was over three years since I had last appeared in Australia; three years since I had last seen my parents, my brothers and sisters, and my old friends. I realized that I wanted nothing more in the world than to go home, at least for a while; and the prospect of writing a new show seemed to dispel all my daemons and provide me with a positive view of the future, not just for me, but for my growing family, for it was at this time that my second daughter, Emily, was born.

Often, I took Tessa for afternoon walks along the Regent's Canal, and on one of these, beside the Edgware Road, I spied a very interesting old house set back behind a neglected garden. An overgrown blue plaque informed the curious – and they were few – that the house had belonged to the Edwardian sculptor Sir Alfred Gilbert, whose masterpiece is the statue of Eros on the Shaftesbury Memorial Fountain in Piccadilly Circus. The house and grounds were in a state of uttermost desuetude, and I wandered up the ruined driveway until I could see a building, slightly separate from the house, which had obviously been the artist's studio. There was not a soul about, so I made a pile of bricks and boxes and, clambering on top of them, I just managed to peep in at the high studio window. I saw an astonishing sight. There, ranged around this enormous room, were allegorical carvings and huge plaster casts, left as if the artist had just walked out of the room; and yet I knew that he had been dead since 1934. But there was one thing which was alarmingly wrong. The sculptures had been horribly vandalized: heads lay shattered on the floor, hands smashed off at the wrist, and there were fragments of stone, plaster and gypsum everywhere, as though some vindictive poltergeist had been let loose in the studio.

I was startled by a man's voice, gruffly reminding me that I was on private property, and asking me my business. It was a grizzled old caretaker who lived in some kind of shed behind a hedge, which I had failed to notice. I apologized for trespassing, but told him of the terrible sight I had just seen through the studio window. Had vandals broken in? I asked. He shook his head. It was the last Lady Gilbert, he explained. For years after her husband's death she would visit the studio every morning, and, with a stout iron hammer, fastidiously mutilate her husband's surviving works. 'She was at it for years, Governor; *at it for years!*'

I felt blenched and shaken as we walked back down Maida Avenue. Why should a woman, however wronged, bitter or envious, murder a man's work? Was it in the hope that by destroying this extension of the man she might somehow succeed in destroying him? But I was young and, happily, still had more illusions than I thought.

At one Christmas during the Little Venice years, I decided, rather magnanimously, to give my bank manager a seasonal gift. I carefully selected a bottle of Black Label Johnny Walker Whisky and had it gift-wrapped for presentation to the unsmiling, silver-haired curmudgeon who presisded over my 'active' account at the local bank. Alas, when I arrived on the morning of Christmas Eve with my tinselled offering, his secretary told me rather sourly that he was engaged with another client. I decided to wait and, instead of loitering in the banking hall, I found a comfortable bench round the corner beside the canal. The time seemed to drag, and I decided without too much deliberation that a very small swig from the bank manager's Christmas present would go unnoticed, especially if I was careful in replacing the elaborate wrapping. This proved easy, and after some fastidious peeling of sellotape and surreptitious uncorking I drank a yuletide toast to Mr Rogerson in his own liquor, with a epiglottal sensation that I imagined to be not unlike that regularly experienced by knife-swallowers.

By the time I got back to the bank the secretary told me Mr Rogerson had waited, but was now with another client and would be free in an hour. From beneath his mahogany door cigar smoke seeped, and I imagined the manager behind his gift-laden desk, sharing a Christmas Monte Cristo with some crass client with an account in obscene credit. Promising to return sixty minutes hence, I repaired to my bench round the corner and gazed on the sparkling canal. 'Why not?' I reflected, once more delicately tackling the gift-wrapped whisky. By the time I had finished the level in the bottle did look distinctly lower than it should, but I decided that was a detail which Mr Rogerson was unlikely to notice in the seasonal excitement. Back at the bank Miss Powell shook her head. I had missed him again. In fact, Mr Rogerson had gone around the corner for a drink with an old client but would be back directly. Would I . . . ? But I was gone.

By now the wrapping round the Johnny Walker bottle looked like last year's Christmas paper. The selloptape had lost its stickiness, and the silver ribbon and the red rosette had blown off into the canal as I sampled more deeply my placatory gift. I had, however, effortlessly crossed that invisible line beyond which such things ceased to matter. Besides, if someone gave me half a bottle of scotch for Christmas I would be exceedingly grateful. It was lunchtime when I returned, and Mr Rogerson, who had been in and who had waited, could wait no more, and had departed for lunch. Quickly I scribbled an effusive and insincere note on a pay-in form, and, thrusting my dishevelled and radically depleted gift into Miss Powell's hands, I dashed out of the bank for my own lunch and some leisurely shopping in the West End.

On subsequent and inevitably tense meetings Mr Rogerson, rather rudely, neither made reference to my gift nor expressed his gratitude for the inch and a half of festive cordial from which I had so generously abstained.

*

At last the time came to embark on the tour. We found an Australian journalist to house-sit our flat, and, with a French au-pair girl called Dominique, we all set off for Australia, this time by aeroplane. Since Qantas then flew on an interesting route via Mexico and Tahiti, I decided to stop off for a few weeks in both places to finish writing my show, which I had already started in Little Venice. It was to be called *Excuse I*, one of my favourite genteelisms, long remembered from talc-scented, Colombine-caramel-rustling matinées in Melbourne, as tardy floral ladies squeezed past our knees; ''Scuse I, 'scuse I, 'scuse I.'

If not completely chastened by the recent events in my life, I may have been more than a little frightened; so I decided not to drink alcohol for a while. In retrospect, I am surprised that I found this so easy, but I see now that I was merely postponing the next inevitable drink. Besides, it was amusing to see the expression of incredulity on people's faces when I sanctimoniously said at dinner parties, 'Not for me, thanks, I don't use that stuff.' That was what teetotallers said all the time, I presumed, but they didn't feel as good as I did because they *meant* it, poor wretches.

None the less, my brain cleared and the ideas seemed to flow. My new stage characters included two outdoor hedonists, a 'surfie' extolling the cult of the waves in his almost incomprehensible jargon, and a loutish Public School skier, pursuing 'snow bunnies' on the slopes and in the chalets of Australia's newly developed Alpine resorts. Another invention was Neil Singleton, a character who gave a party on stage and did a lot of talking to invisible acquaintances. It was a good acting exercise and was bound to impress people, even if I did not perform it all that well. You don't really have to try very hard for critics to write: 'He peopled the stage.'

Some insisted they knew Neil Singleton. He was a left-wing academic, not very high up in his department, an advertising executive perhaps, or a journalist with literary aspirations that never quite came off. Longish hair, and that fringe of beard around the chin, *sans* moustache, identified him very precisely according to my 1965 audience at the old Theatre Royal, Sydney. Someone else in Melbourne was positive that Neil was inspired by an annoyingly successful art critic, whilst the art critic in question asked me confidentially if a tall, bearded radio playwright had recognized himself yet, or was going to sue.

I had no idea how many Neil Singletons would emerge from the woodwork. Until the mid-sixties Neil's class of puritan, querulous, turtle-necked, elbow-patched, pipe-sucking, wife-cheating, wine-buffing, abstract-art-digging highbrow had been amongst my most enthusiastic fans, eager for a chuckle at the middle-class effusions of Edna, Sandy and the other Australians they never met at their own parties. Deep chagrin greeted this impersonation; and it was only after the birth of Neil Singleton that the arty periodicals began to launch upon me their rather snide attacks.

There was an uncanny moment after a matinée in Sydney when an importunate journalist, complete with fringy beard, muscled his way into my dressing-room dragging a reluctant and waif-like spouse. He *was* Neil Singleton, my fictitious character, dreamt up, or so I thought, whilst taking the waters at Puruandiro, in Michoacan. He seemed to be actually *imploding* with rage, which I gathered from his hostile and confused manner, had something to do with me living in England and having the cheek to write rude things about contemporary Australia.

'There's a cultural renaissance going on here, y'know,' he declared truculently. 'Things don't just stand still here because guys like you piss off to the bright lights and easy money in England. You're living in the past, mate, and so are your characters.'

'But surely the reaction of that audience out there today showed some recognition?' I interjected. 'I mean, would they laugh so much at people they didn't know?'

'They weren't all laughing, mate,' said the clone with a

complacent smirk. 'A lot of people I know are very worried about the direction your stuff is taking. We think it lacks ...' He seemed to be searching for a word, and, when he finally found it, he spat it out so violently a little geodesic dome of spittle hit my nose '... *relevance!*'

I never saw this captious fellow again, but over the intervening years he has regularly flown into print with the same old carpings, to which have been added the fashionable accusations of racism, sexism, élitism, Fascism and misanthropy. I took to quietly observing this man's journalistic career, and when a novel failed and then a rock opera, I saw the full extent of his tragedy. He wanted so very much, I realized, to be an artist; a part of the Cultural Renaissance he was always on about. There is, perhaps, no more dangerous man in the world than the man with the sensibilities of an artist but without creative talent. With luck such men make wonderful theatrical impresarios and interior decorators, or else they become mass murderers or critics.

Excuse I seemed to hit the spot with Australian audiences and there were, indeed, long queues for tickets at the box offices in Sydney and in Melbourne. Edna, the character I had once thought of dropping altogether, had come up in the world. It was almost as though she were developing a life of her own, over which I had little, if any, control. She was also building up her part. On my first tour she had appeared on stage only once, but this time she opened and closed the show. In *A Nice Night's Entertainment* she had treated the audience to an old-fashioned slide evening, but this time she showed a short home-movie of her peregrinations around London, drawing attention as often as possible to Royal edifices.

Edna wore a different dress in the second half to the first; a long blue satin number, and a hat with one of those short projecting veils known as a 'fascinator'. She had also made a significant change in her appearance, by adopting a pair of upturned *diamanté* spectacles. These had no lenses and were as cosmetic as the moustache of Groucho Marx, but they suddenly invested her face with a sharper, beady-eyed and predatory look. They were also the kind of glasses which more fashionable ladies in the audience wore. From then on Edna's 'look' began slowly to converge with that of her better-dressed patrons. From having been, at her beginnings, a comical frump, she was now almost as attractively attired as the ladies at her matinées. Today – though this would have been beyond her wildest dreams – she is better dressed than the richest and most fashionable women in her audience.

It was during my extended season at the Theatre Royal in Sydney that Mrs Everage took pity on a woman in the front row who had been covetously eyeing the vase of 'gladdies' on the piano all night. At last, in exasperation, Edna hurled the dripping blooms with full force at their sedentary admirer, who unselfishly passed them to her neighbours down the row. It was the sight of an audience spontaneously wagging these evocative flesh-pink spears in time to the final number that inspired Edna to 'keep it in'. No show of hers is now complete without ritualistic gladdie-waving in the finale, and sometimes as many as two hundred gladioli, imported from plantations as far distant as Brazil, Queensland, Malta and Mexico, are showered nightly on the stalls, or catapulted by giant slings or cannons into the dress circle.

'Our Joan' Sutherland had just toured her homeland, and after singing through a comparatively highbrow repertoire, had endeared herself to those who might otherwise have pigeon-holed her in the expatriate 'traitor' category, by singing 'Home Sweet Home' as an encore. Edna did the same, and it was to this sentimental air that the sea of glads so suggestively oscillated. The standing, saluting, the trembling and the twitching and all the other virtuoso variations were to come in later years.

Although my recent compilation, *Bizarre*, was available in Australian bookshops, *Private Eye* was not. It was banned. The reason it was banned was because it contained my comic strip, Barry McKenzie, which was officially deemed obscene. Barry's occasional expletives, which were never worse than 'shit', were none the less thought to be demeaning to Australia's international image as a *nice* country. The word 'image' was just beginning to be bandied around, and in some prudish circles there was a fear, amounting to paranoia, that the closely guarded secret of Australian vulgarity might leak out.

But it had happened already. In 1946 a traumatic event had taken place. Debates and Question Time from the House of Representatives in the Australian capital, Canberra, were for the first time broadcast to the Nation. With shame and horror, Australians heard the voices and vocabulary of their governors.

Initially, this was thought to be a radio hoax perpetrated by students or some antipodean Orson Welles, in order to frighten listeners into thinking their country was run by yahoos and guttersnipes, but slowly the truth dawned. This was what our elected politicians and their opposition really sounded like! *This was us.* There were a few parliamentary pansies, it was true, who spoke in more expensive and grandiloquent tones, but they were a drop in the ocean. The enormous and prospering Middle Classes were appalled. What was the use of teaching the kiddies nice manners when our politicians carried on like that, squawking and braying like livestock? It was a crime against Niceness.

So was Barry McKenzie. Yet, despite the ban, the comic strip already had a large underground popularity; Bazza talked dirty with lyricism; he revived a dialect that had been vitiated by respectability, he was the Voice of Vulgarity.

After a triumphant tour, we returned to London slowly via Bangkok, Beirut and Prague. In Bangkok I committed a terrible gaffe by buying a durian fruit at the market and bringing it back to our room in the hotel. Supposedly an aphrodisiac, this fruit has a strong, gamey odour, or, as I preferred to imagine, the odour of the hircine bed-linen of an imaginative couple. I was not aware that durian was strictly banned in all good hotels, and, having been sniffed out by the management, we were, *en famille*, asked to leave.

Back in London at last, we settled into our lovely, if rented canal-side house, the walls of which were soon covered with pictures, many by our Australian friends. Throughout the mid-sixties I wrote a weekly column for Rupert Murdoch's national newspaper, the *Australian*. It was dispatched, often precariously close to its deadline, from London, but often too from wherever I happened to be, like Lisbon or Beirut, Vienna or Mexico City. But now I wondered what my next real job would be, and I did not have to wait long.

The Satire Movement, launched so brilliantly in the early sixties by Peter Cook, was by now showing signs of enervation, but late-night television 'satire' continued. I was invited by the BBC to join the cast of a new weekly programme to be called *The Late Show*. The other actors and writers were veterans of the Establishment like John Bird, Eleanor Bron and John Fortune, or *Private Eye aficionados* like John Wells and me, and our little troupe was supplemented by two Americans, Andrew Duncan and Tony Holland. A further and most unlikely addition to the cast was Malcolm Muggeridge, like a satyr in a dog-collar, who delivered a weekly sermon on some topical theme.

The programme was live and very uneven in quality and the producers had some difficulty in fitting me in to sketches, so that I mostly delivered songs and monologues, hastily written and often ill-rehearsed. The BBC Club was also a trap for people with my susceptibilities, though in retrospect it is extraordinary how many drunks, and convivial folk like myself, were officially tolerated, and managed to hold down respectable jobs.

The largesse of the BBC in this period was legendary, and for those of us without Jaguars, there was always a black radio cab at our disposal to take us to work, and to bring us home.

On leaving Television Centre at Shepherd's Bush for Maida Vale every evening, I was inclined to take advantage of the comfortable transport provided and break my journey at various places, not all of which were on my direct route home. Sometimes, for example, I might be so engrossed in some urgent discussion in a Soho bar that I would temporarily forget the black vehicle ticking away outside at the British taxpayer's expense. At other times I might call in at art exhibitions or late-closing secondhand bookshops, where time, so often, stands still. So long as the taxi was there, my conscience was salved; *I was on my way home.*

One evening, slumped in the back of the cab reading the *Evening Standard*, I half overheard the driver's radio broadcasting an emergency. Some child, apparently, had accidentally swallowed poison, and a driver in the vicinity of the accident was urgently needed to rush the victim to a hospital. The cabbie looked over his shoulder: 'Not far from your gaff, Governor,' he said. 'What's your number in Maida Avenue again?' I told him. 'Christ,' he said, stepping on it, 'looks like that kid's in one of your flats.' Then terror struck me. 'It's not a block of flats,' I said. 'It must be one of my daughters!' We screamed to a halt outside the house a couple of minutes later, and Dominique and Rosalind were outside the gate with little Emily, white-faced in a bundle. She had been prescribed some fancy anti-colic remedy with a strong sedative constituent, and had grabbed the bottle, carelessly left at child-level, while the nanny was out of the room. She must have guzzled most of it because she was unconscious as we rushed into the nearest hospital on the Harrow Road.

The poor little girl was there all night under observation, which gave me plenty of time to pace the floor and wonder what might have happened if my cab had not been a few short blocks from the emergency. I could easily have been on one of my selfish jaunts across town. *What if . . .?* I anguished. But Emily recovered and the au-pair lost her job. And yet the whole episode, which could have had such a tragic outcome, left me with an uneasy mind. *'I must remember I have a family, I must remember I have a family, I must remember I have a family,'* I said to myself, *'and not hear about it on a cab radio!'*

After a typical morning at the BBC, larking about the office, the cast of *The Late Show* would all wander down to Shepherd's Bush Green, where an old-fashioned Italian restaurant called Bertorelli's still stood. There we would have a long 'working lunch'. It was at one of these that I astonished my colleagues by drinking, at a single draught, a pint of crème de menthe, and being none the worse for it afterwards. I had secretly warned the waiter of my intention by phone, so that when I, amongst protests, demanded the drink, he brought me a pint glass brimming with water which had been thickened with sugar to give it a syrupy consistency, and to which a few drops of green vegetable dye had been added. After this feat it was generally thought that I had a remarkable head for strong drink, which was of course far from the truth, since I had begun to notice that my tolerance was waning.

I made two great friends on *The Late Show*, the composer Stanley Myers, and a young comedy writer called Ian Davidson with whom I work to this day. Stanley and I wrote what must have been the very first ecological song in history; it was dedicated to the Thames and it was called 'Filthy River'. Stanley arranged the song for a large string orchestra and choir – the BBC seemed to offer us unlimited funds – and I sang the refrain;

> River, Filthy River
> flowing,
> down to the filthy sea.
> Alone I stand
> gazing down at you,
> filthy river,
> you remind me of me!

The lyric rambled on in much the same manner as its subject

and there were lines like 'children paddle in you', rhyming with 'cattle straddle in you'.

But the sketch to which that cant word 'controversial' most aptly applied was a potted musical on the subject of the Pre-Raphaelite Brotherhood; an esoteric theme, even for a *very* late show. A young pianist and adroit lyricist called Richard Stilgoe collaborated with me on a scandalous segment in which the painter Millais, hearing a knock on the door, opens it to reveal a blow-up of Holman Hunt's famous painting, *The Light of the World*. Holding a lamp aloft, Jesus's lips suddenly animated, and he delivered a well-known commercial for pink household paraffin. Witless though this reads, it was visually very amusing to those unperturbed by blasphemy. However, the matter was raised in the House of Lords by the Archbishop of Canterbury, there were outraged letters to *The Times*. *The Late Show*, which was watched by so few, enjoyed a fleeting notoriety.

One evening after work, Stanley Myers and his girlfriend, and Rosalind and I, dined at a smart new restaurant in Holland Park called Chez Moi. The evening was going very well until Stanley suggested that it might be amusing if I did the trouser trick. This was a simple, and perhaps juvenile, stunt which worked only in a dignified or pretentious ambience. All that happened was that my pants fell down, apparently by accident, at a conspicuous moment. The 'trick' was that I should exhibit a high degree of embarrassment. That night, on my way back from the gents, I timed it to perfection. Barely a diner in that crowded restaurant could have missed it, and with a tremendous show of shame and apology and much bowing and shrugging I retreated to our table, where Stanley, at least, sat convulsed with laughter. Soon the maître d' was at our side, his lips to my ear. 'I am sorry, sir, but we must ask you please to leave the restaurant *immédiatement*. Lord Snowdon over zair is most offended by what just 'appen.' I had no time to protest, or even to get a view of Princess Margaret's outraged husband. Two burly waiters lifted me bodily from my chair and propelled me out the door into Addison Road, where I was obliged to loiter, undined and unwined. All I had to nibble were a few stale sponge fingers left over from my luncheon zabaglione at Bertorelli's, the kind which are sometimes known, rather suggestively, as Boudoir Fingers.

I attempted to get back into the restaurant, but the door was locked, and through a chink in a curtain I could see my wife and my friends enjoying a delicious meal as if nothing had happened; relieved, no doubt, that I was out of the way. On the corner of Addison Road was a telephone box and, after consulting a dog-eared directory, I dialled the number of the restaurant. The maître d's voice answered, ''Ullo, 'ullo?' I assumed the fluting tones of a middle-aged, upper-class Englishwoman. 'This is the Countess of Rosse speaking. My son Lord Snowdon is dining in your restaurant tonight. May I speak with him urgently please?' There was a long pause on the line and then a man's voice. 'Mother? How did you track me down here?' 'Tony, darling,' I trilled, 'there is a lovely and talented man in your restaurant tonight who has been far from well, his name is Barry Humphries and he has been accidentally locked out in the street. Please buy him and his party a large bottle of champagne and get the management to apologize.' On the other end of the line I could hear a voice cry: 'What, Mother? Who is this? *Who is this speaking?*' I rang off.

The door of Chez Moi, much to my chagrin, was not immediately thrown open, until Rosalind, Stanley and Yvonne at last emerged, but there was a sequel to this sorry incident, which will be told later.

Paint Over Rust

> Food glorious food
> Hot sausage and mustard
> While we're in the mood
> Cold jelly and custard . . .

The maddening chorus of small boys' voices leaked out of the tannoy in my dressing-room. Carefully I dabbed some spirit gum under my ginger moustache, which had come adrift after the last generous sip of South Australian claret. It was hard to believe I was back in the same old show, but this time I was Fagin – the lead! It seemed poetically just that I should accept the offer when it came along, and it was satisfying to have my name up there in lights in Piccadilly Circus.

The revival of Lionel Bart's classic musical at the Piccadilly Theatre suited me in every way, and now I even had two small daughters who were old enough to enjoy it. What a relief not to have to attend understudy rehearsals! The young actor who played Mr Sowerberry, the Undertaker – my old role – was no doubt dragged in to the theatre every day to rehearse with the boys, just as I had been, and no doubt also he watched me like a hawk – as I had watched Ron Moody – for signs of flagging health or laryngitis.

The so-called 'swinging sixties' were at their height. A few yards from the theatre, Piccadilly Circus in mid-summer was thronged with hippies from all over Europe, and on the steps surrounding Sir Alfred Gilbert's Eros, with nude, reasty feet the tie-dyed, patchouli-drenched girls from Holland and Germany and Denmark and North Finchley sprawled provocatively beside their unsuitable male companions. Gaudy, bell-bottomed tatterdemalions with guitars strummed plaintive songs about remote wars as tourists swarmed into Soho in search of Union Jack T-shirts, granny glasses, old ceremonial uniforms and Doors' albums.

During my season as Fagin I heard that auditions were being held down the road for the musical *Cabaret*, based on Christopher Isherwood's Berlin stories. I had listened to the Broadway recording, and rather fancied myself as the sinister Master of Ceremonies which Joel Gray had played in the original production. It would have been imprudent to inform my management that I was trying for a role in another show whilst I was still working successfully for them, so I enrolled for my audition under a false name.

I had not been to an audition for years, and I was as nervous as hell, but I launched into my big number 'Willkommen', with baleful energy, focusing my eyes on the small row of tiny red lights that winked in the blackness of the stalls; the terminal embers of the producers' cigarettes. At the end I just stood there as a disembodied voice reached me from the darkness. 'Thank you so much, Mr Harrison,' it drawled. 'Very nice interpretation indeed. I'm sorry we can't offer you anything in this particular show but please let us know when you have had some experience. NEXT!'

'*Experience!*' I muttered to myself, skulking angrily back up the Haymarket, to a position where I could see my own name up there in neon on the *Oliver!* sign. 'I'm only playing a West End lead, for Christ's sake! How much experience do these bastards want?'

My morale was greatly boosted when a letter arrived from Bernard Miles, who had launched the Mermaid Theatre.

This lead directly to my next engagement, the role of Long

MERMAID THEATRE

PUDDLE DOCK BLACKFRIARS LONDON EC4 CITY 6981
BOX OFFICE *Telephone* CITY 7656   RESTAURANT BOOKINGS *Telephone* CITY 2835

August 10th, 1967

Barry Humphries, Esq.,
25 Maida Avenue,
London W.2.

Dear Barry,

    Brought grandchildren to see "Oliver" and
must congratulate you.   You are superb, incisive
totally audible, finely characterised, larger
than life and bursting with personality – and the
voice!

          Congratulations!

          Yours,

          Bernard Miles

John Silver in a stage adaptation of Stevenson's *Treasure Island*. Miles had created the role, and appeared in it every year, except for one winter season when the part was taken by Sir Donald Wolfit. In this new production Spike Milligan was to play Ben Gunn, and William Rushton, Squire Trelawney, so I would be amongst friends. As soon as my *Oliver!* contract ended, I started rehearsals at the Mermaid, but it was a long part, and I was a poor learner of lines. Spike suggested a brilliant hypnotherapist he knew in Harley Street, and in desperation I went to see this 'alternative' physician. I was wary, however, half expecting to find Spike in a white coat and a wig posing as a hypnotist.

I explained my learning block to the doctor, who told me to

lie comfortably on a table while he tried to put me under. Staring at the ceiling, and extremely sceptical, I felt not the least sleepy sensation. All I could hear were the rumblings of the doctor's stomach. Rather begrudging this old charlatan his exorbitant fee, I hurried back to the Mermaid for the afternoon rehearsal. I knew every line.

Knowing the lines, however, was only half the battle. Acting on one leg with a parrot on one's shoulder, and participating in a frenzied cutlass fight, was almost beyond human endurance. The parrot, a pet of Bernard Miles', hated me. It also had a keen appetite for human flesh, and when it was not flying into the auditorium and screaming indecencies at the children in the audience, it was pecking at my ear until the blood flowed.

We did two shows a day, and the weather was bitterly cold. After the first week I slipped on some ice outside the theatre and sprained my one good leg; the leg on which I so heavily relied every day for five hours of solid hopping, while the other leg was strapped up behind me. Switching legs was strangely disorientating, and far from being Stevenson's nimble old amputee, I developed a tendency to fall over rather too often. But since rum was Silver's preferred tipple, it became, in the interests of literary verisimilitude, my own. It was remarkable how little pain I felt, or how much manic energy I seemed to release, after a few breath-taking tots of this powerful Jamaican beverage.

As the season wore on, so did I. I seemed to need less and less character makeup, as my face began naturally to assume the lineaments of a ravaged old sea-dog, and a magenta hue that would formerly have taken me some time to achieve artificially.

As I became Long John Silver, I felt an increasing licence to take my own liberties with the text. Was it not possible that Silver was an escaped Australian convict? Why not introduce a few echoes of Barry McKenzie? Perhaps even a chunder scene from the poop? When Bernard Miles, returning from a holiday, looked in at a matinée he failed to recognize the show he had created. There were some acerbic notes, but a kind of anarchy had been set in motion, which could not easily be curbed. Long John Silver, being the ship's cook, occasionally produced his own specialities, and one of these proved to be a giant quivering pavlova which was sometimes accidentally planted on the face of Squire Trelawney or the dignified Dr Livesey. Spike was without reticence when it came to pantomimic anachronisms. When Ben Gunn appeared with a blunderbuss and fired, we were all showered with a great cloud of white flour. 'What was that?' said Squire Trelawney. 'Flour-power,' replied Milligan, topically.

In the midst of this highly professional jollity, the stage doorman told me he needed a word with me. In a quick break between scenes, and rums, I limped to his cubbyhole. He pointed to a large suitcase to which was affixed an envelope. It was a note from Rosalind. She was sending the rest of my clothes and personal effects to the theatre in the next few days. An anonymous member of the *Oliver!* cast had told her all she needed to know about my relationship with Delia, the assistant stage manager, and she hoped I would be very happy. It seemed to have gone very quiet on stage. 'My God!' I thought. '*I'm on!*'

'I hope you realize I'm just putting paint over the rust.' It was an offensive thing for anybody to say, let alone a doctor. And a doctor I was paying good money. I was in Sydney again, backstage at the old Tivoli Theatre, presenting yet another one-man offering, this time entitled, with mock modesty, *Just a Show*. The doctor was giving me a powerful shot of vitamin B_{12} and my cheeks were burning with the characteristic 'niacin rush'.

There is a type of medical practitioner I particularly loathe. The smug type. I had consulted just such a doctor a few months before in London, when Rosalind presented me with a legal ultimatum.

MERMAID THEATRE

PUDDLE DOCK BLACKFRIARS LONDON EC4 CITY 6981
BOX OFFICE *Telephone* CITY 7656   RESTAURANT BOOKINGS *Telephone* CITY 2835

8th February, 1968

Barry Humphries Esq.,
25 Maida Avenue,
LONDON W.2.

Dear Barry,

      Just a word of profound thanks for your
work in Treasure Island - you have enormous capacity
as an actor - most of all a life-enhancing vitality
and energy which is a gift from the Gods - besides
your intelligence and ready wit.

      You also have what I think is almost the
greatest gift of all, namely determination not to
give in.   I know you were often feeling down and
hard-pressed and the three performances on Saturday
(I did them myself three years ago so I know what
I am talking about) are really like total war.

      A thousand congratulations and Bless
you Barry.

               Yours ever,

P.S. Do give me a ring as soon as you are in
circulation again and come and have lunch. Bring
your beautiful wife.

The late Dr Lászlo Zadór had rooms in Harley Street at the top of three flights of stairs, but I had to spend a long time in the waiting-room first, examining his other patients. They looked awful. 'Who the hell recommended that I see this quack?' I thought. 'Probably that smooth lawyer who is winding her up!' I felt angry, and completely sane. Hadn't I agreed to keep everybody happy by doing another Australian show?

One of the girls in the waiting-room was muttering to herself. Was she drugged? I had seen the junkies queuing up outside Boots the Chemist in Piccadilly Circus. It was a sickening sight to behold all those young people who had completely lost their will-power. Often, gazing at them pityingly from my comfortable seat in the back of a cab, I would need to take a quick swig of scotch from the half-bottle in a Harrods' bag.

I told the doctor a long and rambling yarn which I felt sure would amuse him, and he took copious notes. At the end of the interview, in his strong Hungarian accent, he asked me only one question: 'Have you ever thought of going to Alcoholics Anonymous?' I felt soiled and degraded. It seemed to me a disgrace that one should actually *pay* to be insulted.

This all came back to me in the dressing-room in Sydney. Paint over the rust? What moralizing shits some of these doctors were. I had agreed, at short notice, to do another Australian tour. Rosalind had magnanimously accepted me back into the fold on condition I got some sort of treatment. I'd seen this phoney shrink in Harley Street. Even done a stint in some private nursing home in North London, God help me. Then we had all gone to Mexico again where I had been a good boy and kept off the tequila, and I had even written an entire one-man show, which was now booked solid. What more did they want?

I was far from paranoid, but I knew that Cliff, the impresario, was having me tailed, if by any chance I managed to slip away from my 'jailers' after the show. Working under the pressure I did, didn't I deserve a few quiet drinks in a peaceful club to recharge my batteries? It was insulting to glance across a dimly lit room, in a louche part of town, and see Don Harris, my poor hard-worked stage manager, *who needed his sleep*, trying to look unobtrusive at a remote table. We never exchanged a word on those embarrassing occasions, but I guessed he was being paid a few dollars extra to snoop on me, though God knows what they thought I was getting up to. A nightcap or two, that was all.

When the doctor had gone, I looked in the mirror. My hair was short and blond for a new character called Brian Graham, a young fertilizer executive in the novel and ludicrous uniform such Australians were beginning to affect: shorts and long white socks worn with a collar and tie. Brian's chief aim was to hide his homosexuality from his tyrannical father and business associates. It was a nice dramatic piece.

Over the blond hair I wore a succession of wigs, including a pale blue one for Edna. She'd gone mauve in the last act, and she now wore Thai silk like every other Edna in Australia, and the audiences loved it. If only they knew the aggravation I was having to tolerate backstage. *Paint over the rust!*

I was rather proud of the richness of my new show, considering the troubles which had preceded it. Apart from Edna and Sandy Stone, there were five other characters, including Rex Lear, a coarse *nouveau-riche* father of the bride stumbling around at his daughter's wedding reception and, like his Shakespearean counterpart, railing against his daughter's ingratitude. It was an experiment to see if I could present single-handed on stage an entire (and invisible) wedding breakfast complete with bridesmaids, vicar, best man, caterers and Italian waiters.

I had made the show a little easier for myself by including a filmed segment. An 'underground' film. One of my new characters was called Martin Agrippa, a hispid Australian movie-maker with pretensions to being a kind of avant-garde Ingmar Bergman. The better half of the sketch was Martin Agrippa's film, which Bruce Beresford had made for me in London before I went out to Australia.

I had always wanted to include short films in my solo shows, both to give me a rest and a chance to transform myself into Edna or some other character who required an elaborate makeup or costume change. Patrick White had recommended a young Sydney film-maker whom he thought was destined for great things, on the strength of having seen one of Beresford's student efforts. When I met him, he was in charge of the production unit at the British Film Institute, and married with one son to a stylish and beautiful Irish girl called Rhoison. He was an enormously bright and attractive character, tousle-headed, opinionated, wittily intolerant and passionately fond of movies and music. Bruce sometimes wore an old-fashioned navy-blue chalk-striped suit which he proudly announced had been bought for £1 off a street vendor. His cars were equally picturesque bargains. It was Bruce, really, who put me on to the Underground Cinema joke, since he knew a lot of people both in England and Australia who had successfully applied for large grants in order to inflict their turgid and pretentious films upon an indifferent public.

Bruce and I created a hilarious and convincing parody of one of these movies; later shown at several International Festivals of Underground Cinema where it was acclaimed as a masterpiece of the genre. In *Just a Show*, following Martin Agrippa's monologue, the film brought the house down.

When Beresford and I were working together in London, I was unsure how much he knew of my domestic difficulties. On the one hand he was an indefatigable, indeed gleeful gossip; and on the other, curiously thoughtful and circumspect. After *Treasure Island*, when I agreed to incarcerate myself in a nursing home for a while, he made the long journey to visit me and never asked why I was there. This struck me as very odd. I managed to do some work in this foetid institution; some book reviews for the *Spectator*, commissioned by a nice-sounding girl called Hilary Spurling. She never inquired, either, why her correspondence was always addressed to me care of a private hospital. Very odd indeed. If Bruce or Hilary, or indeed anyone else, had asked me what a perfectly sane, talented and perhaps over-sensitive person like me was doing virtually locked up, I would have had to express myself very delicately – perhaps even pretend to be depressed – so that they would not think too unkindly of my wife.

I remember very little about this interlude in the nursing home, except that one day when I had been 'a good boy' for several weeks I was granted permission to go for a walk. I dressed excitedly, and set off into the nearby woods. Half an hour later I was still in sparse woodland and obviously lost. I increased my pace until I came at length to a large tract of common land, with a few houses in the far distance. I was running now, though not sure why. I reached the houses and at last came upon a small parade of shops. Breathless from my exertions I ran past them, around the corner and straight through the doorway of an off-licence. I had to lean on the counter for a few minutes to regain my breath. A friendly Irishman smiled at me interrogatively.

'Ahem, twenty, er, no, forty Dunhill please . . . and, er, a couple of boxes of matches, thank you.'

The Irishman smiled again, and put the cigarettes on the counter, and the matches, and then a package containing six miniature bottles of Smirnoff vodka.

'What are these for?' I asked, flabbergasted.

'You're up at Elm Hill, aren't you now?' he said.

I nodded.

'That's what they all order.'

I quickly paid my money and bolted out of the shop. A minute later I was back on the common beside a very large bush. I ripped the lid off one of the miniatures and held it to my lips. Nothing came out. There was an air lock in the neck. I gave the bottle a little shake and, with a glug, the entire contents poured down my throat with a sharp burning sensation. I took a deep breath before tackling the lid of the second miniature, at the same time tossing the empty bottle into the bush. There was a loud clink. I parted the foliage, and peered inside. There was a considerable pile of empty vodka bottles. Others had been this way before. I had the sudden, if fleeting, impression that I was not entirely alone.

There were flies everywhere. Australians are used to them of course; even in restaurants where they grow to the size of hummingbirds, but it was unusual to find them in an art gallery, and in such numbers. They crawled around the picture frames, they supped at the eyes and briefly formed loose scrums at the corners of people's mouths. High up, against the white ceiling, thousands of them moved ceaselessly in a decorous holding pattern.

The cause of this muscarious invasion seemed to be a large, circular, blue plastic paddling-pool in the centre of the gallery floor. It appeared to be filled with some clotted and pus-coloured substance which already bore in places the blue-green bloom of mould. Here the nimbus of flies was thickest, for the glutinous yellow liquid in the pool was custard, gallons of it; and here and there, projecting through its coagulating surface, were the corners, spines and covers of books. It was laced with dozens of books, which I had bought as a job-lot from a Salvation Army depot. This 'sculpture', for sale at $6,000 (with a discount to museums and learned institutions), was an inflated recreation of my notorious work from the early fifties: 'I was reading these books when I felt sick.' Unfortunately it was an exhibit that attracted more attention from the flies than from the public.

I had decided to hold this art exhibition to run concurrently with my Sydney theatre season. It was to be pretentiously called a 'Retrospective', in mockery of the retrospectives every young artist in Australia under the age of twenty-five seemed to be having. An old friend, Kym Bonython, had opened the smartest new gallery in town and he offered it to me for my show. In spite of performing solo for three hours every night, I had somehow managed to assemble enough 'works of art' to fill Kym's large gallery. There were a lot of my early landscapes of Mornington in an amiable fauvist style, some reconstructions of Dada objects of the early fifties, like 'Books', as well as a series of large and realistic portraits of Australian prime ministers, some of whom were wearing real suits, glued on to the canvas. I had also executed a series of monumental 'Bigscapes', mainly to fill up empty spaces in the gallery. These consisted only of the word 'Big', fastidiously painted on canvas in huge letters.

The show attracted large numbers of people who did not normally frequent art galleries, but sales were few. One of the portraits was bought by a Sydney collector and someone else bought a drawing. The rest of the exhibits either got lost, rotted or were thrown out with the garbage. Kym told me years later that after my show the flies never forsook his gallery but loitered in their hundreds in the hope, no doubt, that in the fullness of time I would be mounting another delicious retrospective.

Just a Show played in all the Australian cities, ending in Perth. By then I was reluctantly beginning to agree with that impertinent theatre doctor in Sydney. The rust was starting to bleed through the paint.

By the light of a trembling match he stared at his watch. It was twenty to two. There was something very important that had to be done but he could not remember what. On the floor of the small unfamiliar room was a puddle of clothes; some were like his, except for the crumpled brown silk dress with an Indian pattern. Nearby in a tangle of linguini laces were a pair of Roman sandals that had fallen in first position. They were like the ones he had seen before, latticing a girl's brown legs. The girl asleep on the bed reminded him vaguely of the student whose eye he had caught in the front row at a talk he had given at the University of Western Australia. When was that? Yesterday? TODAY? The match had gone out, burning his fingers. He lit another and looked once more at his watch. Was it upside down? The time now seemed to be twelve minutes past eight.

By the time he got to the theatre, fortunately only a few blocks away from the shabby private hotel where he had found himself, the audience — in varying degrees of puzzlement, impatience and jocular irritation — had been seated for over thirty minutes listening to a jolly medley of recorded music. His hair was glued to his scalp with sweat from the mad dash across town, and the manager kept refilling a cup of black coffee which rattled on the saucer as he stabbed at his face with

*makeup and stumbled into the gaudy costume. Somewhere
nearby, white-faced, stood his wife; but he looked no one in
the eye that night, and felt at home and safe only when he
had burst on to the stage, and for the next two hours struggled
for the forgiveness of laughter. It was an evening which,
for years afterwards, if he ever thought about it, made his flesh
crawl.*

During the Melbourne run I had a visit from a London producer, Peter Bridge. He was convinced that the show would be
a huge hit in the West End and he told me he wanted to
produce it himself. I patiently explained that no one in London
really got the point of my Aussie act, except homesick Australians and English people who had been down there on a visit. I
had even tentatively introduced Edna a few times on *The Late
Show*, but the BBC switchboard had not exactly been jammed
with calls from ecstatic viewers; nor had the mailbags
overflowed with fan letters hailing a great new comic creation.
Only Malcolm Muggeridge seemed to have found Mrs Everage
risible. I also told Mr Bridge that my earlier attempts to win
over a British audience to my essentially regional material had
met with stony indifference. Better, I said, to stick to my comic
strip, which I had heard had quite a few distinguished fans, like
Kenneth Tynan, Bernard Levin, John Osborne and Alan Sillitoe.
Bridge disagreed, and told me to let him know when I got back
to London so he could present me at the Fortune Theatre,
where *Beyond the Fringe* had been triumphantly launched six
years earlier.

I heard a shrill cry of 'Daddy!' and, turning sharply in surprise,
I saw little Emily running towards me along the pavement with
her arms outstretched. I felt a tremendous surge of joy as I
stooped ready to snatch the child up into my arms. But suddenly,
only a couple of yards off, she stopped, and looked at me with
horror. At the same moment I realized that it was not Emily at
all; just a little girl who looked like Emily. The child was crying

now and running towards a woman outside a fruit shop, who gathered her up and glowered at me resentfully. 'What have *I* done?' I thought, with a thumping heart and tears in my eyes. It was hardly my fault that the child mistook me for her father.

Of course it could not possibly have been Emily or, for that matter, Tessa, for I was now in London, and they were 13,000 miles away in Melbourne with their mother. When the tour of *Just a Show* had ended, or petered out in illness and disarray, Rosalind had moved into a flat and not disclosed the address.

For a while I had dossed down in a suburban motel, making a few desultory excursions to Sydney in search of consolation. But when they went to New Zealand to stay with Rosalind's parents, I followed, checking into a mean room, not normally rented, above an Auckland pub. By having my bed only a few yards from my chosen drinking haunt I had hoped to avoid the pitfalls and dangerous distractions which seemed always to entrap me when these two polarities of my life were widely separated. It was, I decided, the *getting home* that was the central problem, not the harmless conviviality which preceded it.

To the best of my ability at the time, I tried to make amends to my family, but to no avail. Rosalind had finally had enough. Briefly, I saw the girls again, and with a heavy heart set off for London, and work.

Peter Bridge was as good as his word, and as I began rehearsing for my first London one-man show, my spirits, and my health, seemed to revive. I had always directed myself in all my solo enterprises, but this time Eleanor Fazan, an old friend, was hired to direct the production, which was to contain most of the elements from the Australian show with a couple of extra ingredients. One of these was my old 'surfie' character, clutching a bucket of prawns and singing Barry McKenzie's legendary drinking song, 'The Old Pacific Sea'.

Oh, I was down by Bondi pier
Drinking tubes of ice-cold beer,
With a bucket full of prawns upon me knee;
But when I'd swallowed the last prawn
I had a technicolour yawn,
And I chundered in the old Pacific Sea.

CHORUS

Drink it up, drink it up,
Crack another dozen tubes and prawns with me.
If you want to throw your voice
Mate, you won't have any choice,
But to chunder in the old Pacific Sea.

I was sitting in the surf
When a mate of mine called Murph
Asked if he could crack a tube or two with me.
The bastard barely swallowed it
When he went for the big spit,
And he chundered in the old Pacific Sea.

CHORUS

There's a lot of ways that you can
Have a ball when you are pukin',
And the secret of it is variety
You can either park a Tiger
From the summit of the Eiger,
Or chunder in the old Pacific Sea.

CHORUS

I've had liquid laughs in bars
And I've hurled from moving cars,
And I've chuckled when and where it suited me.
But, if I could choose a spot
To regurgitate me lot,
Then I'd chunder in the old Pacific Sea.

CHORUS
Drink it up, drink it up,
Crack another dozen tubes and prawns with me.
Why kneel there all alone
By the big white telephone
When you can chunder in the old Pacific Sea.

On the opening night my producer Peter Bridge was very excited by the 'buzz' in the foyer, and even I, nervous and still sceptical, felt a frisson of hope as I hid in the manager's office next to the box office in my Edna disguise of cyclamen-and-peacock Thai silk. The show always opened with an overture on the Hammond organ played by my female accompanist in the orchestra pit. As she took her bow, Edna would enter shrilly from the back of the stalls, an ordinary member of the audience wishing to address publicly several popular misconceptions about the Australian way of life. That was the reason I was huddled in the manager's office and not waiting in the wings.

The audience was settling down. The house-lights dimmed, I took a discreet but fortifying nip of brandy from a small flask in Edna's purse and crept out of my hiding place to peer through a crack in the doors at the back of the stalls. Beside me, in black tie, and perspiring with nerves, was Peter Bridge. The organist he had hired seemed an apposite choice; Josephine Bradley. In Edwardian evening dress and wearing a feather boa, she looked like a musical Lady Bracknell. She got a large and encouraging round of applause too as she sat down at the electric organ, but she seemed a long time starting the overture, a medley of early fifties novelty numbers. Beside me Peter muttered profanely, but Miss Bradley's problems with her instrument, which had somehow become separated from its source of electrical power, seemed to amuse the audience, who tittered, as audiences do, at shows where things are *meant* to go wrong.

After an eternity, during which the sweat must have washed

all traces of Edna's makeup off my countenance, the Hammond organ was reconnected, and the show began. I tensed for my entrance, but it was that moment that Mr Bridge chose to inform me of a minor adjustment he had made to the props in the finale. He hadn't worried me about it before because I had a lot on my plate, but the wholesale florists at Covent Garden were out of gladioli due to some bug that had attacked the crop, so he had taken the liberty of buying five dozen daffodils instead. I could throw those at the audience at the end of the show and they would be none the wiser.

'But, Peter,' I hissed, 'what about the song?'

'What song?'

'The song I sing at the end,' said Edna, frantically. 'To the tune of "Coconuts"!' With five seconds to go before her entrance, she sang a few bars:

> '. . . I've got a lovely bunch of gladdies,
> See them all awaving in the stalls
> Big ones, small ones, some as big as your thumb
> Give 'em a twist, a flick of the wrist
> – There's lots of different ways of arranging them,
> Just remember all you mums and daddies,
> There's lots of flower power to be had
> All you need's a lovely bunch of gladdies
> And you'll never be sad, as long as you wave a glad!

Try getting "daff" to rhyme in *that* number,' I yelled over my shoulder as I bolted through the door and down the aisle to the point, just against the stage, where the spotlight hit the flurry of Thai silk and the sparkle of *diamanté*, and Edna trilled: 'Excuse I!'

I have a clear memory, however, of Peter's face as he got the message and his lips mimed the word 'Jesus!'

At the end of the show there were gladioli. Dozens and dozens of them. Poor old Peter must have dragged every florist in London away from his dinner to provide an Australian housewife with what remaining stocks they had of this endangered species.

Next day, we had some nice publicity. RARE PLANT INSECT THREATENS WEST END SHOW. Qantas Airlines must have read this because for the next few weeks they flew, from far Australia, large quantities of glads of a hue, size and succulence never before seen in London.

The papers also published the reviews. They were not all bad, but they were not all good. Harold Hobson dourly said, 'Most of Barry Humphries' *Just a Show* will give pleasure to most Australians living in London.' And Herbert Kretzmer wrote: 'The mood of those [last] ten minutes cannot be produced in words. It was one of those magic moments in the theatre where the audience becomes truly happy.' But, as I had feared, the show was ultimately a provincial curiosity; admired by a few, shrugged off by most, and attracting too few patrons for my valiant producer to be able to keep it going for more than six increasingly difficult weeks.

As we limped on, I viewed the attraction across the road at the Theatre Royal, Drury Lane with mounting envy and resentment. It was *Mame*, starring the already legendary Ginger Rogers. Even before I opened, Miss Rogers' renovations to her dressing-room had received more publicity than our modest production could ever hope to attract. Edna countered with a piece about *her* gorgeous improvements to her backstage accommodation, but as Miss Rogers' box-office queues lengthened, Mrs Everage's dwindled. Every night as I left the theatre I cast a jaundiced eye across the road at the stage door of the 'Lane', where Ginger's many fans were waiting for a fleeting glimpse of the star. When we finally knew we had only a few more performances to go, I decided to capture Ginger Rogers' audience, if just for a few minutes. Carefully timing the end of my show to coincide precisely with the end of hers, I dashed out the stage door the instant my curtain fell, so that Edna, in all her finale finery, was outside the Fortune Theatre before my audience had found their coats. Leaping on to the roof of a parked car, Edna executed a lively tap routine just as both theatres, Ginger's and mine, disgorged their patrons. My own meagre followers were, of course, dumbfounded to see the artiste they had just left behind performing an encore in the street, and the throngs evacuating the Theatre Royal stopped in their tracks as Edna shrilly exhorted them to come back tomorrow and patronize 'the Ginger Rogers of the sixties'.

Two weeks later, after we had closed and I was out of a job, I received a nice fan letter from a woman who had witnessed this event. She enclosed a large invoice from a North London firm of panel-beaters who had encountered extraordinary problems in removing the indentations of stiletto heels from the roof of her Jaguar.

Don't Wake Me For Cocktails

THE ONLY REALLY hostile review *Just a Show* received was in Australia. I was now living in a small private hotel on Westbourne Terrace, and one night the telephone jangled at about four a.m. It was, of course, an Australian journalist under the impression that the time in London is identical to the time in Sydney, although such intrusions – and they still occur – always begin with the phrase: 'Sorry mate, what time is it there?'

The reason for this call was that a New Zealand impresario called Harry M. Miller, of whom I had vaguely heard, had come back to Sydney after a quick shopping expedition in London, and attacked my show on the grounds that it was unpatriotic. In Australia, a foolproof means of grabbing publicity and appearing to be a fine fellow is to impugn another man's patriotism; and no doubt Mr Miller hit upon this method to liven up his press conference. 'What did he say?' I sleepily challenged the transmitter. The journalist gleefully quoted:

'That man Humphries is an idiot ... We have enough trouble convincing the world Australia is sophisticated, yet we have this idiot ruining the country.'

I had a brief and comic vision of Mr Miller convincing the world of Australia's sophistication, where I had patently failed. Luckily, despite the hour, I managed to think up a few vaguely amusing ripostes to the charges levelled by this scurrilous Kiwi, who had, it emerged, not even been to see my show. In the intervening years, however, and as regular as clockwork, I have had to reply to – or ignore – similar charges; usually from disc jockeys and tenth-rate academics with chips on their shoulders. As a recipient of these attacks I have always been in excellent company. There is not one Australian singer, artist, writer, actor or film director whose success abroad has gone unpunished by an envious minority of his countrymen. A few of our film directors had quite recently been fulminating against their colleagues who had 'sold out to Hollywood'. They wanted to ban foreign actors and directors from working in Australia. One or two of these same film-makers are a little more circumspect now, I notice, as they recline beside their pools in Beverly Hills.

Someone at the BBC had seen *Just a Show* and I was offered my own TV series, *The Barry Humphries Scandals*. It was to be produced by a man called Dennis Main Wilson who, I was told, was one of those BBC comedy veterans who 'could do no wrong'. He had initiated many famous television shows, and he seemed very enthusiastic about my series.

Gradually I learned to live with that dull ache of loss over my little daughters back in Australia, and I felt a resurgence of energy as I started work again at Television Centre. It was as if my way of doing things, of living even, had been vindicated after all. Considering the way in which my life had been sliding out of control over the past couple of years, I seemed to have landed up on my feet again, so to speak. And my feet stood nonchalantly at the important end of the long bar at the BBC Club, where I could smile and nod to people like Frankie Howerd, Harry Secombe, Morecambe and Wise and Marty Feldman. I was back in the world of black taxis, too, which would whisk me 'as directed' around the West End of London, and wait obediently for hours outside smart Mayfair pubs as I purchased cigarettes, sampling a few Fernet Brancas and large Teachers while the bartender fetched them.

We now lived in Mayfair, that is to say, Roslyn Mackrell

and I, in a tiny flat in Park Street. Roslyn was a beautiful girl from Sydney who deserved a great deal better than the sporadic companionship of a dissolute, guilt-ridden, self-obsessed boozer, whose own definition of himself would have been *very* different. To cheer myself up, I had got a lot of books and pictures from the old house at Little Venice out of storage, and had stuffed them into our cramped accommodation; ballast from the past. On the mantelpiece and on the crowded tops of tables stood my collection of Gallé cameo glass, mostly assembled whilst browsing in junkshops during Australian tours, long before art nouveau had returned to fashion.

The *Scandals* were written by me and my old colleague from *The Late Show*, Ian Davidson, though the tapes of the series no longer exist, having been destroyed by the BBC to save space. This may not be a tragic loss to the world's archive of funny material, but the show had its felicities. There was an elegant film set in a 1930s nightclub in which I, disguised as Jack Buchanan, sang my own loosely autobiographical composition, 'Too Drunk to Dance', and a musical based on the career of the Australian bushranger, Ned Kelly. Various actor friends made guest appearances in the series, including Dick Bentley, June Whitfield and Michael Palin.

One of the most successful sketches concerned an unmarried man who, as he rushes out the front gate to work, is always intercepted by his mother with the question: 'I hope you're wearing clean underwear this morning, darling. No man knoweth the hour!' Of course the tardy commuter, summoned back to his bedroom to change his underpants, saves time by merely stuffing a clean pair into his briefcase, pecking his mother on the cheek and running to the bus stop.

In our film he could be seen crossing the road just as an enormous lorry bore down upon him at high speed. Seeing his peril too late, he becomes rooted to the spot as the camera goes into slow motion. Then, methodically, he puts the briefcase down on the road, removes his trousers and underpants, dons the clean pair, places the old ones in the briefcase, pulls up his trousers, straightens his bowler hat and stands to attention, only to be flattened by the lorry, as his mother's words echo through his brain: *No man knoweth the hour!*

This short film ended with a scene in which the old lady answers her front doorbell. A policeman stands in the porch looking grim. 'I'm afraid I have some very bad news for you, madam.' 'It's Basil, isn't it?' says the sweet old lady presciently. 'Tell me, officer, was he . . . was he . . .?' 'I'm happy to say he was, madam,' replied the policeman, handing her a small package. 'You'll be relieved to hear they were *absolutely spotless.*' The bereaved woman fell into the policeman's arms with the words, 'Heaven be praised, heaven be praised!'

A song I had written called 'True British Spunk' proved to be the swansong of the series. A swansong, moreover, that was never transmitted, though an audio-tape miraculously survives. 'Spunk' was a party turn of mine at the time, ostensibly about British courage and fortitude down the ages, but its humour resided, of course, in the equivocal meaning of the word, with its sticky schoolboy resonances, which nobody at the BBC dared to point out at that time.

Dennis Main Wilson, with his usual flair and extravagance, commissioned a large orchestra, and a chorus of soldiers, sailors, airmen, nurses, air-raid wardens and land-army girls to harmoniously ejaculate, in stirring Elgarian style, the rousing and spunky chorus. I might add that I sang the song myself, as Edna impersonating Vera Lynn. But it was only after the whole thing had been expensively recorded in the presence of a large and enthusiastic audience that a senior member of the BBC Board found the courage to draw me to one side, and attempted to explain to me that the title of my song had, in some circles, an alternative and unacceptable meaning, of which I, as a Colonial, was naturally ignorant. This was elucidated with much beating about the bush, which I suppose was appropriate under the circumstances.

*

No one ever saw the final episode of *The Scandals*, which remained, at the last, true to their title. Yet when the series ended and there seemed no immediate prospect of work, my morale quickly faded. I spent money as fast as I earned it, and my health seemed to be failing.

A doctor told me that my liver was inflamed and asked me how much I drank. It was a difficult question to answer. Did he mean, for example, before or after breakfast? Did he mean wines or spirits? How could a professional man expect me to know how much I drank, when much of my drinking was performed unconsciously and in those reaches of the night that were becoming increasingly blank.

In the small hours of the morning I would wake up in a cold sweat, with feelings of impending doom. I was convinced something terrible was about to happen, but could not possibly explain what it was that I feared. The sounds of cars outside in the street became ominous; would they stop at my house? Were they coming for me?

In the mornings, on waking, I would need to lie for several minutes with my eyes squeezed shut before daring to examine my surroundings. Was it my own bed? Was this my girlfriend? The relief at discovering that I was at least in my own flat would lend me the courage to examine my discarded clothes. Were they neatly hanging in the wardrobe or folded over a chair, or were they strewn, inside-out, on the carpet? If the latter were the case, as it all too often was, I would then begin an agonizing reconstruction of the night before. Where had I been? The stubs in my chequebook might hold an answer to this mystery. Feverishly I would riffle through them. Three were blank. My God! I must have cashed some cheques – but where? There was one cheque stub across which was scrawled, in unfamiliar writing, the cryptic word 'entertainment'. The pocket of my jacket yielded a clue: a book of matches which advertised the Blue Parrot Club. Where was that? There was a sordid-seeming address off the Harrow Road. A few smudgy memories filtered back, but not many. I vaguely recalled dinner in Soho. A room somewhere, ruddily lit, with a lot of people. Where had the evening gone wrong? I must have changed my drinks, I decided. If I had only stuck to whisky, and a little wine, everything would have been all right. Or I must have run into some boring crowd who insisted on pressing on somewhere else, and then somewhere else, ruining my plans of an early night. But I would not be so easily led astray next time. It would never happen again. *Never again*. They were the two words I repeated every morning of my life like a mantra.

This mental and physical anguish did not, fortunately, last for too long. A Radox bath, a sanguineous shave, a clean shirt, too much cologne and I was ready for the short stroll from the flat in Park Street to the Red Lion, which, miraculously, threw open its doors at the precise moment of my arrival, to permit my thirsty ingress. As I walked towards the bar the barmaid, without any command from me, placed a large glass of bitumen-coloured Fernet Branca on the bar. I had discovered this powerful Italian *digestif* and tonic several years before, but had only lately taken to imbibing it before breakfast. Politely, Veronica turned her back as I picked up the glass with an unsteady hand and contrived to steer it towards my lips without spilling too much on the way. Fernet Branca stains on ties and lapels defy the efforts of even the best dry-cleaners. Several deep gulps of air usually persuaded me that the balsamic cordial had been permanently ingurgitated, and I could safely order a little whisky and mineral water to banish, for the day at least, the phantoms of the night before.

Often across the bar I noticed a trembling copy of the *Daily Telegraph*, opened to its full extent. I never once saw the reader, only his right hand, which from time to time darted beneath the newspaper towards a large glass of clear and rapidly diminishing liquid, which it then withdrew behind the quivering screen of newsprint. Who was he, I often wondered. And how did he sneak into the saloon bar before me? Hadn't I arrived on the dot of opening time? Had he, perhaps, been there all night? Sadly, I made my own diagnosis: the poor man behind the paper must be an alcoholic.

One morning, with a worse attack of amnesia than was customary, and a conviction that some catastrophe had occurred that I would rather not know about, I wandered into our sitting-room. As usual, the telephone was off the hook and growling resentfully. I had come to dread this instrument, and the bad news it must invariably communicate.

Something in the room seemed to be missing. Where was my precious glass collection? The slender vase by Daum with its shouldered, swollen, cylindrical form and gently everted rim, on knopped stem and bun foot, acid-etched and enamelled with poppies in orange, black and green on a yellow acid-textured ground? The Gallé mould-blown triple-overlay vase, with acid-etched crocuses in pink and mauve, in frosted opalescent glass with the artist's intaglio signature? And where was the Gallé lamp with its hemispherical shade and double-overlay carved and acid-etched decoration of clematis, blue and amethyst, on a ground shading from yellow-amber to frosted coral, with Gallé's cameo signature on the base and shade? There were half a dozen more pieces which also seemed to be missing. I asked Roslyn if she had put them somewhere safe and out of range of the cleaning lady's duster. She gave me a look of incredulity. 'Don't tell me you don't remember what happened last night?' Of course I didn't. 'You just came home and threw them at the wall; every single one of them. I couldn't stop you. But surely you remember that?'

It appeared that my father had arranged my rescue, for I was back in my hometown of Melbourne. Back with Rosalind and the children. With my father's support, she had just turned up, minutes, it seemed, after sending me a telegram, and the next thing I knew was that there was a furniture van in Park Street, loading up the contents of the flat to be shipped back to Australia. The scene reminded me, dimly, of my expulsion from the artist's garret I had rented years before, when my father had unceremoniously packed my bags with the words 'Why the dickens do you want to live in a dump like this when you've got a perfectly good home to go to?' It had a kind of logic, too, if one wasn't an adult. Now, I felt I had forfeited all will of my own, and I was almost relieved to be a person to whom things just happened.

I remember little of the flight back to Melbourne, much of which I spent at the back of the plane obtaining furtive drinks from the obliging Qantas stewards, who always had a fund of amusing gossip. In the maroon leatherette wallet, containing my in-flight toiletries, sockettes and slumber-shades, was an adhesive disc intended to be stuck, if necessary, on the back of one's seat. It said: DON'T WAKE ME FOR COCKTAILS. I screwed it up and stuffed it into my air-sick bag.

My mother's arthritis, which she was convinced was an unavoidable and hereditary complaint, seemed much worse when I saw her again. She rarely went out, preferring the company of her domestic helpers, and communicating daily on the telephone with all her sisters. It was darkly hinted that her health was none the better for my antics. My father was working even more frenetically, and obsessed by golf, his only recreation. However, at this time he confided to a friend: 'I was so worried about Barry, I couldn't even play golf last Thursday.'

A quantity of my books, many purchased years before when I was a schoolboy in Melbourne, arrived from London in large crates. Because I had been the compiler of a lewd work, *Bizarre*, and since I was also the author of the banned comic strip, *Barry McKenzie*, the Australian Customs authorities took an interest in this much-travelled library, and when it finally arrived and was unpacked in Rosalind's sitting-room, there was a senior official from Customs in attendance over a period of several days, who gravely examined every volume for obscene illustrations and equivocal texts. Every now and then, having stolen a few drinks from a carefully hidden cache, I would put my head around the corner of the room in which this custodian of decency ponderously laboured, and make matters worse with smart quips and sarcasms. In the end the poor old dunce got his own back by confiscating a couple of books; one a

Victorian treatise on morality, misleadingly entitled *A Book of Strange Sins*, and the other a tame translation of a nineteenth-century adventure story with a North African setting called *Musk, Hasheesh and Blood*. It is amusing to think of these anodyne works sitting on his suburban bookshelf between *Arthur Mee's Encyclopaedia* and *Whitaker's Alamanack*.

On the Queen's birthday weekend, after a period of good behaviour, I was allowed to take the car to a nearby shopping centre to buy some groceries. On the way I stopped at a pub and drank several glasses of schnapps in quick succession. The local doctor had put me on a course of so-called anti-depressants, which doubled the effect of the alcohol. I returned to the car and was just about to turn the key in the ignition when two policemen appeared from nowhere. Some years before, in London, I had had brushes with the law, and I had once lost my licence for a year for driving in the wrong direction up the Tottenham Court Road in a state of chemical exaltation, but at least the London bobbies called one 'Sir'. Their Melbourne counterparts were less polite. I was hustled to the Camberwell police station, a stone's-throw from my parents' house, where I most unwisely muttered the word 'fascists' within earshot of my apprehenders. Seconds later I was in a cell.

My appearance in court the next day attracted a great deal of what is now called 'media attention', so that my poor family must have deeply regretted the part they played in my extradition from London. A lawyer friend, armed with medical reports that emphasized my 'depression' and its chemical antidotes, cleverly got me off most of the charges, so that I escaped with only a light fine. The police glared across the court-room, and I smiled back.

Two days later, my medication doubled, I was in town to discuss the possibility of writing a regular newspaper column for the Melbourne *Age*. I managed to slip out of a side door of the building and into a nearby bar frequented by journalists. Only very vaguely do I recall somebody saying, 'There are

some friends of yours in a car outside who want to talk to you.'
My next recollection is of distant lights and mud. It was night
and for some reason I was lying face down in some kind of
waste land surrounded by rubble and broken glass on which a
fine drizzle descended. I tried to crawl, but there was an
excruciating pain in my abdomen and I collapsed back into the
mud. Slowly, however, I dragged myself towards the edge of a
desolate road and, at length, attracted the attention of a passing
car which dumped me off, like a severely damaged parcel, at St
Vincent's Hospital. As I lay in Casualty, shivering in my ripped
and mud-soaked suit, my face swollen and bleeding, I heard
one of the doctors saying '. . . they must have given him a real
going-over. Could be some internal bruising . . .' Sick and sore
as I was, I remembered that scene in the court-room two days
earlier. Had I been entirely wise in beaming quite so broadly at
my captors?

I opened my eyes and saw my father beside my bed. He was
weeping.

I must have spent many months in the Dymphna Ward of St
Vincent's Hospital. John Betjeman wrote me a long and comforting letter containing much information about the life and good
works of St Dymphna herself. My father called regularly to see
me in my private room, bringing cigarettes and nougat, and
Rosalind came a few times without the children. I learned that I
was in the psychiatric section of the hospital and a very softly
spoken doctor saw me daily for a chat. I was constantly being
woken up and given tablets of various colours and quantities,
but they did little to alleviate my self-pity. I spent a lot of time
weeping into my pillow and thinking to myself, 'Why should a
thing like this happen to a nice person like me?' After a long
time I was allowed out to visit my children, but I had no sooner
left the hospital than I felt a craving to use the telephone. The
nearest telephone was in the nearest pub, so that I returned to
St Vincent's, in a sorry state, without having glimpsed my
daughters. 'Who's been a naughty boy?' said Sister Mann when

I had been put to bed and sedated even further. I liked that. I preferred to be thought of as a child. Children have only to close their eyes for problems to go away.

Somehow, I began my column for the *Age*, which I could spend the whole week polishing in the seclusion of my cell. I must have been one of the few patients in the psychiatric hospital who was earning a living. But my friends and most of my family had disappeared, or withdrawn from the danger zone. Still, I had other visitors.

Nuns popped their heads round the corner of my door and smiled compassionately. Salvation Army officers looked in and passed the time of day. I was a sitting duck for bores. Couldn't they see I was busy? *That I was an artist?* Hadn't they noticed that I had a portable typewriter on my lap? The fact that it contained a blank page was neither here nor there. Doctors of course were always barging in, and they were very interested in finding out what childhood events had led to my present predicament. I did not mind doctors so much, because it was their job to listen, and I was happy to talk to them endlessly on my favourite subject – myself.

One morning a man in a suit walked straight into my room without knocking, and sat on the end of my bed. I assumed he was a new psychiatrist, and I prepared to launch into another impressive monologue of self-justification, but he cut me short. He explained that he was a prosperous real-estate agent. It occurred to me that he was probably another psychiatric patient, and possibly dangerous. Then he began to talk about himself. His background was not unlike my own; respectable, Melbourne, middle class. His parents had given him everything on a plate, and he had been very successful in his work, but things had started to go wrong. His drinking had slowly and insidiously changed, so that alcohol, once a delightful adjunct to his life, had gradually destroyed him. He told me that only a few years before he too had been a patient in the Dymphna Ward.

I told Tony that I didn't believe a word of his story, hair-raising though it was. He looked far too well, he had made affectionate references to his family and he drove a Mercedes Benz. He then explained that he no longer drank, and that he was a member of something called Alcoholics Anonymous. I winced with embarrassment at the mention of those two words, and at my own plight, lying there helplessly in hospital, a prey to ratbags like this; salesmen and evangelists for some kind of temperance society, or middle-class Salvation Army.

Tony took all this with infuriating good humour. 'How can you be so sure you know how boring an AA meeting is if you have never been to one?' he asked with a reasonableness that I failed to perceive. 'I could, of course, get permission to pick you up from here next Thursday night, take you home for dinner and off to the Sandringham meeting; you could see for yourself then.'

It sounded deathly, and Sandringham was a bayside suburb of Melbourne I had always thought to be mind-numbingly boring. Still, I reflected, with the cunning of the crazy, what could be more boring than this hospital? Here was a simple-minded do-gooder, willing to sit me in his Merc, give me dinner and take me on a suburban drive. There were worse ways of spending an evening, and when his car stopped at the traffic lights, I would only have to turn the handle on the door to be off into the night to liberty . . . *to freedom!*

On the following Thursday evening, between St Vincent's Hospital, Fitzroy, and the Anglican church hall at Sandringham, six miles down the coast, there were green lights all the way.

My experience in that smoke-filled hall that evening, where I saw a number of people that I had known years before whom I had assumed must be long dead, had a profound effect on me. Although I had never thought seriously about Alcoholics Anonymous, I had pictured the gathering in my mind on the journey to Sandringham in Tony's car. A grim prayer meeting of derelicts, probably all wearing army-surplus overcoats and thumping tambourines. Doom, gloom, ginger-ale and Jesus. I was completely unprepared to find a large crowd of well-dressed people, many my own age, and younger, and women – some very pretty – and to hear laughter; gales of it. If you had seen that diverse group of people leaving the hall after their meeting you would not possibly have guessed what they could have had in common. As Lola said to me over coffee later, 'The only thing we've all got in common is that we don't need to drink anymore. If you can't smell us, you can't tell us!'

I wish I could say that my life changed immediately thereafter. In a sense it did, since, after a few meetings – and to Tony's alarm – I became a world authority on Alcoholics Anonymous. At the drop of a hat I would stand up at a meeting and give everyone the benefit of my insights – at length. I discharged myself from St Vincent's Hospital, and I decided that it was time to resume my trade as a comedian; time to do another show. But who would produce it this time? Why not Harry M. Miller, the New Zealand impresario who had attacked my London show in the Australian press? It was a piquant idea, and of course this fellow would jump at the chance of presenting someone like me, and of being photographed shaking hands. It was *delicious!*

Christmas was approaching, and I was still writing my weekly column for the *Age*, but the editor was being difficult over petty things: cutting out my best jokes, censoring my more outspoken material. I was in an irritable frame of mind when I caught the flight to Sydney for my historic *rapprochement* with Mr Miller. While I was in Sydney I thought I might even telephone Roslyn, whom I had rather caddishly abandoned in London, and tell her I was 'on the wagon'. She would be so pleased that she would undoubtedly fly out to Australia on the next plane. The stewardess asked me if I would like a drink. 'No thanks,' I smiled smugly, 'I don't use the stuff.'

'That's funny,' she said, pointing to the little plastic tray that unfolds from the seat in front, 'you've just had one.' I looked at the tray. There was an empty glass, and a miniature bottle of brandy. I must have drunk that automatically, unconsciously, I thought with more curiosity than alarm. An AA phrase came back to me: *It's the first drink that does the damage.* Well, it seemed that I had had the first, so a second would do no harm so long as I kept it at that. I thanked God that I had rediscovered my will-power.

He checked in to the Gazebo Hotel in Kings Cross, a brand-new cylindrical building, rather like a cocktail-shaker. The room was large, with a view of Sydney Harbour, but he telephoned the desk and asked to be moved to a suite. Then he telephoned a florist and ordered lilies, dozens of them. It was so exciting to be back in Sydney, with all those hospitals and doctors a thing of the past. A relief too, not to have to go to those AA meetings any more – he had helped those people enough.

The doorbell rang and a room-service waiter pushed a jingling trolley of champagne and glasses into the suite, followed by another waiter bearing oysters and lobster.

Harry Miller was not returning his calls. It was disgraceful under the circumstances, and he decided that it was demeaning to be always ringing those patronizing secretaries. Who did that shaygets and schlockmeister – he relished the Yiddish epithets – think he was? Instead, he would call around to Miller's apartment in person.

A housekeeper opened the door, Irish, and, he suspected, very slightly drunk. Mr Miller was not at home, she explained, and he couldn't come in. What nonsense. He pushed past and took a comfortable chair in the sitting-room. The pictures looked to him as though they might have been hired, and he mentioned this to the agitated woman who hovered in the background. He demanded a cocktail, but after several of these it was apparent that his unwitting host was not immediately returning.

Back in his suite at the Gazebo, heavy with the intoxicating efflux of too many lilies, he decided to have a party to celebrate the resuscitation of his career, and his new sobriety. He telephoned Patrick White and left an urgent message for him to come to dinner at his hotel. He telephoned his old girlfriend Margaret, who was now married to a charming property tycoon, and invited them both. He called all his old girlfriends. He telephoned everyone he could think of, he even telephoned the Sydney switchboard of AA. Someone there could surely do with a party, he thought.

But nobody came. He nibbled the oysters, drank some more champagne and obscurely wondered how he would ultimately pay for all this, for he had absolutely no money. No more, in fact, than his return ticket to Melbourne, and a chequebook on a bank account that no longer existed. He was sick a few times, unfortunately into the sunken bath, or as near to it as he could manage. It must have been nerves, he reflected. Nervousness from being in the world again after so many months 'inside'. The doorbell rang and a stranger called Guy stood there looking embarrassed. He said he was a member of AA, a pretty new one, too, but he had been told about a phone call, and did he need help? The man in the suite with the lilies, and the trolley laden with half-opened wine bottles, and the debris of several seafood suppers, laughed. 'Do I look as though I need help?' he said.

All night long, and well into the next day Guy sat there watching the man make phone calls, sleep, drink, weep and vomit. A secretary phoned to say that Mr Miller's housekeeper had been insulted yesterday and that Mr Miller never wished to hear from him again. The man then telephoned the florist and ordered twelve dozen gladioli to be delivered immediately to Mrs Nora O'Sullivan, care of Mr Miller's residence.

At some point he went off in a taxi to visit his friend Patrick (see Asides), and at another time Margaret arrived and fed the man with some potent vitamin B compound. Late the next afternoon a psychiatrist turned up and persuaded him to go to hospital, but at the very gates of the institution the man escaped and thumbed down a car-load of students whom he conned into buying him a bottle of vodka. With this in his pocket he somehow found the airport, and was reluctantly admitted on to a flight to Melbourne. There, it seems, some plans had been laid, by persons he did not know, for his admission to a small hospital called Delmont, run by a Dr John Moon. It was a hospital for 'thirsty people'.

After the doctor had been to see him, he was given, at his own importunate request, a large glass of brandy. It was his last drink.

As he sank deeper and deeper into sleep, he felt like a character in a remembered story by Kafka, who, as he dropped into the river Moldau, cried softly: 'Dear parents, I have always loved you, all the same.'

Rest for the Wicked

I WAS AT the very entrance to the departure lounge when I heard my name being called. A small bald man in a fawn suit was running across the terminal waving frantically. As he drew nearer I saw it was Jim Preston, from the Australian Film Development Corporation. He must have been in rather bad shape because he was panting heavily and gulping for air by the time he drew level with me.

'Just one thing, Barry, before you go, and can you pass this on to Bruce when you get to London.' A Qantas steward in his coral-pink blazer was standing only a few inches away looking interested. Jim stepped nearer and lowered his voice: 'I've been talking to the Board, and we all hope there won't be too many . . . er, *colloquialisms* in the fillum.'

I assured him, on my honour, that any 'colloquialisms' that might be in the script would be reduced to an absolute minimum. Jim, having done his duty by the Board and risking coronary occlusion on his dash through the airport, mopped his brow and looked relieved. 'It's not me, Barry,' he explained rather sheepishly. 'But Barry McKenzie does get a bit on the *permissive side* every now and then, and the blokes upstairs – who I have to keep sweet – are keen that we don't do anything to ruin Australia's overseas' image.'

On the long flight back to London I could still picture Jim

Preston's touching expression of simple gratitude. It seemed strange that the Film Development Corporation should have given Beresford and me $250,000 to make a film about Barry McKenzie, and then have last-minute scruples about the propriety of his language! If we cleaned up the dialogue there wouldn't be a movie; but with one foot on the aeroplane and the cash in my pocket I didn't dare tell old Jim that.

It was Bruce Beresford's first big feature, and my first film, not counting 'cameos' in a few movies during the sixties. Bruce had been talking about a Barry McKenzie film for several years, and in the end he had, with a little help from me, actually written a script in which Mrs Everage appeared, as Barry's aunty from Melbourne. I was not totally convinced that Edna would acknowledge such a common nephew, let alone fly with him to England as the script required, but we thought we could make it plausible enough, within the manifold implausibilities of our narrative. Apart from the role of Edna I was also going to play two other parts, a hippie and Dr Meyer de Lamphrey, the psychiatrist on whom Barry chunders.

The drawings of Nicholas Garland for the original comic strip largely governed our casting. My old manager, Clifford Hocking, had, years before, drawn my attention to an uncanny resemblance between Barry McKenzie and a talented Australian singer, coincidentally also called Barry – Barry Crocker – now renowned as the singer of the *Neighbours* theme. Crocker was engaged to play the eponymous Bazza. The cast also included Dennis Price, in his last performance, Dick Bentley, Julie Covington and my old friends Peter Cook and Spike Milligan.

Our producer Philip Adams had rented a small production office in Soho, not very far from the offices of *Private Eye* where Barry McKenzie had been born. It was a strange but exhilarating experience for me to be back in London after such a long absence – and not drinking. I would find myself walking past pubs in which I had formerly spent countless hours, and a great deal of money. Where on earth did I find the time? Or the money? Two years before, after a meeting at Delmont Hospital, I remembered asking Dr Moon a question over which I had long agonized: 'Now that I have stopped drinking, John, what am I going to do with my time?' He had smiled patiently. 'As you get well, a person like you will find more than enough to do. The danger is getting too busy.' But I had persisted: 'What takes the place of alcohol in a man's life?' Dr Moon said, 'How about gratitude, and concern for others?'

At the time, they were the most novel concepts I had ever encountered.

Two years before, I had resumed my acting career in Sydney on a modest scale. It was an anthology of early material, and my old adversary Harry M. Miller produced it. For reasons not totally unconnected with the desire for financial gain, we had succumbed to each other's charm. After the big theatres I had played in the sixties, I now adjusted myself to smaller venues, and rediscovered an intimate connection with the audience. Above all, my confidence, which had been badly shaken, returned.

In Melbourne I got to know my daughters Tessa and Emily again, and we spent weekends together in the countryside not far from Healesville, where I had had so many happy childhood years. Rosalind had divorced me, citing her near-namesake Roslyn, who had bravely returned. Then came the news about the Mckenzie film.

We were at first amazed that a new Government film-funding organization should have chosen, as its first project, a picture based on a comic strip which another Government organization had banned. However it was not for us to question the byzantine workings of the Australian bureaucracy. A few months later when we returned from London with the finished picture, yet another Government department – this time the Censor's Office – gave the film its most restrictive classification. Adams, Beresford and I appealed, and we got to meet the custodians of Australian morality themselves; an unprepossessing trio consisting of a one-armed functionary, a schoolteacher and a retired Olympic athlete. Root-faced, they watched the film again and delightedly reconfirmed their original classification.

Happily, far from sabotaging the success of the film, the Censors only gave it the allure of the forbidden. It enticed into the cinemas of Australia a totally new class of youthful hedonist, who ecstatically identified with McKenzie, imitated his habits and 're-cycled' his dialect.

The world première of *The Adventures of Barry McKenzie* took place in Melbourne and was an immediate success. This, however, was in spite of its reviews, which were almost universally disparaging. Like the Parliamentary broadcasts of the fifties, the film exposed an aspect of Australian speech and behaviour that many preferred to think did not exist. Australian journalists, never renowned for their refinement, sensitivity or temperate habits, went apoplectic with rage and denial at this jolly little picaresque saga. 'The worst Australian film ever made', shrieked Max Harris.

The manufacturers of Foster's Lager, that obscure beverage which the comic strip character had been cheerfully guzzling for nearly a decade, viewed the success of the film with mixed feelings. They had recently spent a large sum of money with an advertising agency to make commercials in which their product was depicted as a rather sophisticated tipple, to be consumed on yachts by men in blazers and girls in pearls. Now here was their beer being drunk directly from the cans, crudely described as 'chilled tubes', and 'ice-cold tinnies'. Worse, its incessant consumption on screen led directly to the film's two major climaxes: Barry's famous chunder attack, and the final scene where a fire at the BBC is extinguished by a group of Australians drinking Foster's Lager and urinating on the flames. For the London première at the Columbia Cinema in Shaftesbury Avenue, we had approached the distributors of Foster's for a couple of free cases of their product to serve VIPs at the party. They refused unequivocally. Our guests drank Carlsberg.

Years later, when Foster's had become available all over Britain, I noticed a television commercial for this frothy cordial. There was no yacht, or blazered gigolo, but a craggy-faced man wearing a wide-brimmed bush hat, exhorting the public, in unmistakably proletarian tones, to 'crack an ice-cold tube'. It had taken the brewery a long time to profit by experience. Alas, it was a profit in which Beresford and I were not invited to share.

When the producer and I had set off for London to make the film, both my parents and my brothers and sister had come to the airport to see me off. It was a touching expression of their new attitude to my work, and perhaps also to me. In the preceding two years we had become closer, and my father had even proudly arranged a special evening at my stage show for all his friends at the Rotary Club.

One evening not long before the film première, I called at our family home in Christowel Street, Camberwell for Sunday tea. As I arrived a dapper figure in a dark suit was climbing into his Mercedes in the driveway. I recognized Sir Clive Fitz, the famous Melbourne cardiologist. He explained that he had just made a professional call on my father, reassuringly adding that things were not serious. But my father looked very grey and older than his sixty-eight years. That night, as I left the house, we embraced. It was the last time.

Neither of my parents came to the film première. I could understand my mother's absence from a widely advertised evening of relentless vulgarity, though she diplomatically declined on the grounds of 'a headache'. My father would have had a wonderful time, but I suspect his last-minute apology was due to some gentle coercion from my mother, who would otherwise have spent the evening alone. He may also have been unduly nervous about critical reaction to the film. My family placed great store on what the papers said. I might have received rave reviews, but if one journalist even *qualified* his praise, my mother would say with a slow shaking of the head:

'I see you didn't get a very good write-up in the *Sun*, Barry.' No reference was ever made to a favourable notice.

A few years later, when I went to New Zealand with a show called *An Evening's Intercourse with Barry Humphries*, we had to cancel the Christchurch season because the local paper refused to publish the word 'Intercourse' on their entertainments page. The result was that the tour was less than financially successful. When I told my mother this news, she brightened perceptibly. 'You see, Barry,' she said triumphantly, 'you're not popular everywhere.' On hearing this, my pianist at the time, Irene Kalinsky, said, 'Are you *sure* your mother isn't Jewish?'

The pompous, outraged reviews of Barry McKenzie were still appearing in the Melbourne press when John Levi telephoned to say that my father had died in the middle of a game of golf, just like Bing Crosby.

With the help of my new manager, Clyde Packer, I launched a new stage show in Sydney called *At Least You Can Say That You've Seen It*. Like many of the titles of my one-man plays, this was inspired by the sort of remark my mother or her friends made after attending the theatre. Again, this contained film segments which Bruce Beresford helped to create. Meanwhile Bruce and I were thinking about a McKenzie sequel, and since the first picture was such a money-spinner (the Film Development Corporation, to its surprise and irritation, recouped its investment five times over) we had no trouble in raising the money. A Brisbane entrepreneur called Reg Grundy backed the sequel and Bruce and I finished the script in a secluded hotel in Tasmania.

Before I left for England I went to see my mother, now alone in the big empty house. 'No rest for the wicked' was a favourite phrase of hers when she was a busy young housewife, invariably uttered with a short self-deprecating laugh. As a child I had found it startling, like a blasphemy against her goodness; worse, really, since spoken against herself. But now that she was widowed, reclusive and increasingly crippled with arthritis and a curious form of self-starvation, I still occasionally heard her use the same words, but this time they described poignantly, her loneliness and guilt.

Flying back to London once more, I took a detour to Prague to visit my old friend Jiří Mucha, the Czech writer, and son of Alphonse Mucha, the great exponent – if not the creator – of the art-nouveau style in Paris at the turn of the century. After his release in 1957 from six years' imprisonment in a Stalinist labour camp, he devoted much of his time to the rehabilitation of his father's artistic reputation, so that those floriated and tendrilled posters, many originally commissioned by Sarah Bernhardt, became a commonplace of the sixties, decorating psychedelic record sleeves and the boudoirs of teeny-boppers.

Until his death in 1991, Jiří lived in some style in a thirteenth-century house near the Castle, surrounded by his father's pictures, sculptures by Rodin and a harmonium that had once belonged to Gauguin. Always hospitable, this dear and loyal friend has been unfairly described elsewhere as an 'orgiast', but if a love of youth, a speculative intellect and a generous desire to accommodate the tastes of his guests, however whimsical, is orgiastic, then so be it. It is true that sometimes in the darker moments of Prague's recent history before the liberation of his country – which happily he lived to see – he choreographed piquant gatherings of the city's Golden Youth for the amusement of visitors; and it was into one of these that I had, it seemed, stumbled late one evening, as I returned from a concert of Mozart and Martinů. As I mounted the stairs, the house seemed deserted, and on entering the large drawing-room I found it to be in pitch darkness, so that I had to feel my way cautiously across its length to get to my bedroom. Slowly, I became aware that the room was not empty. There was a palpable warmth, a faint susurration and a musky atmosphere suggesting invisible human presences; and here and there, as my eyes became accustomed to the intense and velvet darkness, I saw the pulsing glow of a cigarette. Just as I was reaching forward to touch what I estimated to be the panelled doors that would lead me to the chamber beyond I froze in my tracks, as a hand – warm, inviting and insistent – closed around my left ankle.

Barry McKenzie Holds His Own, starring Barry Crocker and Donald Pleasence, was, very loosely, a vampire story set in Transylvania, where the vampires, for the first time in the history of this genre, were Communists, determined to kidnap the Queen of England in order to attract tourist dollars. Edna Everage is mistaken for the Queen, and Barry McKenzie for Prince Philip. Soon after this the complex plot lapsed from plausibility; due, no doubt, to the insidious Tasmanian influences that surrounded its writing. There was a funny scene in the film when Edna, Barry and his twin brother, the Reverend Kevin McKenzie ('Kev the Rev'), visit Paris and meet Colonel 'the Frog' Lucas, an Australian intellectual long expatriate in France. This bereted, goateed and French loaf-toting personage – played by Dick Bentley – was based on Alister Kershaw, a Sydney writer whom I had met on my hectic visit to Paris years before with Arthur Boyd. Barry's rare filet mignon ('just knock off its horns, wipe its arse and bung it on the plate, *garçon*') is drugged by the Transylvanians, and 'calls Ruth' from the top of the Eiffel Tower. Although this film did not attract the audiences of its predecessor, it is memorable for this scene alone. The minor character of a drunken film critic was movingly played by Clive James, an author who has had the acumen to distribute his reminiscences over several volumes.

But at the end of this uneven film there was a moment which could truly be described as Epiphanic. It is the moment when Edna and Barry return triumphantly to Australia after their adventures. The script demanded that they be met at the airport by the Prime Minister of Australia, and we had difficulty finding an actor with sufficient grandeur to impersonate the

Right Honorable Gough Whitlam. I chanced a phone call to Canberra and Mr Whitlam himself, and his wife Margaret, agreed to appear as themselves in the climactic scene. As Edna emerges from Customs she is stupefied to behold the Whitlams awaiting her with open arms. As she fell into an embrace with the Prime Minister, Gough improvised: 'Arise, *Dame Edna*!' he intoned, as the camera rolled until Beresford cried 'cut'. Edna obviously took this accolade as a legitimate citation, and has ever since appropriated the title. The Prime Minister was later heard to mutter to an aide, 'She certainly picked up on that one.'

Not long afterwards, Whitlam's Labor Government ignominiously fell and, after the two Barry McKenzie pictures, Bruce Beresford, the future director of *Driving Miss Daisy*, dismissed as a director of vulgar comedy, found it impossible to get work in pictures for the next two years.

One afternoon I found myself a passenger in a London taxi travelling from Chelsea to Hampstead, and as we turned into Park Lane I had a sudden and curious impulse to see the house in Mayfair where I had lived five years before, at the nadir of my career. The driver, surprisingly, protested that Park Street was well off the direct route to Hampstead, but on my insistence he turned right at the Dorchester and into Mayfair. I cannot explain why it then seemed to me so important that I glimpse once more the uninteresting house in which I had so briefly lived, but as we neared it I remembered with a shudder the shattered Gallé, and my old pictures. Most of them were now back in Melbourne, at Rosalind's house; all except one, I recalled, a big oil I had bought in the early sixties from an art student in New Zealand, that had never turned up in the shipment. Lost forever.

Now we were in Park Street and travelling north. I leaned forward as we passed the Grosvenor House, and there ahead, on the right, I saw scaffolding outside my former flat. There was a pile of rubble on the pavement also, and I realized that this gloomy abode was at last being renovated. Just as the taxi drew level with number 62, two workmen strode out of the door, holding between them a large unframed canvas, the painted surface of which directly confronted my approaching cab. *It was my picture!* At that instant the two men tossed the painting on to the pile of rubble and went back inside. Several yards further on, at my urgent command, the taxi screamed to a halt and I leapt out, ran back to the building site and entered the derelict house. 'Where did you find that picture?' I said to the men. I must have been rather wild-eyed, because they looked at me oddly. 'That's our Gainsborough, isn't it, Terry?' laughed one of the men. 'We found her flat on her face on top of that wardrobe.' Terry chimed in, 'It's our table, too, Guv, we've been having our tea off it for the last few weeks, haven't we, Len? You can see the rings.' '*It's mine*,' I blurted. 'I used to live here once.' The men looked at each other sceptically, but I led them out into the street and pointed to my name on a torn label on the canvas stretcher. Then I showed them my passport. A decent tip, and the picture and I were back in the cab, and I vowed, then and there, that in future I would pursue as many impulses of that kind as I possibly could.

In Melbourne not long afterwards, in yet another taxi, I experienced again that mysterious prompting to diverge from the normal route, which on that day took me from the airport to my mother's home. Motoring down an unfamiliar street I saw, outside a terraced house, a shingle that bore the legend ART GALLERY in sign-writers' gothic. I stopped the cab, got out and, still yielding to impulse, knocked on the door. It was opened by a bearded young man who, when he saw me, stepped back with a gasp. 'Who told you to come here?' he asked rather rudely. 'Is this some kind of joke?' 'I just arrived from London this morning,' I replied calmly. 'I have never been in this street before, but I like pictures and I saw your shingle.' The young man looked confused. 'But I've just put it up. I mean to say, I've just opened the gallery this morning, you're my first customer.' 'Perhaps that's lucky,' I said. 'What can you show me?' But he was shaking his head and looking at me oddly. 'I believe I know who you are,' he said at length, 'and it's not quite true to say that you're my *very* first customer, because a man was here an hour ago who sold me a picture that might interest you.' He was leading the way up a narrow staircase, but said over his shoulder, 'You'll see what I mean when you see the picture, Mr Humphries, but I still don't believe nobody put you up to this!' Together we entered a bare, recently decorated room. One large painting stood against the wall. It was a picture which I knew had been missing since 1958, and had long been thought lost or destroyed. When I recovered my composure I asked him his price, which was not, under the circumstances, extortionate. I paid it and, still in a great agitation of spirit, took the picture home. It was a portrait in oils by Clifton Pugh, of myself. It is the frontispiece to this book.

In 1976, at the end of my Australian tour of *At Least You Can Say You've Seen It*, I took my daughters on a long holiday to California and Mexico. On my return I began living with a gifted young surrealist artist called Diane Millstead. Some months later she joined me in London where Michael White, the wunderkind of West End producers, had invited me, as Peter Bridge had done in the sixties, to present my Australian show.

This time it worked. At the unusual hour of eleven p.m., on Tuesday, 16 March 1976, at the Apollo Theatre, Shaftesbury Avenue, *Housewife-Superstar!* opened. It was an abridged version of *At Least You Can Say . . .*, with the addition of a new character called Les Patterson, the self-proclaimed Cultural Attaché to the Court of Saint James's.

Les had been invented in the previous year when I had ventured once more 'to do my act' at a Sydney football club. I still had grim memories of the Granville Returned Servicemen's Club on a far-off morning in 1956. But Clyde Packer urged me to invent a new character suited to the rougher milieu of a

Sydney Leagues Club. I decided that Les, with his nicotine-stained and snaggled teeth, padded stomach, powder-blue suit and stacked Engelbert Humperdinck shoes, could pose as the Club Secretary, and could in that way deflect possible audience hostility towards the next act – Edna.

Les Patterson was, perhaps, an oblique and long-delayed revenge on the Club Secretary at Granville who had, all those years before, thrown me a damp and grudging fiver, and shown me the door.

Leslie Colin Patterson inherited the Language of Barrington Bradman Bing McKenzie, although his discourse is today a great deal closer to that of real people; especially the more eloquent and verbally inventive Australian Politician, although, needless to say, Les Petterson's cheerful vulgarity is condemned on all sides in his homeland and is dismissed as a scurrilous anachronism. Les is by turns long-winded and laconic, and he has a knack of stating the obvious at length, which is particularly Australian.

Soon after the Berliner Helmut Newton, a fugitive from Nazism, arrived in Melbourne, he and his wife June were in bed one morning reading the newspaper. It was a warm day and the curtains were open on their ground-floor city flat, affording curious pedestrians a glimpse of the bedroom. Two men walked past, glanced in the window and stopped in their tracks. One said to the other:

'Jeez! Look at that fuckin' man and that fuckin' sheila lyin' in that fuckin' bed, reading the fuckin' newspaper!'

After this reflection they continued on their way with great merriment. Certainly the pedestrian's observation appears, at first sight, to be merely a brutal statement of fact, but it is more subtle than it seems, for it conceals an acrostic message; an oblique speculation on how Mr and Mrs Newton might, under the circumstances, more appropriately occupy themselves. Helmut remembers this as his first baptism into Australian culture. Without doubt it is a classic example of the art which conceals art in our vernacular.

In *Housewife-Superstar!* Les entered through the audience, as Edna had in the late sixties, and as he blundered on to the London stage on the first night, I realized, by the hush that had fallen over the audience, that they all believed Les to be a genuine Australian diplomat, the worse for liquor!

To the padding which constituted his false stomach I had added a large upholstered phallus, the contours of which were unmistakably discernible beneath the taut fabric of the diplomat's stained blue trouser. As Les rambled on discursively on cultural topics, I noticed women in the audience slowly becoming aware of the pendulous yet frisky protuberance which extended to a point only a few inches above the diplomat's knee. Deep within Les Patterson, I hoped at least one highbrow critic, whatever he thought of the show, might mention the persisting influence of Aristophanes' *Lysistrata* – or at least Brecht's Mr Punt.

Yet for all his gross ventripotence, some women love Les Patterson. His involuntary habits of projectile expectoration do not dismay them, for as he says: 'Don't worry, ladies, Les Patterson's saliva is *safe*!' One evening a very attractive, if chemically elated, young woman sat sprawling in the middle of the front row, legs akimbo. 'Spit on me, Les,' she cried imploringly, 'spit on me!'

It was strange, after all those years, to find London audiences laughing just as loudly, and in just the same places, as audiences in Melbourne. The penny, it seemed, had dropped at last. Soon there was a show album, and, thanks to my old publisher friend Ken Thomson, *Dame Edna's Coffee Table Book* was launched upon the world. 'Is it *meant* to be vulgar?' asked Harold Acton ingenuously.

After the show had been running in the West End for several weeks, *Vogue* magazine, I was told, wished to interview me, and they were sending a photographer to meet me at the theatre. When I turned up, as usual slightly late to the appointment, I was considerably taken aback to see that the photographer was already waiting at the stage door. It was Lord Snowdon.

Remembering a distant and acutely embarrassing incident, I effusively apologized for my lateness. But he was exquisitely polite. He didn't mind in the least, he said, because it gave him a chance to think about the pictures he was planning to take. 'I'd like to take up most of your day on this job, if you can spare the time,' he said. 'Perhaps we could break somewhere for lunch?' I told him I knew a good Italian restaurant near the theatre, and would be delighted if he would be my guest. 'Oh no, thank you,' replied Lord Snowdon. 'I want you to be *my* guest. There is an excellent French restaurant I know in Addison Road, Holland Park, called Chez Moi. I wonder if you know it?'

He gave me a broad Royal Doulton smile, and I think he might have even winked. Otherwise, no subsequent reference was ever made to that evening, so long ago, when for two minutes I had been his Mother.

Talking Back

F ANNY, MY EDITOR, was briefly out of her office, and I noticed, upside-down on her strewn desk, a letter, still warm and gently undulant, freshly extruded from her groaning facsimile machine. I perceived that it was from her Australian counterpart, and concerned this book. Unhesitatingly, I read it. '... Thank you for sending me those sample chapters of Humphries' book. It is perhaps more serious than I imagined, but just as self-centred as I expected ...'

I wish I knew how to give an account of my life that was less egocentric, but the art eludes me. Perhaps it is because, in the theatre, I am always a one-man band; my supporting cast is the audience.

Throughout the seventies and the eighties I continued to work in the same vein, commuting between England and my homeland, without ever being quite sure where I really belonged. In all my travels, but especially in Portugal or Tasmania, I went on searching for that familiar fronded gateway, the tunnel of trees, and beyond, in the folding hills by the still, argent sea, a house that seemed to say: 'Here, live your life out!'

In 1977 Michael White decided to present *Housewife-Superstar!* in New York, in association with Arthur Cantor, a fine producer, especially of solo performers, but a man, none the less, who could be said to give Melancholy a bad name. The theatre selected for my off-Broadway debut was Theatre Four, a long way from the beaten track. I asked Mr Cantor why he felt this was such an ideal venue, and he disarmingly replied: 'The Boys in the Band was a hit here for years. It's a good theatre for fag shows.'

But Mr Cantor poured a great deal of energy and optimism into the promotion of my show, and with Brian Thomson's sets, help from Ian Davidson in adapting the London production and moral support from Diane Millstead, I began to feel encouraged. The previews went wonderfully well. Stephen Sondheim forced all his friends to attend, and Charles Addams sat in the front row – and laughed. On the first night everyone was suitably embarrassed by Les Patterson, who had now become Australia's Cultural Attaché to the White House. Edna's beady eye fell on several choice victims, including the inimitable Earl McGrath, former president of the Rolling Stones' record company, art dealer, *flâneur*, wit, host *extraordinaire* and, in 1992, Dame Edna's godson.

After the show there was the traditional party at Sardi's, where the mood was cautiously ebullient. An hour or so later I went upstairs to read the notices. Arthur Cantor's offices were conveniently above the restaurant, but, when I opened the door and saw Michael White and Mr Cantor slumped silently over the early editions, I knew the worst. So did the guests at the party. By the time I had gone downstairs again, the restaurant was deserted.

A Jaffa is a popular Australian confectionery; a small sphere of solid chocolate, coated with a brittle orange-flavoured shell. At the time of my New York débâcle, an Adelaide newspaper carried the following banner headline:

BAZZA GOES DOWN IN NEW YORK LIKE A JAFFA DOWN THE LIFTWELL OF THE EMPIRE STATE

For its imaginative ingenuity, and as a classic illustration of Australian *Schadenfreude*, I was almost proud to have inspired it.

Oscar & Rupert

A sketch by the author

Diane Millstead and I were married in June 1979 and in the ensuing years she presented me with two wonderful sons, Oscar and Rupert. The marriage lasted nine years. Now I am very happily remarried to the writer and actress Lizzie Spender. My daughter Tessa is a successful young actress, and Emily is an artist now living in Melbourne. (See forthcoming volumes.) I still paint cheerful landscapes in oils, during rare holidays abroad, except that I am never quite sure what is abroad.

A few doors from my dentist's surgery in Mayfair I had for several years noticed a doorbell above which was the label: Spoliansky. Could it, I wondered, belong to Mischa Spoliansky, the Russian-Berliner who had written the first songs to bring fame to Marlene Dietrich – the composer whose insouciant music had, more than Kurt Weill's pervaded the whole Weimar period? It was. During our brief friendship we spoke of collaborating on a *Songspiel* for Dame Edna, but this gentle, cordial and humourous man died in 1985, at the age of ninety-one. Three years later Sacheverell Sitwell also died, a very different artist, but one whose rich creative life spanned the same period as Spoli's, and who like him, had remained artistically prodigal since his early fame in the far-off twenties.

A far cry from Mischa Spoliansky and the *Goldenen Zwanzige Jahre* is Mr Barry Manilow, the popular singer, who has expressed a desire to write a musical comedy based on the memoirs of Dame Edna. It seems strange that I am now making television programmes for the National Broadcasting Corporation of America, and planning new and energetic amusements in the land where, not long ago, I was convinced that my act was 'too British'. But I believe, as Gabriel Dalzant once wisely said to Vernon Lee, that 'one must be prepared to begin life many times afresh'. If I were granted one wish, I would ask to be a cocktail pianist.

Some of my friends are now retiring; a few, like me, remarrying, and others, sadly, have died. Since my father's death, my mother had increasingly withdrawn from life, though she still enjoyed family holidays in Mornington. She and I had long and affectionate international telephone conversations; her brain was active, and her sense of humour remained as sharp as ever. But the day we brought little Oscar to meet his grandmother for the first time stays in my memory. When we arrived on the back terrace of Christowel Street, my mother could be seen through the french doors in her usual chair, listening to a portable radio. As we entered, she pointed to the radio and with her finger to her lips made a gesture of silence. It was a 'Talk-back' programme, in which listeners are invited to contribute their views on a topic dictated by the announcer, and on this occasion, by a macabre coincidence, the topic was me. In the fruity tones adopted universally by all afternoon radio 'personalities', Patrick Tennyson was asking his female listeners whether or not they thought Barry Humphries was 'selling Australia short overseas'. Then came the phone calls, as one by one the ladies of Melbourne expressed their opinions.

'I've never seen any of Brian Humphrey's shows, Pat, and I don't want to. Australia is a beautiful country, and we don't need people like that Dame Edith and that horrible Len Peterson giving the world the wrong idea.' And so it went on.

My mother was listening intently, and only once looked up at us all. She was obviously quite distressed. 'You see, Barry,' she said, 'that's what they think of you.'

I felt helpless. I went into my father's old den, and after looking in the phone book I dialled the number of the radio station.

'This is Dame Edna here, I want to be put straight through to Mr Tennyson.' I was. I was on the air.

'Is that you, Pat, darling? It's Edna here. I *adore* your show, especially today. How I agree with all those wonderful women who are ringing you up. I know Barry Humphries better than anyone, and he is dragging Australia through the mud as often as he can, for base financial gain. The millions who laugh at his shows should be ashamed of themselves, and I HAPPEN TO KNOW THAT HIS MOTHER AGREES WITH ME!'

Trembling, I put down the phone and returned to the sun-room. As I entered, my mother switched off the radio and shot me a dry smile, as if to say '*touché*'. Then, as though nothing had happened, she held out her arms towards Oscar and said: 'Don't just stand there, I want to see my grandson.'

In 1985, in a private hospital in Melbourne, my mother died. I was in London, and unable to fly home in time. Shortly before the end I spoke to her on the telephone. Later, she said to her nurse: 'Look at the beautiful carnations Barry has given me.' But the nurse could see no flowers.

Twenty years ago, when I returned to London sober, I walked one sunny morning down Lower Regent Street to meet my old friend Paul Oppenheimer for lunch at his club. Half-way down the hill, I had to stop and sit on the doorstep of a shop. I had the most extraordinary sensation that something was seriously wrong, and I was convinced that I was having some kind of heart-attack. For a while I sat there, panic-stricken, breathing deeply and wondering when I was going to pass out. In front of me the legs of pedestrians endlessly scissored past. Which leg, I wondered, would I grab, and cry to its owner: 'Quick, for God's sake, get a doctor! On this sunny day in London, I am dying.' But I did not do that; I sat a while longer on my doorstep until I decided I was not dying at all. With a rush of joy I found at last the label to my strange and alarming condition. I realized I was happy.

Santa Fe, 9 May 1992

ASIDES

from
Colin Munro
Bruce Grant
C. K. Stead
Patrick White
John Betjeman
Julian Jebb

Dada days

W**HEN BARRY WAS** at Melbourne University doing a combined Law and Arts Degree he stood for SRC. His election speech in the Public Lecture Theatre was an extraordinary theatrical event. Immaculately attired, he appeared in what might be described as his persona of 'Dr Humphries'. Behind him on the dais sat a committee of friends wearing academic gowns and 'Tid' masks, large and vaguely circular disks of white card on which were drawn the childishly minimal features, dots for eyes and a single line each for nose and mouth, of a variety of cretinously vacant faces. Each performed throughout the speech some infantile repetitive task, such as the piling up and toppling of children's blocks. A toaster, despite audience protests, filled the theatre with the pungent fumes of burning toast. One of his election purposes seemed to be the deregulation of medical services. He described how a 'little tot' had written to his organization and had been supplied by post with surgical instruments which enabled her to perform a very delicate operation on her mother's eye. Humphries also advocated the rebuilding of the University 'along the present lines of Wilson Hall'. The speech, it must be explained, occurred shortly after the fire which had left Wilson Hall a smoking ruin. Referring to his well-known artistic talents, he admitted that he had received many requests to execute a painting before an audience. An ancient framed oil was then produced, and Humphries proceeded to chip it to pieces with an axe. At the end of the speech, perhaps fearing audience reprisals, Dr Humphries appeared to experience some kind of seizure, took pills and fled the hall to be whisked away in a waiting car. Despite the pure Dada of this performance, he attracted a large number of votes.

Another University event was the Dada Exhibition. This was held in the Women Graduates Lounge, rooms of the old Union which were transformed by the renovations of the sixties. I recall three of the exhibits. One was a glass retort whose bowl had been filled with cooked spaghetti coloured with blue dye. It was entitled 'Spaghetti Head'. Another was a drawing in which the letters of the word BOY had been arranged so that the inverted Y formed the body and legs of a stick figure, the O the head and the B, on its side with slightly projecting stem, the genitals. It was entitled 'What we are'. The third consisted of a large box containing old books with worthy titles, such as *The Book of Beauty*. Over them had been poured a tin of thick vegetable soup. The caption read: 'I was reading these books when I felt sick'.

Barry was at this time producing a variety of Dada works, notably the '-scapes' in various media. Cakescapes, Forkscapes, Shoescapes and Rubbishscapes. There was also a project, perhaps never actually realized, for abstract sculptures, even an entire exhibition of them, constructed from broken glass. Long, dangerous slivers of glass were to protrude from these works, and a trained nurse was to be in attendance to give first aid to viewers mutilated by too close an inspection.

An exhibition in which many of these varieties of artefact appeared was held at the Victorian Artists Society Gallery. The show was opened by the artist himself at twenty-minute intervals throughout the first afternoon. One exhibit, shown in this or more probably the University exhibition, caused consider-able controversy. It consisted of a beer bottle around whose neck was an Old Melburnian tie. The title was 'Old Fool's

Tie'. As a result Barry was evicted from the Old Boys' Association. He claimed at the time that he had appeared, dressed in a pin-striped suit and homburg, and bearing a calf-bound edition of Burke's *Trials*, at the offices of the Association, where he threatened to subpoena the minutes of the decisive committee meeting.

No account of Barry's extra-curricular activities at the University would be complete without mention of the Dada Revue. This was a lunch-hour performance in the Union Theatre, and in many of its sketches the distinctive form of his later satire was already present. There was, I recall, a long, excruciatingly funny conversation about nothing between two solemn suburbanites, both named Jim. There was also the notorious final sketch, later to be included in the 'Wubbo Recording'. My memories of the stage performance are now inseparable from the recorded version.

The scene is a mission station somewhere in Bengal. The Reverend J. Big and his wife, Mrs Tum, are at breakfast. The minister reads from his newspaper descriptions of heart-rending incidents arising from the current famine. There is a picture of an old woman being eaten alive by a starving child. Suddenly Mrs Tum (played by Barry) interrupts him to shriek: 'I couldn't care less!' Before her on the table for some reason there is an incongruous pile of vegetables, cake and raw meat. In a kind of paroxysm of jubilation at her own sufficiency, she springs to her feet and begins to pelt not only her husband but also the audience with the contents of the table.

This was too much, even for the most devoted supporters of Dadaist subversion. The audience began to assail the stage.

Barry, fleeing to the dressing-rooms to hide from attack, euphorically quoted historical precedents for such events in the original Dada movement.

Colin Munro, 12.10.91

A Bunyip comes to Melbourne

The Bunyip and the Satellite, which can be enjoyed for only a few more days at the National Theatre, must be added to the growing list of original work which is contributing to Australia's theatrical renaissance.

The Bunyip, the strange likeable character which Mr Humphries presents with such sensitive artistry, is the Australian relation of the Harlequin, Pierrot, Joey, Touchstone and even Lear's Fool. I think we should rejoice at this. We might easily have had as our national Fool a swaggering bandicoot or a Koala footballer.

Here instead is a delicate hero. A courteous, gay, troubled creature who admires wit and intelligence and has no material ambition except the discovery of his identity. It is the touch of pathos – the sad, white face framed with a gumleaf wreath, the essential loneliness – which gives the Bunyip the power to inspire us with feelings that are too deep for laughter. This is not only good theatre, which can never afford to forget the heart of man. It also represents a fresh Australian line of heroes.

Barry Humphries has a voice with a range and melodic sharpness of a violin; he sings as he looks – angular, uncomfortable, determined on cheerfulness.

He also dances. Jean-Louis Barrault said that for grace, actors should walk 'with the pit of their stomachs'. Mr Humphries walks with the top of his head, as graceless as a pair of hedge-clippers.

Bruce Grant, *The Age*, January 1958

A Kiwi remembers

I FIRST SAW Barry Humphries on stage in the Phillip Street Theatre in Sydney in 1956 or 1957, and got to know him in Auckland in the early sixties after we had both come back from our first visits to London. Barry's second wife, Rosalind Tong, a dancer, was an Aucklander. Sometimes Barry would put on a lunch-hour show at the University, which was where I first encountered the then rather down-market but already very funny Edna Everage. There was an evening when Barry and Rosalind took my wife and me to a sort of teen-club under the street where there was a band and dancing. We were all aged about thirty and felt out of place; my inclination was to be inconspicuous, but with Barry Humphries for company it was impossible. The Beatles hadn't yet begun the fashion that allowed men to grow their hair long; and in Australia and New Zealand the short-back-and-sides was almost a moral obligation, as was the jacket and tie. Barry's hair was long, partly as a protest (his headmaster in Melbourne was given to saying, 'Long hair is dirty hair'), and partly because at that time this was the hair that came out from under Edna's hat. He wore an overcoat and no tie, and looked rather like a tramp, and we hadn't been long at our table before he had made everyone aware of his presence. When the band began something with a strong beat he suddenly launched himself backwards into the crowd.

His dance was extraordinary, jerky, almost spastic, yet perfectly rhythmical, with something of that physicality with which Dame Edna still reminds her audience that she's really a big energetic male. Someone shouted angrily at Barry, calling him 'Jesus'; there was a precarious moment in which the mood might have turned hostile; and then by some magic of facial expression he swung it entirely in his favour. The crowd pressed around him clapping rhythmically and cheering him on, while Barry, still leaning backward in his dance and with the bewildered expression of someone not quite sane, but benign, danced with prodigious vigour. When he sat down I felt as if I'd watched someone go over Niagara Falls in a barrel and survive.

Not long after, I wrote a fantasy called 'A Fitting Tribute' about a character I called Julian Harp, who solves the problem of engineless flight. The figure of Julian Harp was modelled on Barry Humphries, and the scene I've described . . . occurs in the story, as does Humphries's remark to me that at night the timber houses of Auckland look like lanterns. The story first appeared in the *Kenyon Review* in the United States, and soon afterwards was translated into Spanish, where it appeared in *Reviste de Occidente*, and into Hungarian for an anthology of 'the world's best stories'. It seemed to me significant that literary persons in a Fascist and a Communist state of that time should both seize on it. New Zealand and Australia were political democracies: but the sense of moral repression, of the crushing weight of propriety, was extraordinarily strong. Barry Humphries's outrageousness – his dandyism, his Dadaism, his various stage personae – were all aspects of the one rebellion against that oppression. Whatever he has become since, that is where he begins.

C. K. Stead, 1990

A letter
from Patrick White

Patrick White to Geoffrey and Ninette Dutton, 27.7.70

... A few days ago Barry Humphries suddenly came up on the
telephone (it turned out he had got my silent number from that
strumpet at the British Council!). He was in Sydney, in a state,
after blotting his copybook in several places. The *Age* had
given him the sack after he had written a column sending up
the rich Melbourne Jews who celebrate Christmas. He had then
rushed (perhaps even escaped) from his hospital in Melbourne
to come to Sydney to ask Harry Miller to take him on. Harry
had given him an appointment at the office but before this was
due, Barry had burst into Harry's flat in Harry's absence and
insulted the housekeeper by saying rude things about the paintings and furniture. According to Barry he was confused by his
first day of freedom after a year of hospital. According to the
housekeeper, he was drunk. Next day he rang up the secretary
and insulted her too, according to Harry; amongst other things
he said, 'I'm trying to get in touch with a friend who's become
an acquaintance: a Christian writer called Patrick White.'
Barry's call to me was to see whether I would try to make the
peace with Harry M. We had Barry out here to lunch. He

arrived an hour late, after two more telephone calls announcing himself, and a taxi-driver at the door to ask whether I still expected to see Barry Humphries. Barry, in a grazier's hat and monocle, was looking rather strange. He says he has been 'weaned off one or two toxic breasts' but I felt he must have got on to at least one of them again on his way to Martin Road. I'd be most interested to see his medical report. He still has flashes of great brilliance, but moments of despair, one feels. Very difficult to assess. He is such an actor one can't decide when the acting has stopped. I spoke to Harry Miller on the phone, and he agreed to talk to Barry. Whether he did, I don't know, and I didn't feel strong enough to ring Barry and ask. He was staying at the Gazebo, in spite of being on the rocks financially, and was planning a party for the following night to which so far he had invited Sculthorpe, Peter Coleman, and Peter Scrivener. He said: 'I suppose you wouldn't care to come?' I didn't feel I wanted to. Nor do I like to think what must have happened to Barry when faced with the toxicity.

Patrick White to Ronald Waters, 8.1.71

[After an abbreviated account of the visit to the flat and the call to the office:]
How insulting the insults were, I don't know. Both the house-keeper and the secretary told Harry that Barry was drunk. Barry comes here and wants me to make the peace. I, in my Martita Hunt role, try to do so. At least I rang Harry and told him he ought to see Barry: although he's crazy, he's a genius and one can't dismiss him just like that. Harry said he would see him. Since then I haven't had a word from either of them. I expect both are angry with me: Harry because I tried to make him do something. Barry because Harry either made no attempt to get in touch, or did and gave him the brush-off.

A programme note by
John Betjeman

I**T WAS IN** the British Council office at Sydney that I first heard of Barry Humphries. Someone there had his records and I played them over to myself dozens of times. I had already realized, as anyone who visits that marvellous and varied continent must realize, that Australia has an exciting and vigorous culture of its own which has more to give the Old World than it can take from it. Musicians, artists and writers from Australia have won international fame and when one considers the size of its population, the number is disproportionately large. It would be invidious to mention names, but you all know them. Barry Humphries is one who, I have no hesitation in saying, will become internationally famous, because he is an artist with words, imagination and mimicry who belongs to the great tradition of music hall and theatre.

I was surprised to find that in his own country he was regarded as a satirist by some people. To me he seems much more than that. He shares the tears of things, as well as the laughter. He has created in Sandy Stone a character for whom one can feel affection and sympathy, while laughing at him at the same time. He is a sort of verbal and Australian Charlie

Chaplin. He is also a figure whose prototype can be found in most parts of the Western World, the decent, honest, kind-hearted but deeply conventional man who takes life as it comes.

Sandy Stone is only one side of Barry Humphries' genius. He can see into the home thoughts and home life of the average housewife or teenage daughter, or tough young man who is little different in England from the Australian counterpart.

There is besides all this the brilliant subtlety with which Barry Humphries portrays his characters and situations. Not a word is wasted. Not a point is missed. He hits the nail on the head every time and his phrases linger in the mind for months after one has heard them.

As soon as I returned to England I made a point of searching him out where he was performing in a successful musical, *Oliver*. I was not surprised to find he was longing to return to his own country, for his inspiration is local and derives from Melbourne in particular. He knew, of course, all about the artists and writers I admired, and we had in common a liking for artists of the nineties and Edwardian times – Conder, Phil May, Streeton, Tom Roberts and the early McCubbin, as well as modern Australian artists and writers, and we shared an enthusiasm for English music hall with its local and broad jokes and moving songs with memorable choruses.

Here is no satirist. Here is a great artist who comes from a country which has grown up and can look back at itself with amusement and affection.

Over in England I thought, in my enthusiasm for all things Australian, that the genius of Barry Humphries might be a bit too local and specialized for my friends who had not been to Australia. Not at all. A course of Sandy Stone enchanted them and has made at least fifty people who have heard the records I have played to them want to go to Australia. That is because of the note of affection implicit in them.

John Betjeman, 1962

Julian Jebb on
Just a Show

'THIS IS the most expensive finale in London, Peter Bridge
will go mad,' shrieks Edna Everage nightly from the
stage of the Fortune Theatre as she hurls armfuls of gladioli into
the auditorium. On a good night she reaches the gallery and,
when all the absurd phallic blooms have found their place,
Edna leads the audience in the Gladioli Song. This extraordinary woman, a vulture in bird-of-paradise clothing, exhorts
the audience to wave, thrust and tremble their gladdies with an
almost spiritual fanaticism. This finale is not only the most
expensive in London: it is one of the strangest and funniest
quarters of an hour you could spend inside a theatre.

Edna's creator is Barry Humphries, a young Australian who
reverses the saw about the prophet not being honoured in his
own land. He has recently returned from a six-month tour of
Australia where he played to capacity houses in theatres nearing
up to 2,000. Now he is playing the same theatre, and under the
same director, Eleanor Fazan, as *Beyond the Fringe*. In spite of a
note in the programme of *Just a Show*, which says he was born
on 'the eve of Munich', he is 35 years old, the eldest son of a
prosperous Melbourne builder. He recalls that the atmosphere
of gross philistinism at his school encouraged him to champion

the cause of minor artists whom he might find precious today –
Denton Welch was one. His image of England came, somewhat
surprisingly, from the music of Vaughan Williams and Delius
rather than from the poets and novelists. The cultural wallpaper
of his own childhood was the Australian commercial radio
stations.

After school he became a repertory actor and played one of
the tramps in *Waiting for Godot*. Beckett is a very clear
influence on the monologues which he started doing in revue
and soon put on records. The most extraordinary of these is
called *Sandy Agonistes*. A drunk old man (one suspects that he
is drunk and old and a man, but the voice is sexless and
ageless with disappointment) speaks a litany of names for
nearly half an hour. Patent medicines, breakfast foods, old film
stars, snatches of popular songs, Melbourne suburban stations,
follow one upon another by every conceivable associative process. The final effect of this poem is anthropological: it is as if
the listener had been present at the construction and decay of a
mythical society.

There are two distinct sides to Barry Humphries's genius as a
performer. The dionysiac reaches its apotheosis in the gladdie-
hurling finale of *Just a Show*; and the introverted in *Sandy
Stone's Wake*. Edna totters dementedly from side to side of the
stage, released at last from the pent-up fears which haunt
Sandy and the other pathetic creations. The doomed farce of
parents' relationships with their children is the chief source of
his inspiration. Rex Lear, lonely and drunk, boasts about how
much his ungrateful daughter's wedding reception has cost
him. Edna is hysterically refined in her vindictiveness against
her son Brucie's mixed marriage (to an English girl). Even little
Debbie Thwaite, the plucky Earl's Court girl speaking her
amazing aria about the comparative prices of meat in London
and Melbourne, is gripped by the fear that Mummy or Daddy
will suddenly turn up. In Barry Humphries's world there seem
to be only two absolutes, family life and death, and only the
latter can free one from the former.

In England he is probably best known as the author of 'Barry McKenzie', the scatological comic strip in *Private Eye*. The fictional Barry is far less ambiguous than any of the characters he has created on stage or record. This mountainously jawed extrovert chunders (or vomits) his way through the kangaroo valley of Earl's Court in pursuit of Sheilas and notes (girls and money) buoyed up by innumerable tubes (bottles) of Foster's beer. He is the embodiment of grossness and anarchic good humour, the child which Edna and Sandy dread they may have borne. Unhappily, their fears are groundless: they could never have conceived a creature so free from repression.

In 1959 Barry Humphries came to Europe for the first time. In 1962 Peter Cook, the owner of the Establishment Club in Soho, heard one of his records and offered him a season in cabaret. He was booked to appear for a month, but closed after a fortnight. The audience, used to jazz singers, satire companies or stand-up comedians, could make nothing of his work. Were they meant to laugh? At that time he left the audience to distinguish between the poignant and the comic in his monologues.

To his admirers the critical reception of *Just a Show* has been dispiriting but predictable. His fans rallied, he made some conversions, while the rest of the critics registered shades of disapproval ranging from terse bemusement to open hostility.

The Listener, 1969

Acknowledgements

The publisher thanks the following for permission to reprint from copyright works: *Mandrake the Magician* comic strip reprinted with the kind permission of King Features Syndicate Inc.; *The Age* for 'A Bunyip comes to Melbourne' by Bruce Grant, 1958; *London Review of Books* and C. K. Stead for 'Here to Take Karl Stead to Lunch'; Barbara Mobbs Agency on behalf of the Patrick White Estate for Patrick White's letters to Geoffrey and Ninette Dutton (27 July 1970) and Ronald Waters (8 January 1971); The BBC for 'Barry Humphries' by Julian Jebb, *The Listener*, 1969; Peermusic (UK) Ltd for 'Oh Mona!' by Weems and Washburn, copyright 1931 by Peer International Corporation, New York; Essex Music for 'Food Glorious Food' from *Oliver!*, 1967 by Lionel Bart; Music Sales Ltd (Campbell Connelly and Co. Ltd) and Carlin Music Corporation (Redwood Music Ltd) and MCA Music Publishing for 'When the Lights Go On Again' sung by Vera Lynn; Charles Osborne for permission to quote Max Oldaker.

PHOTO CREDITS: 'Marriage' – Bruno Benini; 'Dr Humphries' – Australian Consolidated Press; 'Wild Life in Suburbia' – The Glenn A. Baker Archive, photo Gerrard Vandenberg; 'The author, 1967' – Cecil Beaton; 'The author in Little Venice with his Conder collection', 'The author', 'The author with hat', 'Moonee Ponds' – Lewis Morley; 'The Surfie', 'The bride's father' – Theatre Museum Crown Copyright, Houston Rogers Collection; 'Sober', 'The author with Mischa Spoliansky', – John Timbers; 'The author with John Betjamen c. 1974, Chelsea' – Don Bennetts; 'The author' – Brian Savron; Melbourne *Herald*; 'Dame Edna, a recent Hollywood study' – Roddy McDowall; 'The author at dinner in Los Angeles', 'With David Hockney in California', 'Oscar and Rupert' – Lizzie Spender/Lewis Morley; 'Drunk' – David Bailey; 'Lizzie, Barry and Stanley' – David Hockney.

Endpapers: *A Nice Night's Entertainment* – John Tourrier; *Isn't it Pathetic at His Age* – Toby Purves; *Just a Show* – Geoffrey Goldie; *Back With a Vengeance* – Dewynters; *Tears Before Bedtime, An Evening's Intercourse With Barry Humphries* – Diane Millstead; *Excuse I* – Colin Munro.

He just wanted a decent book to read ...

Not too much to ask, is it? It was in 1935 when Allen Lane, Managing Director of Bodley Head Publishers, stood on a platform at Exeter railway station looking for something good to read on his journey back to London. His choice was limited to popular magazines and poor-quality paperbacks – the same choice faced every day by the vast majority of readers, few of whom could afford hardbacks. Lane's disappointment and subsequent anger at the range of books generally available led him to found a company – and change the world.

'We believed in the existence in this country of a vast reading public for intelligent books at a low price, and staked everything on it'
Sir Allen Lane, 1902–1970, founder of Penguin Books

The quality paperback had arrived – and not just in bookshops. Lane was adamant that his Penguins should appear in chain stores and tobacconists, and should cost no more than a packet of cigarettes.

Reading habits (and cigarette prices) have changed since 1935, but Penguin still believes in publishing the best books for everybody to enjoy. We still believe that good design costs no more than bad design, and we still believe that quality books published passionately and responsibly make the world a better place.

So wherever you see the little bird – whether it's on a piece of prize-winning literary fiction or a celebrity autobiography, political tour de force or historical masterpiece, a serial-killer thriller, reference book, world classic or a piece of pure escapism – you can bet that it represents the very best that the genre has to offer.

Whatever you like to read – trust Penguin.